Marketing That Works

Second Edition

Marketing That Works

How Entrepreneurial Marketing Can Add Sustainable Value to Any Sized Company

Second Edition

Leonard M. Lodish
Howard L. Morgan
Shellye Archambeau
Jeffrey A. Babin

Publisher: Paul Boger
Editor-in-Chief: Amy Neidlinger
Executive Editor: Jeanne Levine
Operations Specialist: Jodi Kemper
Cover Designer: Alan Clements
Managing Editor: Kristy Hart
Senior Project Editor: Lori Lyons
Copy Editor: Karen Annett
Proofreader: Chrissy White
Indexer: Lisa Stumpf
Senior Compositor: Gloria Schurick
Manufacturing Buyer: Dan Uhrig

© 2016 by Pearson Education, Inc.
Old Tappan, New Jersey 07675

For information about buying this title in bulk quantities, or for special sales opportunities (which may include electronic versions; custom cover designs; and content particular to your business, training goals, marketing focus, or branding interests), please contact our corporate sales department at corpsales@pearsoned.com or (800) 382-3419.

For government sales inquiries, please contact governmentsales@pearsoned.com.

For questions about sales outside the U.S., please contact international@pearsoned.com.

Company and product names mentioned herein are the trademarks or registered trademarks of their respective owners.

Printed in the United States of America

45 2023

ISBN-10: 0-13-399333-7
ISBN-13: 978-0-13-399333-2

Pearson Education LTD.
Pearson Education Australia PTY, Limited.
Pearson Education Singapore, Pte. Ltd.
Pearson Education Asia, Ltd.
Pearson Education Canada, Ltd.
Pearson Educación de Mexico, S.A. de C.V.
Pearson Education—Japan
Pearson Education Malaysia, Pte. Ltd.

Library of Congress Control Number: 2015937237

NC 01.05.2023 1608

The authors dedicate this book
to our best venture partners:
our spouses who have supported us in so many
ways for over 150 years of happily married life—
Susan Lodish for 50 years,
Eleanor Morgan for 48 years,
Scotty Scott for 31 years,
and Kathy Babin for 22 years.
We love you.

Contents

Acknowledgments

This book is an outgrowth of the Entrepreneurial Marketing Course that Len Lodish teaches in The Wharton School MBA program. Aside from the invaluable help and wise counsel of Howard Morgan and Shellye Archambeau, there are many people who have helped the course and this book. Amy Kallianpur administered the questionnaire and tabulated the results, as well as developed some of the content on franchising. Jill Beraud, the former chief marketing officer of Limited Brands, and Len's student, was very kind to be interviewed about the marketing strategies that made Victoria's Secret so successful. Yosi Heber provided some very interesting conceptual structure for our discussion of Web search advertising.

The Wharton MBA students who participated in the class for the past 18 years have been inspirational to us all. The entrepreneurs who have either spoken to the class or helped the book by sharing their real-world experience have been invaluable to this effort. A partial list of those entrepreneurs includes Mark Stiffler of Synygy, Inc.; Craig Tractenberg, the franchise law guru at Nixon Peabody; Gary Erlbaum of David's Bridal and other ventures; Eric Spitz of Trakus, Inc., and the Know Fat Lifestyle Grill; Mel Kornbluh of Tandem's East; Bob Tumulo of Rita's Water Ice; Steve Katz of SEI Corp and many ventures; Jim Everett of Country Junction; Bill Gross of Idealab; Alan Markowitz of many ventures; Ralph Guild of Interep; Ken Hakuda of Allherb.com; Dwight Riskey of Frito Lay; Barry Feinberg of many ventures; Chuck Holroyd and Mike Perry of IndyMac Bank; Barry Lipsky and Mort David of Franklin Electronic Publishing; Bob Brisco of Internet Brands; Andrew Beebe of Energy Innovations; Jim Simons of Renaissance Technologies; Gerry Shreiber of J&J Snack Foods; Marc Lore of Quidsi, Inc., and diapers.com; Brett Hurt of Coremetrics and other ventures; Angelique Irvin of ClearAlign; Don McLagan and the management of Compete, Inc.; Max Lodish of Aerial-Media Services; Jake Lodish of Papa Jakes Subs; Steve Woda of Buy Safe; Lucinda Duncalfe of Monetate; Jon Sobel of Sight Machine; Andy Kohm of Vendop; Jack Abraham of Atomic Ventures; and Josh Kopelman of half.com and First Round Capital. Tovah Feldshuh, the actress, demonstrated to Len how valuable excellent sales execution and dedication are to a successful venture.

The Wharton Global Consulting Practicum has also been a source of rich entrepreneurial and strategy experiences of foreign companies entering the United States. Over the years, this book has benefited from the insights of Therese Flaherty, Guri Meltzer, Shlomo Kalish, Yuval Dovev, Ron Waldman, and David Ben Ami of that program, as well as all of the MBA students and faculty in Israel, Africa, Australia, Chile, China, Colombia, France, India, Mexico, Peru, and Spain, who have added their insights.

Many colleagues at Wharton and other academic institutions, and other marketing scientists, have helped with concepts, method-ologies, and paradigms. In particular, John Little, Pete Fader, Magid Abraham, Gerry Eskin, Abba Kreiger, Jerry Wind, David Reibstein, Russ Palmer, Terry Overton, Erin Anderson, C. B. Bhattacharya, David Aaker, Robert Nason, Irwin Gross, Raghu Iyengar, and David Bell have been very helpful over the years. The participants in the Wharton-Insead "Leading the Effective Sales Force" program, which was codirected by Erin Anderson and is now codirected by Paddy Padmanhaban and Len, have also contributed many valuable ideas and insights over the years.

Len has been coinvesting and advising many ventures and venture capital funds in San Francisco, Philadelphia, and Israel. He acknowl-edges the very valuable ideas of his Musketeer Capital partners, Alan Markowitz, Steve Katz, and Marty Lautman as well as his capital part-ners, Alan Feld, Martin Gedalin, Jon Soberg, Mitchell Green, and David Blumberg.

Thirty years of experience working with Information Resources, Inc., has helped Len Lodish with significant learning about how consumers react to advertising and other marketing mix elements. Working with the entrepreneurs of the more than 400 companies of Idealab and First Round Capital has given Howard Morgan many exciting experiences with all types of marketing, both consumer and industrial. Working with entrepreneurial founders such as Bill Gross and Josh Kopelman has shaped many of the insights in this book.

We want to also thank Charlene Niles and the staff of *Inc. Mag-azine* and Ian MacMillan, Greg Higgins, Mark Dane Fraga, Emily

Cieri, Clare Leinweber, and the staff of Wharton Entrepreneurship and the Wharton Small Business Center for developing and running programs that help us learn and explore from today's entrepreneurs. In particular, the entrepreneurs of Wharton's Venture Initiation Program continue to be an inspiration and source of innovation and experience.

Howard Morgan wishes to thank his mentors through the years: Jim Simons of the Simons Foundation, Bill Gross of Idealab, and his partners at First Round Capital—especially Josh Kopelman—who have helped him pursue the continuing passion of startup investing.

Shellye Archambeau would like to acknowledge the value of the experience gained working with the entire MetricStream team, especially Gunjan Sinha, chairman and Gaurav Kapor, COO. Her mentors and advisors over the years have helped shape her approach to marketing and sales. Special thanks go to Bill Campbell, Tim McChristian, Vinod Khosla, Ben Horowitz, Robin Sternbergh, and Ken Thornton.

In addition, Jeffrey Babin would like to thank the hundreds of employees, clients, and students with whom he has had the pleasure of working over the years and with whom he has learned (and lived) effective marketing and innovation. Jeffrey also would like to thank Rob Weber and Ellen Weber and offers special thanks to Tom Cassel, Joe Sun, Eduardo Glandt, Ian MacMillan, Wendell Dunn, and of course, Len Lodish for initiating and encouraging an unexpected third career in academia that has been nothing but joy.

About the Authors

Leonard M. Lodish, Ph.D., is Samuel R. Harrell Professor Emeritus of Marketing at The Wharton School. He is cofounder and Leader of Wharton's Global Consulting Practicum, and innovator of Wharton's MBA Entrepreneurial Marketing course. His research focuses on marketing decision support systems, marketing experimentation, and entrepreneurial marketing. As an active venture advisor and investor, Len was the first outside board member and helped raise the first investments for Quidsi.com (diapers.com) and Milo.com, and other very successful ventures. He is a cofounder of Musketeer Capital and advisor to a number of venture funds.

Howard L. Morgan is cofounder and Partner of First Round Capital, a venture capital investment firm, and founding investor and board member of Idealab. He has served as Professor of Decision Sciences at The Wharton School, as Professor of Computer and Information Sciences at the University of Pennsylvania, as Assistant Professor of Operations Research at Cornell University, and as Visiting Professor at the California Institute of Technology and Harvard Business School.

Shellye Archambeau is CEO of MetricStream, Inc., a recognized global leader in Governance, Risk, and Compliance. She also serves on the boards of directors for Verizon Communications and Nordstrom. She previously served as CMO and EVP of Sales for Loudcloud, Inc., responsible for all global sales and marketing activities. There, she led Loudcloud's transformation into an enterprisefocused company while growing sales by 50% year over year. As President of Blockbuster, Inc.'s e-commerce division, she was recognized by *Internet World* as one of the nation's Top 25 click-and-mortar executives.

Jeffrey A. Babin is Associate Professor of Practice & Associate Director of Engineering Entrepreneurship at the University of Pennsylvania, and founder and Managing Director of Antiphony

Partners, LLC, a strategy consulting firm that helps companies create sustainable value through innovation. He is Senior Project Advisor and Regional Manager of the Wharton Global Consulting Practicum, Advisor for the Wharton Venture Initiation Program, and founding member of the Mid-Atlantic Angel Group.

For more information about Marketing That Works, visit www.marketingthatworksbook.com.

Introduction

The Book's Mission

Truly successful businesses over the long term have achieved greater-than-market levels of profit return to their investors because they have been able to somehow insulate themselves from competitive pressures. If a company cannot insulate itself from competitors, it becomes doomed to market-level rates of return as competitive forces continually attack its profit margins and revenue sources. In this book, we show how entrepreneurial marketing can help firms both large and small to differentiate themselves and insulate themselves from some competitive pressures. The entrepreneurial marketing techniques, concepts, methods, and paradigms we provide will help your venture make more money—extraordinary money—on a sustainable basis. Not only will you be able to position your product/service offering to leverage your firm's distinctive competencies and potential sustainable competitive advantages, but the way you do marketing will make you more efficient than your competition as well.

Marketing, more than technology, is most often the reason for the success or failure of new ventures or new initiatives of mature corporations. Yet there are few detailed guides, and fewer serious studies, on what does and does not work when dealing with these situations. This book is designed to help marketers make the best use of their time, money, and effort in growing their businesses in a way that gives them some competitively sustainable differential advantage. The book is itself the product of cost-effective, entrepreneurial marketing thinking. There is a target market that has a need for help that we hope to provide. We have seen no books that combine conceptually sound marketing concepts and paradigms with practical guidance on how to apply them in real situations in order to leverage the resources used for marketing and attain sustainable competitive advantage.

This book has a very pragmatic objective. We are not trying to deliver a complete compendium on marketing or on entrepreneurship or intrapreneurship (entrepreneurship within a larger corporation). We cover only marketing concepts, methods, tactics, and strategies that "work"—that is, can add value to real ventures regardless of the ongoing changes in technology and economy. We have been guided in our thinking, not only by our academic research and practical experience with dozens of companies, but also by studying what the most successful companies (as well as those that do not perform as well) are doing to create sustainable competitive advantage. These results provide new insights into what types of marketing programs and channels are most effective in diverse business settings.

You, our target reader, are someone who needs to get results quickly, and has limited financial resources and people resources— you are someone who often does not have any staff to help with speculative research or analysis. Although some bigger, older companies may have the luxury of waiting for longer-term impact of their marketing and sales strategies, the company we write for has to worry about the short term. Like it or not, for many managers today, and for all start-up firms, without a short-term cash flow, the longer term is impossible. Even if you work for a large, "deep pockets" organization or have significant funding reserves, acting as though resources are limited often produces the best results. No matter what size your entity, your responsibility is to get the biggest return from your resources that you can. One of the ways this book can help you to be better than your competition is that your competition will still be thinking in outmoded, less-productive ways about marketing. You will be much more able to get increased productivity from your marketing budget and will be able to develop offerings that are part of sustainable competitive advantage.

The Authors' and the Book's Heritage

Marketing That Works is possibly the best of both the academic and practical approaches to marketing issues—it comes from the intersection of both approaches.

This book's intellectual parent is *Entrepreneurial Marketing: Lessons from Wharton's Pioneering MBA Course*, by Len Lodish, Howard Morgan, and Amy Kallianpur. The book got started as a by-product of the entrepreneurial marketing course that Len Lodish developed at The Wharton School of the University of Pennsylvania. In the class, MBA students worked in groups to develop marketing plans for entrepreneurial ventures they were possibly starting. Along with the instructors' comments on how marketing could be used to help entrepreneurial ventures, the students were exposed to success-ful entrepreneurs who spoke and answered questions.

Since the course was begun and the first book was released, we have expanded the experience base from which we draw beyond the classroom. Len Lodish has over 40 years of applying marketing and strategic thinking to entrepreneurial ventures. One of Len's early entrepreneurial ventures has become Information Resources, Inc. (IRI). As a corporate director and consultant to IRI, Len has worked with many of the major packaged goods firms to improve their mar-keting productivity—including Procter & Gamble, PepsiCo, and Campbell's. Len was also the Founding Vice Dean and advisor to the Wharton Venture Initiation Program in San Francisco. He has been a director, advised, and/or invested in over 40 ventures, includ-ing some that have had exits in the hundreds of millions. Howard Morgan brings more than 35 years' experience with over 300 high-tech ventures as a consultant, director, sometimes executive, and financial resource. Shellye Archambeau was one of the first entrepre-neurs to speak with the entrepreneurial marketing class when it was given at Wharton's San Francisco campus. Shellye was really elegant in showing how basic entrepreneurial marketing concepts, methods, and paradigms are useful at both large and small firms—from IBM to MetricStream, where she is currently the CEO. As an educator, practitioner, and investor in entrepreneurship and innovation, Jeffrey Babin has worked with Fortune 100 companies as well as technol-ogy start-ups to create value through new products and marketing strategies. Our team of authors brings a unique combination of proven experience in the classroom, in the field, and in the board rooms of many companies. The results reflect both academic rigor and high returns on marketing investments.

This edition of *Marketing That Works*, like the best marketing programs, has been tested, adapted, and restructured in order to deliver the greatest value. We have added and updated many of the concepts, methods, and paradigms that deliver results and expanded them for application by any size firm that wants to make more money by acting like a successful entrepreneurial marketer.

The Importance of Marketing

Marketing, depending on how broadly you define it, is becoming the most important way many firms differentiate themselves. As you will see, marketing's biggest job is impacting how your product offerings are perceived by your target market(s). What's the difference between Jet Blue, Southwest Airlines, or American Airlines Group (American Airlines & US Airways)? Although they all fly customers from one location to another, which customers they fly and the perception of what it is like to use their services are very different. Other examples are Apple, Samsung, and Xiaomi. They all sell smartphones. Apple's positioning is elegant design and usability within the Apple ecosystem; Samsung develops innovative products for the high-end market; and Xiaomi offers high-quality technology at competitive prices to the largest markets. Mistargeted marketing would spend dollars attracting low-end buyers to Apple, when they are unlikely to buy. Proper targeting would focus on bringing Xiaomi phones to the fast-growing mainstream consumer of Asian markets, which has been extremely successful.

> Because the purpose of business is to create a customer, the business enterprise has two—and only two—basic functions: marketing and innovation. Marketing and innovation produce results; all the rest are costs. Marketing is the distinguishing, unique function of the business.
>
> —Peter Drucker, *The Practice of Management*, 1954

These words, written more than a half-century ago, are just as true today. Marketing is of critical importance to the success of a company. In a recent survey, 14 venture capitalists that backed more than 200 ventures rated the importance of business functions to the success of the enterprise. The marketing function was rated 6.7 on a scale of 7.0, higher than any other business functions, in terms of importance to success of entrepreneurial ventures. In-depth interviews with the same venture capitalists concluded that venture failure rates can be reduced as much as 60% using pre-venture marketing analysis. Too many ventures are focused on the technical superiority or inventiveness of their product, but "build it and they will come" often fails because the customers need to be educated with new products.

Entrepreneurial marketing is the tool that every manager needs to help her product or service offering be perceived as more valuable than the competition by target segments. Marketing strategies and tactics help guide the development of offerings that the market wants, help target the firm's offering to the right customers, get the product or service to the customer, and help ensure that the customers perceive the incremental value of the offering better than the competition and will pay for the added value.

Entrepreneurial marketing is also geared to make the resources supporting marketing go as far as possible, squeezing every penny used for marketing to make it as profitable as possible. We will show how to balance incremental lifetime revenue with incremental lifetime costs to be more efficient with marketing activities such as sales forces, advertising, promotion, and public relations. We will also show how in marketing, *adaptive experimentation* can be a very efficient way to estimate the incremental revenue and incremental costs of many marketing activities. Many executives feel that they have to decide "once and for all" how best to get to market. However, the reaction of the marketplace is often very difficult to forecast in advance. Many times, it is preferable to try two or three different ways to get to the market, measure the incremental impact of each method, and then roll out the one that works the best.

One Positioning, Multiple Stakeholders

Marketing is important, but not just in its traditional role of aiding in developing, producing, and selling products or services that customers want. We will demonstrate in the first chapter that *positioning*, the combination of *segmentation* and *differentiation*, are the real core of what makes ventures financially successful or not successful and provide the basis for sustainable competitive advantage.

Positioning is how the product or service is to be perceived by a target market compared to the competition. It answers the question: "Why will someone in the target market(s) buy my product or service instead of the competition?" An equivalent question is: "What should be the perceived value of my offering compared to the competition?" Positioning is intimately related to core distinctive competencies that the firm has or can develop.

The marketing plan—including appropriate pricing, public relations, promotion, advertising, distribution channels, and sales efforts—flows directly from the positioning decision. The positioning sets the vision for the offering in the marketplace and must be unified, consistent, and clear to gain market acceptance, increase perceived value, and gain purchase. However, the tactics and media of communicating the positioning may vary as they focus on other stakeholders who may be at least as important as the end customer:

- *Investors* and potential investors in the venture
- *Market intermediaries* between the company and the end customer
- *Employees* and potential employees
- *Strategic partners*
- *Users*, the nonpaying parties who may influence customers (for example, viewers of advertising-supported programs)

Each of these stakeholders is concerned about the end customer product positioning, but they are also concerned about other issues that are at least as important to them—the *equity* and *image* of the venture. The successful cost-effective marketer has a big job. He needs to manage how his venture is perceived on all three issues—its *product offering, corporate image,* and *equity*—by all of the different constituencies. The positioning challenge is even more daunting because all the stakeholders have different values that they typically seek in the venture's product offering, image, and equity. Throughout this book, we consider all of these stakeholders in the concepts and methods described.

As Bo Peabody points out in his book *Lucky or Smart*, an entrepreneur is always selling her stock. In the early stages of almost every venture, there is no revenue coming in, and expenses are covered by loans or equity. Marketing to investors requires a different approach than marketing to customers, because to them, the product is those shares they're buying. How will they become more valuable? And hiring needs a different way of communicating because getting the best and brightest to work with your venture, a task on which companies such as Microsoft and Google have focused, requires them to believe in your mission, people, and image, as well as the value of stock options. Even in the product area, the customers (those who actually pay for the goods and services) are often not the same as the users (those who consume the goods or services). In many Internet companies—whether a new information site, product-focused company, or service provider—advertisers may be the paying customers, while these customers can only be drawn in by having lots of end users of the company's offering. The plan for marketing to the paying customers needs to be quite distinct from the one designed to draw users.

Challenges of the Next Decade

The Internet began as a network of connected computers that could share information. Today, the devices connected by internetworking technologies extend well beyond the desktop-bound boxes of the late twentieth century. The nodes of the Internet are devices of all types, which are sending and receiving data. The Internet of Things is only the latest term describing the type of connected devices. We are currently experiencing a proliferation of sensors that gather data about location/position, movement, environment, and any number of measurements about changes in state of ourselves as well as our devices. We have only begun to figure out how to capture value from this massive and dynamic source of information.

For years, we have been gathering information about online behaviors to better refine our marketing activities. Now, *Big Data* is the phrase used to describe the analysis of the stream of data we are now gathering from all sources. Making this information actionable is our latest challenge. We have yet to imagine the new products and services that will deliver value from these data streams. We do know that industry sectors will continue to be redefined by disruption of the traditional rules and structures in health care, education, retail, security, transportation, and others.

On March 10, 2000, the NASDAQ index hit a (then) lifetime intraday high of 5,132. Fifteen years later, the NASDAQ is back at (or near) those highs, yet the complex of the leading NASDAQ companies has changed (see Table I-1). Most notable (other than 6 of the 10 in the 2000 top ten are no longer in the top 10) is the shift of companies from hardware and infrastructure to services and more consumer orientation. This is a direct result of the increased value in consumer and information-based services. This trend will continue.

Table I-1 Top 10 NASDAQ Components by Market Cap (Carew, 2015)[1]

March 10, 2015	March 10, 2000
Apple $724.6 billion	Microsoft $525.4 billion
Google $382.3 billion	Cisco $466.4 billion
Microsoft $347.4 billion	Intel $401.3 billion
Facebook $218.7 billion	Oracle $232.4 billion
Amazon $171.9 billion	Sun Micro.$164.5 billion
Intel $151.3 billion	Dell $131.5 billion
Gilead $147.8 billion	Qualcomm $96.4 billion
Cisco $147.2 billion	Yahoo $93.7 billion
Comcast $125.8 billion	Applied Materials $74.6 billion
Qualcomm $119.3 billion	JDS Uniphase $68.9 billion

Technology development and the Internet of Things will also cause changes in policy and regulatory environment. Once the stuff of science fiction, drones and driverless cars are not only a reality, but market-leading companies like Google and Amazon are pursuing business strategies and models based on these technologies. The implications of this for logistics and transportation is only outweighed by regulatory, security, and societal impact these technologies will have. All of this change will occur in a world of changing governments, shifts in control and availability of natural resources, and never-ending advancement of technology and capital markets from many different countries around the world.

Whereas the previous two decades saw the Internet and internetworking technologies accelerate globalization, change how business relationships work, and drive business model evolution, today we no longer distinguish between Internet-based businesses and business. All businesses are and will be technology-enabled and technology-enhanced. The more things change, the more they stay the same, and Peter Drucker's adage that "Marketing is the distinguishing unique function of business" will be as true 50 years from now as it was 50 years ago. The key to any marketing that impacts sustainable competitive advantage is an understanding of "What am I selling to whom?" and "Why do they care?" These are the key questions we address in this book.

Section One, "Marketing Strategy—Refine Your Offering and Positioning," explores how to refine your offering and positioning. Section Two, "Demand-Generation and Sales—Lead Your Customers to Your Offering," focuses on generating demand for your offering. And Section Three, "Execution—Cultivate the People and Resources to Make Your Marketing Work," presents the key resources, including the most important resources of people, to drive your marketing efforts to successful outcomes.

Endnotes

1. S. Carew. *NASDAQ Looks Different 15 Years after Its Peak: Then and Now.* (2015, March 11). Retrieved from Reuters: http://blogs. reuters.com/data-dive/2015/03/11/nasdaq-looks-different-15-years-after-its-peak-then-and-now/

Section One

Marketing Strategy—Refine Your Offering and Positioning

Great companies have a clear vision and the leadership to organize their teams in all functional areas to drive the company toward that vision. The equivalent of that vision in marketing is positioning. Positioning is the foundation upon which you build all marketing activities, and all marketing activities must reinforce the positioning.

Positioning is a combination of two key marketing themes: segmentation and differentiation. Segmentation starts with focus on the customers (or combination of customers) that derive value from your product-offering bundle (offering). Segmentation allows you to organize the total customer population for your offering into discrete segments, each of which share key attributes. In his landmark book, *Marketing High Technology*, Bill Davidow offers one of the most insightful definitions of a market segment:

> A market segment is a group of customers sharing common desires, needs, and buying patterns.[1]

The savvy marketer understands that finding the best segment for his offering means engaging a group of customers who respond to products, services, messages, and almost any situation in a similar manner. Offer a product that resonates with a segment, and you will quickly grow sales of your offering. Marketers have two challenges. The first challenge is to identify and reach a segment, and the second is to ensure that the offering is perceived as delivering a strong value proposition to the segment. Differentiation is the key to achieving a sustainable value proposition.

---

[1] Bill Davidow, *Marketing High Technology* (New York: Simon, 1986), 17–18

Regardless of how new a technology or product offering is, customers have something that performs the same function. The status quo is one of the strongest forces against which marketers must battle and differentiation is the key. You must offer an alternative to the status quo, which delivers a sustainable competitive advantage over existing offerings. You can reinforce your positioning by communicating and allowing your target segment to experience your distinctive advantage.

This section explores the key marketing concept of positioning. Because positioning is so instrumental to successful marketing, it is difficult, if not impossible, to get it "right" on the first try. Luckily, you have the ability to test and learn from the market as you develop your offering and bring it to market. Adaptive testing allows you to invest modest amounts to maximize learning and, most important, to avoid mistakes. Successful marketers test and adapt all aspects of marketing to optimize results.

We also discuss testing in the context of product concept development to ensure that customers respond to and engage with your offerings as you expect and desire. Product concept testing allows you to test the elements of your marketing plan to ensure that you both understand the key messages that resonate with your segments and drive them to purchase. The final chapter in this section explores the key concepts of value and pricing, which allow you to capture the greatest returns from your marketing efforts..

1

Marketing-Driven Strategy to Make Extraordinary Money

Orvis Company—Excellent Entrepreneurial Positioning

The Orvis Company has done an excellent job over the years of capitalizing on a unique positioning in a very competitive industry. They sell "country" clothing, gifts, and sporting gear in competition with much bigger brands like L.L. Bean and Eddie Bauer. Like their competitors, Orvis sells both retail and mail order. How is Orvis differentiated? They want to be perceived as the place to go for all areas of fly-fishing expertise. Their particular expertise is making a difficult sport "very accessible to a new generation of anglers."[1] Since 1968, when their sales were less than $1 million, Orvis has been running fly-fishing schools located near their retail outlets. Their annual sales are now over $350 million. The fly-fishing products contribute only a small fraction of the company's sales, but the fly-fishing heritage adds a cachet to all of Orvis's products. According to Tom Rosenbauer, beginner fly fishermen who attend their schools become loyal customers and are crucial to continuing expansion of the more profitable clothing and gift lines. He says, "Without our fly-fishing heritage, we'd be just another rag vendor."[2]

The Orvis positioning pervades their entire operation. Their catalog and their retail shops all reinforce their fly-fishing heritage. They also can use very targeted segmentation to find new recruits for their fly-fishing courses. There are a number of targeted media and public relations vehicles that reach consumers interested in fishing. Their margins are higher than the typical "rag vendor" because of their unique positioning. The positioning is also defensible because of the consistent perception that all of their operations have reinforced since 1968. A competitor will have a very difficult time and large expense to reproduce the Orvis schools and retail outlets. It also will be difficult for a competitor to be a "me too" in an industry where heritage is so important. The positioning decisions Orvis made in 1968 probably added close to $1 billion of incremental value to their venture since that time. That value is our estimate of the difference of Orvis's actual profit since 1968 compared with what the venture's profitability might have been had they just been "another rag vendor." Victoria's Secret is another company that has really leveraged excellent positioning, as discussed later in this chapter.

Positioning to Enhance the Value Proposition

"What am I selling to whom, and why will they buy?" Determining the answers to this seemingly simple question will have more impact on the success of your venture than anything else. The answers will drive the essence of your unique perceived value proposition to your customers.

What is a unique perceived value proposition, and why is it important?

First, a perceived *value proposition* is the promise of intrinsic worth that your product, service, or offering can provide to customers as perceived by those customers. It is the statement of benefits a customer can expect when buying from you. Simply stated, it's what they perceive they get for their money. A *unique value proposition* is one that is distinguished from the value propositions offered by competitors.

Value is usually created along three dimensions:

- Performance value (superior functionality)
- Price value (low cost)
- Relational value (such as personalized treatment or how the customer will feel or perceive herself because of product/service purchase)

Value is also relatively *perceived.* For instance, one company will place more weight on low cost, whereas another will place it on reliability. For example, Cisco will charge over ten times the price as former competitor and now subsidiary Linksys will for wireless routers that have the same operating characteristics but higher perceived (and actual) reliability. For IT buyers to whom reliability and system uptime are crucial, the Cisco value is there. The home wireless networker is much more concerned about the price paid and will sacrifice some extreme reliability for a significant price reduction. Therefore, it is critical to know to whom you are selling to position your venture to provide a unique value proposition.

Positioning represents the foundation of the venture and its marketing. It is on this foundation that the unique value proposition is built and upon which the customer-oriented marketing plan is based. All of the venture's important decisions and tactics are critically dependent on these basic elements. However, determining positioning is not easy. If other marketing decisions are made before the positioning is defined, there is a danger that resources such as money and time will be poorly used and that expected results will not be realized. The customer-oriented marketing plan must be based on the positioning of the venture, which is to say the target market(s) and the unique and differentiated value proposition offered.

Segmentation answers the first half of the question: *"What am I selling to whom?"* It is through segmentation that the market is divided into categories of like-minded buyers. Once the categories are determined, the target market can be determined.

Differentiation answers the second half of the question: *"...and why will they buy?"*

Positioning is determining how the product-offering bundle should be perceived by the target market as compared with the competition.

Every word in this positioning definition has been chosen carefully. The words *determining* and *should* imply that positioning is an active management decision, not a passive taking of what is given. The words *product-offering bundle* are used instead of product or service because the consumer buys a bundle of perceived attributes when they make a purchase. Everything that a venture does that affects the perception of attributes affects the positioning. Things like how the venture responds to inquiries, to the look of their stationery, to the feel of their website, can all impact the perception of the product-offering bundle. The word *perceived* reinforces that consumers as people only make decisions based on their perceptions as opposed to reality. The *target market* shows that the venture's positioning needs to impact those people who are most likely to value the positioning the highest. *Compared with the competition* reinforces that the target market's perceptions are all relative to competition.

Getting Started: Segmentation and Targeting

In reality, the segmentation and differentiation decisions are typically developed together. However, for ease of communication, we will take them one at a time and consider the interrelationships as we go. Conceptually, segmentation is a process in which a firm's market is partitioned into submarkets with the objective of having the response to the firm's marketing activities and product/service offerings vary a lot across segments, but have little variability within each segment. For the entrepreneur, the segments may, in many cases, only amount to two: the group being targeted with the offering and marketing activity and "everyone else." The targeted segment(s) will obviously be related to the product/service offering and the competitive strategy of the entrepreneur.

There are some important questions that need answers as part of the selection of target market segment(s):

1. The most important question is: *Does the target segment want the perceived value that my differentiation is trying to deliver more than other segments?* Sometimes targeting may involve segments that differ on response to other elements of the marketing mix. However, many successful ventures differentiate target segments on the value they place on the differential benefits they perceive the firm to deliver. If a firm can target those people who value their offering the highest compared with competition, it has many benefits, including better pricing and

higher margins, more satisfied customers, and usually a better barrier to potential and actual competition.

2. Almost as important to profitable segmentation is: *How can the segment be reached? And how quickly?* Are there available distribution or media options, or can a self-selection strategy be used? Are the options for reaching the segment cost effective? Can enough of the segment be reached quickly enough so that you can be a leader before competitors can target the same segment?

3. *How big is the segment?* If the segment is not big enough in terms of potential revenue and gross margin to justify the cost of setting up a program to satisfy it, it will not be profitable.

4. Other questions to also keep in mind include: *What are likely impacts of changes in relevant environmental conditions (for example, economic conditions, lifestyle, legal regulations) on the potential response of the target segment? What are current and likely competitive activities directed at the target segment?*[3]

Virtual Communities: The Ultimate Segment?

The Internet has fostered thousands of virtual communities. These are made up of groups of people who are drawn together online by common interests. Just as enthusiasts for certain activities such as hobbies, sports, recreation, and so on have gotten together in metropolitan areas for years, the Internet lets enthusiasts from all over the world "get together" virtually. The same phenomenon holds for business users of certain software or specialized equipment. Users or potential users like to get together to help each other with mutual solutions to common problems, helpful hints, new ideas, or evaluations of new products, which might help the community members. It is much easier to post notices on a blog or a forum than to physically go to an enthusiast's meeting. A virtual community member can interact with his counterparts any time of the day or night and reach people with very similar needs and experiences.

These virtual communities can be an entrepreneur's penultimate segment. In terms of the preceding segmentation selection questions, the answers to the first two questions are almost part of the definition of an online virtual community. If your product or service offering is tailored (or as importantly, *is perceived to be tailored*) to the members of a virtual community, then it will be positioned as very valuable to that segment compared with any other group. The size of the segment is easily determined as the size of the virtual community.

The incentives for entrepreneurial companies to get involved with virtual communities are great, but it is not a one-way street. All elements of the marketing program need to be cleverly adapted to the new segmentation environment. The challenges of marketing in virtual communities are summarized nicely by McKinsey consultants John Hagel III and Arthur G. Armstrong:

> Virtual communities are likely to look very threatening to your average company. How many firms want to make it easier for their customers to talk to one another about their products and services? But vendors will soon have little choice but to participate. As more and more of their customers join virtual communities, they will find themselves in "reverse markets"— markets in which customers seek out vendors and play them off against one another, rather than the other way around. Far-sighted companies will recognize that virtual communities actually represent a tremendous opportunity to expand their geographical reach at minimal cost.[4]

An Entrepreneurial Segmentation Example— Tandem's East

A clever entrepreneur can use target segmentation as a prime reason for beginning a venture. An example is Mel Kornbluh, who began a company called *Tandem's East* in his garage in the late 1980s. Mel is a specialist in selling and servicing tandem bicycles—bicycles built for two (or three or four). Mel realized there was a segment of bicycling couples that would appreciate the unique benefits of tandeming. It is the only exercise two people can do together, communicate while they exercise, appreciate nature together, and do all this even though they may have very different physical abilities.

When he began his venture, intuitively Mel had very good answers to the previous questions. There were actually two target segments that Mel could target. The first was existing tandem enthusiast couples—those who already had a tandem and would need an upgrade or replacement. The other target segment was relatively affluent bicycling couples who had trouble riding together because of differences in physical abilities. The couples needed to be affluent because tandems are relatively expensive when compared with two regular bicycles. They are not mass-produced and do not take advantage of mass scale economies.

At the time Mel started in 1988, there was no one on the East Coast who had staked out a position as a specialist in tandems. As tandem inventory is expensive and selection is very important to potential buyers, he could establish barriers to potential competitors by being first to accumulate a substantial inventory. He was also able to establish some exclusive arrangements with some suppliers by being first in the area and offering them a new outlet.

Mel also had invented a better tandem crank extender to make it easier for the stoker (the rear rider and typically the female of a couple) to reach the handlebar comfortably. He has patented the design and still sells over 600 pairs per year almost 25 years later.

It was relatively easy for Mel to reach both of his segments. Existing tandem enthusiasts were members of the Tandem Club of America that has a newsletter they publish bimonthly. It is relatively inexpensive to advertise in the newsletter that reaches his first segment precisely. Not only does it reach the segment, but because the readers are already enthusiasts, they pay attention to every page of the newsletter. Over time, Internet user groups dedicated to tandeming were also formed. They are also natural vehicles for effectively reaching the segment.

His second segment was also relatively easy to reach cost effectively. Affluent bicycling couples read cycling magazines—the major one being *Bicycling Magazine*—and specialized websites and blogs. Again, because they are enthusiasts, the target segment pays a lot of attention to even small ads. This segment also attends bicycling rallies and organized rides. Mel still attends many rallies that his target customers will attend.

Both segments were much larger than Mel needed to make the business viable. With small response rates in either segment, he could afford to pay his overhead and to begin to accumulate a suitable inventory. In fact, his advertising costs are significantly under 10% of revenue, indicating that reaching the segments is extremely cost effective.

Thus, Tandem's East was begun and flourished by creatively seeing target segments that valued what Mel was selling. The segments were substantial and easily reached cost effectively, and competitive barriers could be erected. In 2014, Mel had more than 100 tandems displayed in stock for customers to try. Since 1988, no one has been able to effectively compete with Tandem's East in the Mid-Atlantic area. A few other entrepreneurs have started similar ventures in other geographic areas, but no one has been able to effectively challenge Mel in his area. If the average tandem sells for about $4,000, having $400,000 of inventory is a substantial barrier to entry.

An Entrepreneurial Segmentation Audit

Figure 1-1 shows a segmentation audit that the entrepreneurial marketer can use as a checklist to make sure that he has not forgotten an element of segmentation to consider. It may not be cost effective to address many of the audit issues with robust quantitative analysis. However, the issues could be addressed qualitatively—not addressing these issues at all can cause big problems.

The goal of the rest of this book is, in fact, to flush out the seventh group of issues in the segmentation audit. How does segmentation relate to all the other elements of the marketing mix for an entrepreneurial venture? Just as fundamental as the targeting decisions, however, are the interrelated decisions about differentiation, to which we turn next.

	Completely Describes Us (A)	Somewhat Describes Us (B)	Does Not Describe Us At All (C)	Don't Know (D)
1. Our business strategies recognize the need to prioritize target segments.	____	____	____	____
2. Our marketing plans include specific plans for each of the selected segments.	____	____	____	____
3. We have specific product and service offerings for each target segment.	____	____	____	____
4. We have detailed information about segments, including:				
• Current size of the segment	____	____	____	____
• Potential size of the segment	____	____	____	____
• Key business needs of the segments	____	____	____	____
• Information systems needs of the segment	____	____	____	____
• Their prioritized needs/benefits sought	____	____	____	____
• Their prioritized preference for product and service features	____	____	____	____
• Demographic characteristics of the segments	____	____	____	____
• Product ownership and usage	____	____	____	____
• Competitor's strength in each segment	____	____	____	____
• Perceived positioning of each competior by the members of the segment	____	____	____	____
5. We have a process for updating the information on our segmento on an ongoing basis.	____	____	____	____
6. Our segments are developed across countries, but recognize unique country requirements and subsegments.	____	____	____	____
7. Information about the target market segments is incorporated effectively into the following categories:				
• Positioning	____	____	____	____
• Product and service offering	____	____	____	____
• Pricing	____	____	____	____
• Promotion	____	____	____	____
• Public relations	____	____	____	____
• Advertising	____	____	____	____
• Distribution	____	____	____	____
• Sales force	____	____	____	____
8. We have an effective process for implementing segmentation research.	____	____	____	____
9. We have an effective process for implementing segmentation strategies.	____	____	____	____
10. We have P&L reports and accountability by segment.	____	____	____	____

Figure 1-1 A segmentation audit

Adapted from correspondence of Yoram J. Wind, 1997.

Gaining the Competitive Advantage: Differentiation

Differentiation answers the question: "Why should a member of the target segment buy my product or service rather than my *competitor's*?" A related question is: "What are the unique *differentiating* characteristics of my product or service as *perceived* by members of the target segment(s)?" The italicized words in these questions are crucial for effective positioning. First, the word *perceived* must be analyzed. It is obvious people make decisions based only on what they perceive. Many entrepreneurial firms are happy when they have developed products or services that are *actually* better than the competition on characteristics that they know should be important to people in their target market(s). What they forget is that the job is not done until the targeted people actually *perceive* the differences between their product and the competitions. In fact, in the Internet space, many companies try to gain the perception that they're better long before they can deliver on that in reality.

One of the hindrances to effective positioning is that most humans cannot perceive more than two or three differentiating attributes at a time. It is important that the differentiation be easy to remember. If there are too many differentiating attributes, the potential consumer can get confused. The marketer's job is to isolate the most important differentiating attributes of her offering and use those in all the elements of the marketing mix. In many cases, it is cost effective to do concept testing or other research with potential consumers to isolate the best combination of attributes (see "Testing Purchase Intention: The Concept Test" in Chapter 2, "Generating, Screening, and Developing Ideas"). In other cases, the entrepreneur can instinctively isolate a good combination of attributes.

Entrepreneurs who have been successful may overstate how easy it was to get a good combination of attributes for differentiation. Companies such as Starbucks (just great-tasting, excellent-quality coffee) or Apple (fun and easy to use) were successful at least partly because of very effective positioning. What has not been documented is how many entrepreneurial ventures failed (or were not as successful as they could have been) because their differentiation and associated target segments weren't very effective. The venture capitalists' estimate (cited in the Introduction)—that as many as 60% of failures can be prevented by better prelaunch marketing analysis—underscores the importance of getting your positioning right and testing with real consumers to confirm that it is right.

A big mistake many ventures make is to differentiate based on *features* of their product offering compared with their competitors. It's amazing how many entrepreneurs we have encountered who have great ideas based on technical features that are somehow better than their competitors'. The fundamental paradigm that "customers don't buy features; they buy *benefits*" has been lost on many entrepreneurs. Even more precisely, customers buy based on *perceived benefits*. Not only does the entrepreneur need to develop the best set of benefits versus the competition; he must also somehow get the customers to perceive these benefits.

In his article, *Look Before You Leap*, Robert McMath also says that communicating features instead of perceived benefits is "one of the most common mistakes marketers make."[5] He describes a training film in which British comedian John Cleese illustrates how a surgeon might explain a new surgical procedure to a patient lying in a hospital bed:

> "Have I got an operation for you...Only three incisions and an Anderson Slash, a Ridgeway stubble-side fillip, and a standard dormer slip! Only five minutes with a scalpel; only thirty stitches! We can take out up to five pounds of your insides, have you back in your hospital bed in 75 minutes flat, and we can do ten of them in a day."[6]

The surgeon is concerned only with technical features that he as producer (entrepreneur) is excited about. The customer has different concerns. All the customer probably wants to know is whether he'll get better, perhaps what his risks of complication are, and whether he'll be in pain.

Distinctive Competence and Sustainable Competitive Advantage

Differentiation, by itself, is not to ensure success in the marketplace. Successful companies are able to leverage their differentiating attributes into a sustainable competitive advantage, the Holy Grail that most ventures continually pursue. If a way can be found to continually be ahead of competition, then the venture will probably return higher-than-normal returns to its owners. Being ahead of competition means that the venture can easily sell more, and/or charge higher prices, and/or have lower costs than "normal" firms. Let's look at competitive advantage from an entrepreneurial marketer's point of view. As you will see, this point of view is the customer's point of view. Your perceived competitive advantage, related to your competitive price, is why the customer or potential customer will more likely buy your product or service. If you can create competitive advantage that is sustainable from competitive encroachment, you are creating sustainable value.

Distinctive competence is how some people refer to the advantage that is the source of the sustainable competitive advantage. If the advantage is sustainable, then your venture has something that is difficult for your competition to emulate and must be somewhat distinctive to your venture. What are sources of distinctive competence for entrepreneurs that might be sources of sustainable competitive advantage? Creative entrepreneurs seem to be finding new distinctive ways to get customers to prefer them to the competition. Here are some of them:

- Many companies use technology to obtain competitive advantage. Patents and trade secrets are weapons that might keep competition from imitation. For software companies, source code for their products may be a key competitive advantage. Priceline.com has a patent on their method for having consumers try to name their own price for goods and services. This is a source of sustainable competitive advantage.

- Other companies may rely on excellent design, perceived high quality, or continual innovation as distinctive competencies. In its prime, Dell Computers, for example, was able to offer the unique value proposition that it would custom build a computer, exactly as and when a customer ordered it, and deliver it at a competitive price. Dell was able to execute on this because its investment in supply chain and order management systems created a "just in time" system, eliminating the cost of overhead, inventory, and mistakes in calculating demand. However, as other competitors, such as Lenovo and Hewlett Packard, have found alternative low-cost manufacturing and distribution systems, Dell's competitive advantage has been eroded.

- Other businesses use excellent customer service by loyal employees who have adopted corporate service values. Southwest Airlines is a great example of a venture that differentiates itself from competitors with both excellent customer service and technology for scheduling and turning flights around. Many customers fly Southwest, not only because it is economical, but also because it is fun. Other airlines have tried to imitate Southwest and have been unsuccessful.

- Reputations and other differences in customer perception of products, services, and companies can be extremely valuable sources of sustainable advantage. If consumers perceive you as being a preferable source, they will more likely choose your products or service. Industry-leading quality of service has always been a Lexus hallmark. Think about how Lexus focuses on providing a great customer experience. They collect lots of information from each customer and use it the next time the same customer interacts with the company to make her experience even better, from service scheduling, to loaner cars, to doing a good job explaining the work that was done on the vehicle, to completing a quality vehicle inspection process. This is a major reason why Lexus became the top luxury import in 1991 and the number-one luxury car overall in 2000, a title it kept until 2010 when the other two big luxury brands began significant programs to compete with Lexus on service, quality, and innovation. Once the European luxury brands (Mercedes, BMW, and Audi) had achieved parity with Lexus on service, quality, and innovation, they were able to differentiate on brand heritage, which was difficult for Lexus to compete with. Lexus did not continue to differentiate itself on service or quality by upgrading its perception versus the competition. The lesson here is that positioning is not static but needs to be constantly strengthened compared with the competition.

- Diapers.com developed a reputation for amazing customer service by making it their highest priority from the venture's beginning in 2005. Everything they did was targeted toward strengthening their desired positioning—prices similar to Walmart; fast, reliable, free shipping; the broadest selection anywhere; and excellent customer service. In 70% of the United States, if a mom ordered diapers or any other baby stuff from diapers.com by 6:30 p.m., she would receive the shipment the next day. Diapers.com was an innovator in using Kiva robots to semiautomate their warehouse/fulfillment function in order to be able to get such fast fulfillment. Diapers.com and its successor websites were bought by Amazon in 2010 for over $500 million. After Amazon saw how successful the Kiva robots were, Amazon also bought Kiva. Even as a division of Amazon, diapers.com was still getting over 30% of new customers via referrals from existing customers.

  The "secret sauce" to diapers.com and its successor websites—yoyo.com (toys), soap.com (health and beauty aids), beautybar.com (upscale cosmetics), and casa.com (housewares)—was the way they handled customer problems. From the beginning of the company, the "complaint department" was in the corporate offices, right next to the CEO's office. All of the firm's managers had to spend time answering complaints from customers. All of the employees in the department were incented in only one way—to delight the customer at the end of the complaint interaction. They had no constraints—and could do anything they wanted to make sure that the customer's complaint was not only solved, but that the customer was delighted after the interaction.

  Marc Lore, the cofounder and CEO of the company, really understood the power of reputation with young mothers. Every time a customer's complaint was turned to delight, they were very likely to want to share their delight with their friends.

All of these are ways that entrepreneurs search for sustainable competitive advantage. They relate to how customers choose one product or service versus another. Key segmentation and differentiation decisions are intertwined with why customers will choose you versus your competition. These decisions, which feed your unique value proposition, are best made to leverage the distinctive competence of the venture.

Tying Together the Value Proposition: Distinctive Competence, Sustainable Competitive Advantage, and Positioning

Now that we have explored segmentation and differentiation and established their relationship to the strategic concepts of distinctive competence and sustainable competitive advantage, we can return to the unique value proposition. The unique value proposition is the public face that is put on the target market and positioning decisions that were based on the venture's distinctive competence and sustainable competitive advantage. We can now determine the answer to "What am I selling to whom and why will they buy" based on the decisions discussed previously. Be careful, however—these decisions are not easily changed. It typically takes more effort to change a value proposition than to attempt to establish a new one in a vacuum. To change a value proposition is more than changing a slogan. It means undoing a market perception that has been established based on how a venture executes and replacing it with another.

For entrepreneurial companies, deciding on the value proposition—the intertwined positioning, distinctive competence, and sustained competitive advantage decisions—is the most important strategic decision made before beginning a new business or revitalizing an older business. Take the time to do it right. If the market doesn't value *what they perceive to be the distinctive competence of your firm versus the competition* (another way of defining *differentiation*), then the positioning will not be successful. If the positioning is not successful, the value proposition will fail to attract customers. Furthermore, because it is difficult to change perception, the perceived distinctive competence should be sustainable over time. Thus, it is crucial to get the positioning reasonably close to right *before going public the first time*. Figure 1-2 shows the logic of our recommended decision-making process of getting the strategy right before the tactics.

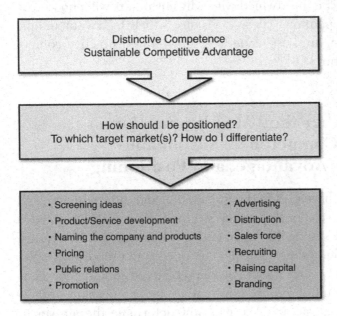

Figure 1-2 Market-driven strategy

By now, this logic should be clear to you. The venture must first assess and creatively identify potential and existing competencies that can be possible sources for sustainable competitive advantage. This assessment needs to be integrated with how the market might perceive the product offerings that may result from the competencies versus how the potential customers might perceive the competition. This assessment needs to be continually re-evaluated as competition and perceptions and consumer needs and wants will change over time. Only after the positioning and the value proposition have been determined, should the tactical marketing elements in the bottom of the figure be decided and executed. Pricing is the only marketing mix decision that should ideally be determined at the same time as the positioning and value proposition. We show in Chapter 3, "Entrepreneurial Pricing: An Often Misused Way to Garner Extraordinary Profits," that pricing is intimately related to and leveraged by the positioning decisions. Customers are willing to pay more for product/ service offerings that are perceived as adding more value than the competition's.

In Chapters 2 and 3, we also explore cost-effective ways of getting market reaction to positioning options before spending a lot of resources.

Victoria's Secret and L Brands—Excellent Integration of Positioning, Segmentation, and Distinctive Competencies[7]

The original Victoria's Secret store and catalog was in Palo Alto, California. In 1982, when L Brands (formerly Limited Brands) founder, Les Wexner, first saw this store, it was very sleazy stuff. However, after seeing the store, Les got the idea to reinvent underwear as lingerie and make underwear emotional—have underwear make you feel good. Les was influenced by how he thought European women viewed underwear much differently than American women. A brilliant idea early on was to use supermodels as part of the public relations (PR) and advertising for Victoria's Secret (VS).

L Brands bought the first VS store for $1 million in 1982. By 1995, they had a catalog, 300 retail stores, and an $800 million business. The catalog was the greatest revenue contributor. In 1995, VS products were perceived by women and men as suited mainly for *Saturday night and special occasions*. In 1995, VS marketers identified an opportunity for a much-expanded positioning for VS—addressing "everyday" needs while maintaining the "special" image. They began the transformation of VS by segmenting by usage occasion. Their first products in the repositioned lines were everyday cotton, but positioned and designed as "sexy." There was a lot of uncertainty in L Brands management about whether it was possible to have women perceive cotton as lingerie. The risk was that cotton underwear might be perceived as comparable to Hanes as opposed to being perceived as sexy lingerie. This was a big communication challenge.

All the elements of the marketing mix needed to be changed to support the new positioning. VS had never advertised before and had only used their catalog as an advertising vehicle. The catalog was low in reach and high in frequency—not suited for getting new people into the brand on a large scale or for changing the perception of the product. Thus, large-scale TV advertising and PR were appropriate, using their successful supermodel icons as part of the repositioning. The supermodels were the embodiment of the emotion of the new VS positioning. The VS supermodel fashion shows on the Internet were extremely effective at reinforcing their positioning. So many people came to their website that they overwhelmed the Internet servers.

In 1995, before the repositioning, VS bras were priced two for $15, and VS was a merchant-driven business. It needed to be made into a fashion business. By 2006, the average price for a VS item had more than doubled, and their revenue had risen by a factor of over four due to the repositioning. One key to the success of the repositioning was that the VS bras were not only sexy, but they were extremely comfortable. The consumer didn't have to compromise between feeling sexy and feeling comfortable. The loyalty levels for VS doubled with the new bras. Increasing loyalty makes the long-term value of a customer larger, thus justifying larger expenses for obtaining new customers—a nice virtuous circle for VS.

The VS stores were an integral element of the repositioning. The in-store experience is designed to be much different from other stores—it is designed to make customers feel special, intimate, and personal. There is much more pampering.

VS has evolved subbrands over time, segmented by lifestyle:

- Provocative—"Very Sexy"
- Romantic—"Angels"
- Girly—"Such a Flirt"
- Clean and simple—"Body by Victoria"
- Younger-flirty-modern—"Pink"

VS has succeeded in doing what Starbucks has also done—changing how people view a commodity—by changing VS into a relatively inexpensive way for women to feel good about themselves. Chapters 2, 3, 6, and 7 go into more depth as to how VS and L Brands were able to use entrepreneurial marketing strategy and tactics to accomplish making VS the crown jewel of L Brands.

Positioning, Names, and Slogans

Many entrepreneurs miss positioning opportunities when they name their products, services, and companies. As we discuss in-depth later, entrepreneurs have limited marketing funds to educate their target markets about the positioning of their products and services. If the names chosen do not themselves connote the appropriate positioning, then entrepreneurs have to spend more funds to educate the market in two ways instead of one. They not only have to get potential customers to recognize and remember their product name, but they must also educate them about the differentiating attributes and benefits of the product that goes with the name. The Please Touch Museum in Philadelphia is a perfect example. Its name tells parents and their children exactly what they can expect. Many new technology and Internet-based ventures have also been very intelligent and creative in their names to connote the appropriate positioning. Companies such as diapers.com ("the best deal on diapers"), Netflix (movie rentals and streaming via the Internet), Salesforce.com (the #1 customer relationship management [CRM] company), and SnapChat (visual conversations) made it easy for potential customers to remember what they do and at least part of their positioning. Although diapers.com may limit customer perception of offerings and allows for minimal expansion beyond diapers, the Netflix name allowed the company to expand from ordering DVDs online and receiving them via the U.S. Postal Service to streaming rental movies and even original content. All of these services clearly connect to the name of the company. On the other hand, all you know just from the Amazon.com name is that it is an Internet company. The fact that it sells a multitude of products via online retail, develops and sells its own consumer electronics, and even offers Internet infrastructure services is not evident from its name. The education of the market needs to be done with other marketing activities.

Some fortunate companies have gone even further by making their names not only support their positioning, but also simultaneously let their potential customers know how to get in touch with them. Examples would be 1-800-FLOWERS, 1-800-DIAPERS, and 1-800-MATTRESS as well as diapers.com and Amazon.com.

Other companies gain leverage by having their product names and company names be the same. Do you know which Fortune 1000 company was named Relational Software? Relational Software's product was named Oracle. To improve market awareness, the company changed their name to Oracle, the name of their popular product. Oracle has become one of the top database software companies in the world. However, the gain in awareness has been a hindrance in diversifying. Oracle is known for its database but, despite large investments and marketing activities, Oracle has been relatively unsuccessful in selling their own application software. Oracle is not perceived as a strong applications software company. Oracle = database.

If the name of the company or product is not enough to position it in the customer's mind, then the next need is for a slogan or byline that succinctly (and hopefully memorably) hammers home the positioning. If the positioning has been done well, then a slogan or byline can in many cases fairly completely communicate the appropriate attributes. One good example is FedEx: "When it absolutely, positively has to get there overnight." The positioning inherent in this byline is a good example of concentrating on only the few, most important attributes to stress in order to position the company. Visa has been using "It's everywhere you want to be" for many years to differentiate itself as a ubiquitous charge card, accepted around the world. On the other hand, Michelin uses "Because so much is riding on your tires" to try to differentiate itself as better on the safety attribute for tire buyers.

Just as brevity and simplicity are valuable in positioning, they are also as valuable in slogans and bylines. The slogan that goes with a company or product name should be one that can be retained for quite a long time, as long as the positioning will be in force. Robert Keidel proposed other ground rules for effective slogans:[8] Avoid clichés, such as "genuine" Chevrolet, Miller, and so on; be consistent; use numbers, but have them backed up; be brief; take a stand; and make it distinctively your own. All of these rules are consistent with our effective positioning paradigm and make good sense.

Hindustan Unilever Limited (formerly Hindustan Lever Limited—HLL) represents an interesting example that illustrates many of the points discussed in this chapter.

Hindustan Unilever Limited: Positioning and Targeting to the Bottom of the Global Pyramid

The positioning should be made like any effective management decision. Develop criteria, generate many decision options (including creative, "out of the box" options), and then evaluate the options on those criteria. The implicit criteria for evaluating positioning decisions are typically related to the long-term and short-term impact on the entity's shareholder value. However, there are also many constraints that may limit the options, such as ethical issues, environmental issues, legal issues, corporate values and culture, and so on. The Hindustan Unilever Limited (HUL) example also illustrates how the positioning decision is deeply intertwined with decisions on how to promote, distribute, and sell the products. C.K. Prahalad in his valuable book, *The Fortune at the Bottom of the Pyramid*, documents the need for the new positioning and how HUL responded to that need with innovative product positioning and marketing mix strategy.

HUL is the largest detergent manufacturer in India, with $2.4 billion in sales in 2001, 40% from soaps and detergents.[9] One constraint that exists on their positioning options is their corporate mission:

> Our purpose at HUL is to meet the everyday needs of people everywhere—to anticipate the aspirations of our consumers and customers and to respond creatively and competitively with branded products and services, which raise the quality of life.

> Our deep roots in local cultures and markets around the world are our unparalleled inheritance and the foundation for our future growth. We will bring our wealth of knowledge and international expertise to the service of local customers.

In their history from 1990 to 2000, HUL had targeted the mass market in India. They developed some distinct competencies that should provide sustainable competitive advantage versus their competition. Products are manufactured in about 100 locations around India and distributed via depots to almost 7,500 distribution centers. HUL reaches all villages with at least 2,000 people. It has a number of innovative programs to involve the rural women in selling and servicing their products.[10] It is difficult for their competition to reach the rural population because of the costs of building the infrastructure and developing products that are appropriate for the rural market.

One of their competencies that they continue to leverage is their ability to introduce and profitably market products that the poorer parts of the society are willing to pay for. Instead of looking at costs first, they look at what the people are willing to pay. This willingness to pay is determined by the perceived value of the product by the potential customers. According to HUL Chairman Manvinder Singh Banga:

> Lifebuoy is priced to be affordable to the masses... Very often in business you find that people do cost-plus pricing. They figure out what their cost is and then they add a margin and figure that's their selling price. What we have learned is that when you deal with mass markets, you can't work like that. You have to start by saying I'm going to offer this benefit, let's say it's germ kill. Let's say it's Lifebuoy. You have to work out what people are going to pay. That's my price. Now what's my target margin? And that gives you your target cost—or a challenge cost. Then you have to deliver a business model that delivers that challenge cost.[11]

Why did HUL decide to use the "germ kill" positioning? They saw a way to fulfill an important unfulfilled need of many consumers. However, they had a number of interacting issues and stakeholders to deal with in order to make the positioning and associated targeting work.

The Unmet Need

Globally, in terms of infectious diseases, only acute respiratory infections and AIDS kill more people than diarrhea, which kills 2.2 million people annually. In India, 19.2% of the children suffer from diarrhea, and India accounts for 30% of all the diarrhea deaths in the world.[12] The solution for this problem is very simple and well known. Washing hands with soap reduced the incidence of diarrhea by 42% to 48% in a number of well-documented research studies.[13] In 2000, the solution was not being used by the masses in India. Only 14% of the mass rural population was using soap and water after defecating and before and after every meal. Sixty-two percent used water plus ash or mud, and 14% used water alone.[14]

There have been a number of attempts to solve this problem globally, but without a lot of success. In India and other developing countries, the problem was seen as too large and costly for a big public health initiative. Additionally, the solution needed to be coordinated among three different government departments—Public Health, Water, and Environment—a daunting task. Because other diseases such as AIDS got most popular attention, there wasn't a champion for diarrhea. Lastly, behavioral change in the diarrhea area is difficult to design and implement. In 2000, HUL was a participant in a public-private partnership for encouraging hand washing. It was a consortium of communities, government, academia, and the private sector and was targeting a pilot in the Indian state of Kerala. However, controversy around the consortium's mission from various community groups hampered its implementation in 2002.

HUL had a long history of marketing 107-year-old Lifebuoy, with a bright red color and a crisp carbolic smell, as "healthy clean." Since the 1960s, they marketed the product using a sports idiom to illustrate healthy clean. Their target market was the Indian male, 18 to 45 years old, with a median income of approximately $47 per month, a semiliterate farmer or construction worker living in a town of 100,000 or less.[15] However, by the late 1980s, competition had also copied the positioning so that health became perceived as the base level of cleaning, and Lifebuoy was not as differentiated. By 2000, in the developed, higher income areas of India (and the world, for that matter), the soap market was saturated and very competitive. Proctor & Gamble and Colgate were world-class competitors for the relatively affluent consumer all over the globe.

Because of this phenomenon, Unilever, the two-thirds majority owner of HUL, as a whole was expecting developing markets to account for approximately 50% of their sales over the next ten years.[16]

If HUL did not have the sales and distribution channels available to deliver the newly positioned Lifebuoy profitably at the price the market dictated, it would not be a good or even feasible strategy. The sales and distribution channel is a unique public/private mix of microcredit lending and rural entrepreneurship that began in 1999. HUL noticed that dozens of agencies were lending microcredit funds to poor women all over India. HUL approached the Andra Pradesh state government in 2000 and asked for clients of a state-run microlending program. The government agreed to a small pilot program that quickly grew. The initiative, now called Project Shakti (strength), has expanded to 12 states, and CARE India, which oversees one of the subcontinent's biggest microcredit programs, has joined with HUL.[17]

The *Wall Street Journal* illustrates the power of this channel by describing the activities and attitudes of one independent microcredit entrepreneur associated with HUL—Mrs. Nandyala:

> When one of Mrs. Nandyala's neighbors, who used a knock-off soap called Lifebuoy that comes in the same red packaging as Unilever's Lifebuoy brand, balked at paying an extra rupee (about two U.S. cents) for the real thing, Mrs. Nandyala gave her a free bar to try. A skin rash caused by the fake soap cleared up after a few days, and the neighbor converted to Lifebuoy.

> When another neighbor asked why she should pay more for Unilever's Wheel detergent than a locally made bar of laundry soap, Mrs. Nandyala asked her to bring a bucket and water and some dirty clothes. "I washed the clothes right in front of her to show her how it worked," she says.

> Project Shakti women aren't Hindustan Lever employees. But the company helps train them and provides local marketing support. In Chervaunnaram, a Hindustan Unilever employee who visits every few months demonstrates before a gathering of 100 people how soap cleans hands better than water alone. Dressed in a hospital-style smock, she rubs two volunteers' hands with white powder, then asks one to wash it off with water alone and the other to use soap. She shines a purple ultraviolet light on their hands, highlighting the specks of white that remained on the woman who skipped the soap. As the crowd chatters, the Hindustan Unilever worker pulls Mrs. Nandyala to the front of the hall, and tells the crowd she has got plenty of soap to sell.

> Mrs. Nandyala wasn't always comfortable with her new, public role. She first applied for a microloan from a government-run agency to buy fertilizer and new tools for her family's small lentil farm four years ago. In 2003, the agency introduced her

to a Hindustan Lever sales director from a nearby town. She took out another $200 loan to buy sachets of soap, toothpaste, and shampoo—but was too shy to peddle them door to door. So a regional Hindustan Lever sales director accompanied Mrs. Nandyala and demonstrated how to pitch the products.

Mrs. Nandyala has repaid her start-up microloan and hasn't needed to take another one. Today, she sells regularly to about 50 homes, and even serves as a mini-wholesaler, stocking tiny shops in outlying villages a short bus ride from her own. She sells about $230 of goods each month, earning about $15 in profit. The rest is used to restock products.[18]

In 2005, 13,000 entrepreneurs like Mrs. Nandyala were selling Unilever's products in 50,000 villages in India's 12 states.[19]

An important reason for the success of this integrated marketing strategy for rural India is the consistency of goals between the private entity (HUL), the government entities, and the NGOs (for example, CARE). Because the Lifebuoy product is positioned and targeted for the socially desirable improved health goal, the other entities are happy to cooperate with HUL. This targeting and positioning is strategically very valuable for HUL. As C.K. Prahalad states:

> Differentiating soap products on the platform of health takes advantage of an opening in the competitive landscape for soap. Providing affordable health soap to the poor achieves product differentiation for a mass-market soap and taps into an opportunity for growth through increased usage. In India, soap is perceived as a beauty product, rather than a preventative health measure. Also, many consumers believe a visual clean is a safe clean, and either don't use soap to wash their hands, use soap infrequently, or use cheaper substitution products that they believe deliver the same benefits. HUL, through its innovative communication campaigns, has been able to link the use of soap to a promise of health as a means of creating behavioral change, and thus has increased sales of its low-cost, mass-market soap. Health is a valuable commodity for the poor and to HUL. By associating Lifebuoy's increased usage with health, HUL can build new habits involving its brand and build loyalty from a group of customers new to

the category. A health benefit also creates a higher perceived value for money, increasing a customer's willingness to pay. By raising consumers' level of understanding about illness prevention, HUL is participating in a program that will have a meaningful impact on the Indian population's well-being and fulfill its corporate purpose to "raise the quality of life.[20]

It is clear that this integrated positioning, targeting, and marketing sales and distribution strategy delivered sustainable competitive advantage for HUL. However, there is one area in which we feel that HUL could have improved the productivity of the whole process—with their newly developed communication channels.

HUL worked with Ogilvy and Mather to develop teams that would visit the villages—targeting the 10,000 villages in nine states where HUL stood to gain the most market share, as well as educate the most needy communities. They spent a lot of effort in designing low-cost ways of communicating with their rural target. HUL grew to 127 two-person teams in 2003 and estimates that the program is reaching 30% to 40% of the rural population in targeted states.[21] Each team went through a four-stage communications plan. Stage 1 is a school and village presentation using an interactive flip chart. At the end of the day, they assign school teachers to work with the students to develop skits and presentations for their next visit in two to three months. Stage 2 is a Lifebuoy village health day, which includes the skits and a health camp in which the village doctor measures height and weight to give "healthy child" awards to those who fall within healthy norms. Stage 3 is a diarrhea management workshop geared toward pregnant women and young mothers who might not be reached by the first two stages. Stage 4 is the formation of the Lifebuoy health club that includes activities on hygiene and keeping the village clean. The two-person team will return four to six more times to run health club activities.

As discussed in more detail in Chapter 6, "Advertising to Build Awareness and Reinforce Messaging," there is a big opportunity for improving productivity of advertising and, in this case, other communications methods, by applying adaptive experimentation. In the HUL case, they assumed that the Ogilvy and Mather-generated communication plan was the best that could be generated, and they rolled it out. However, given that each village or state could be an experimental unit, and given that some other way of efficiently communicating with the targeted rural villagers could have been more effective, there was an opportunity cost of not developing and trying and measuring the impact of other communications methods in different villages as they rolled out the program. Chapter 6 goes into more detail on how this might have been done.

Summary

Each venture must answer the "What am I selling to whom, and why will they buy?" question before it can create a successful marketing strategy and plan. Positioning combines the important elements of segmentation and differentiation. Segmentation selects the subgroup of all consumers to whom you think you can sell your products. Differentiation tries to inform members of the segment of the benefits of using your product or service, vis-à-vis any competitors. The unique value proposition is the public communication of the promise of intrinsic value that customers will receive from your products and services that they won't receive from others. All of these are based on the venture's distinctive competence and sustainable competitive advantage. These important concepts provide the strategic platform on which to build a marketing plan.

This chapter focused on the foundation for the customer-oriented marketing plan, which is the first priority. However, the marketing challenge today expands beyond customers. All of the venture's other stakeholders—such as users, investors, supply chain/channel partners, and employees—care about the customer, but they are also concerned with equity and image of the venture. Each stakeholder needs a relevant value proposition on why to stay engaged with the firm. So the same concepts of segmentation and positioning apply to them.

Endnotes

1. Susan Greco, "Reeling Them In," *Inc. Magazine* (January 1998): 52.
2. Ibid.

3. Some of these segmentation questions come from personal discussions and correspondence with Professor Yoram Wind of The Wharton School, University of Pennsylvania.

4. John Hagel and Arthur G. Armstrong, *Net Gain: Expanding Markets Through Virtual Communities* (Cambridge: Harvard Business School Press, 1997).

5. Robert McMath, "Look Before You Leap," *Entrepreneur*, (April 1998): pp. 135–139.

6. Ibid., 135.

7. This section comes from two interviews done by Leonard Lodish with Jill Beraud, the EVP Marketing of Victoria's Secret from 1995 to 2005 and the EVP/COO Marketing and Chief Marketing Officer of L Brands (formerly Limited Brands) from 2005 to 2008, on July 8, 2004, and April 6, 2005.

8. R.W. Keidel, "Manager's Journal: Say It with a Slogan," *Wall Street Journal*, June 16, 1997, p. A12.

9. C.K. Prahalad, *The Fortune at the Bottom of the Pyramid* (Upper Saddle River: Wharton School Publishing, 2005), 211.

10. Ibid., 213.

11. Ibid., 222.

12. Ibid., 207.

13. Ibid., 209.

14. Ibid., 209.

15. Ibid., 220.

16. Ibid., 214.

17. Cris Prystal, "With Loans, Poor South Asian Women Turn Entrepreneurial," *Wall Street Journal*, May 25, 2005, p. B1.

18. Ibid.

19. Ibid.

20. C.K. Prahalad, *The Fortune at the Bottom of the Pyramid* (Upper Saddle River: Wharton School Publishing, 2005), 229–230.

21. Ibid., 226.

2

Generating, Screening, and Developing Ideas

Idea Generation and Testing at Idealab

At Idealab, a generation of new ideas and companies has turned into a multihundred-million-dollar business. Bill Gross, who had created a number of companies since his early school days, realized that his skills at generating ideas (from speakers, to Lotus Hal and Magellan, to the extremely successful Knowledge Adventure's Jump Start learning series) could be codified and used to incubate many successful companies. Since 1996, almost 500 ideas have been tried, leading to dozens of successful companies, including CitySearch, Overture Services (the creator of the paid search market), and Internet Brands (CarsDirect.com and other Internet services).

The key methodologies used are trend analysis, brainstorming, filtering, and "sense and respond." Let us examine each one. Groups at Idealab regularly discuss large-scale trends in technology and markets. One such analysis led to work in the alternative energy space. At regular intervals, small groups of people (six to ten), including Bill Gross, have brainstorming sessions focused on an area of interest. During these half-day sessions, the first hour is spent discussing the problem area. People are encouraged to generate ideas, with no criticism permitted. The ideas are then grouped into themes, and each theme is pursued for a few minutes. Finally, and key, someone needs to stand up with the passion to take the ideas forward. That is the key first filter in creating a project.

The next filter is a quick market analysis—with the focus on the potential overall size of market. In creating risky ventures, it is often more valuable to have a few percent of a watermelon-sized market, than 100% of a grape-sized one. Big-enough markets create enough opportunity for several companies, reducing one set of risks any new venture faces.

Finally, a small project is started to do a paper or Internet prototype that can be shown to "real" customers to test the product concept. This use of the Internet for concept testing is discussed more fully in the following sections. The results create a feedback loop where reaction to the concept is sensed (measured) and small or large changes are made (response) to hone into what customers will actually buy. This type of adaptive testing is key to successful idea generation, idea screening, and marketing.

Evaluating Specific Venture Ideas

To obtain sales, every product or service idea has to be wanted by some market segment more than competitive products or services. Very simply, if customers won't choose your new product or service over the existing product or service, then you won't make any sales. It is amazing to us that so many entrepreneurs and managers do all kinds of analyses of the costs, patent protection, possible competition, and market potential (if everyone who could use one of my widgets bought one, we would have sales of five billion dollars!). What they don't do is get actual reaction from real customers to the product or service concept. The entrepreneur just doesn't know all of the factors that the end customer will consider when she evaluates the new product or service.

Most entrepreneurs or strategic business unit (SBU) managers have at least one product or service concept in mind when they begin planning new initiatives. This chapter describes some helpful methodologies and concepts, as well as codified entrepreneurial experiences that can help generate and screen new product and service concepts. This chapter then describes cost-efficient methods for getting marketplace and channel participants both to help improve the design and to gauge the potential sales outlook for the idea. The main objective of these methods is to significantly reduce the risk of venture failure or new product offering failure because, as the venture capitalists like to say, "the dogs won't eat the dog food." The old stock market adage of "cut your losses and let your profits run" applies equally well to the development of new ideas. Strong filtering is essential if long-term success is to be achieved. The following section first reviews some very interesting research that helps the entrepreneurial marketer choose a better battlefield to enter if he has the option of choosing different kinds of products or services to consider.

Finding More Receptive Battlefields

Are there better markets for entrepreneurial survival? Are there characteristics of products/markets that make them more likely to be receptive to successful entrepreneurial activity? Are there differences in these characteristics when the new initiative is from a big corporation versus an entrepreneurial venture? When evaluating new opportunities, look for ways to evaluate a large number of opportunities to focus your resources on developing those that have a higher probability of success.

Three European researchers, Hay, Verdin, and Williamson, analyzed 30,000 new U.S. businesses to find characteristics that were more likely to be associated with entrepreneurial ventures that would survive for ten years or more.[1] The researchers developed measures of three groups of characteristics: The first was customer buying patterns, the second was competitors' marketing and channel strategies, and the third was production requirements. They performed a statistical analysis of the relationship of survival rates of independent start-ups and the preceding product/market characteristics. Their main results are summarized in Figure 2-1,[2] which shows hostile and fertile product/market segments for independent start-ups.

Source: Hay, Verdin, and Williamson, "Successful New Ventures: Lessons for Entrepreneurs and Investors," *Long Range Planning* 26 (5), 1993, 31-41

Figure 2-1 The impact of product and market characteristics on the survival of independent start-ups

The data showed that entrepreneurial start-ups had significantly better chances of survival in two product/market segment types: those that had *high service requirements* and those that had *low purchase frequency*. The high service requirements results imply that the greater attention to customer needs and flexibility an entrepreneurial start-up can offer can give it an advantage over less-attentive established vendors for that product/market segment.

The results that product/market segments that made infrequent purchase decisions are also more fertile are consistent with other theories of business-to-business marketing. Infrequent purchases typically involve the customer reassessing the attributes of product or service offerings. In this circumstance, there is a higher likelihood of attending to new information and possibly trying a new alternative product offering.

The figure also shows four product/market characteristics that an entrepreneur should avoid, all other factors being equal. Those segments that require high employee skill and made-to-order supply are harder for entrepreneurs to succeed in. These segments may require extensive employee training and big investments in production assets—both luxuries that are difficult for a new entrepreneur to supply. The other two entrepreneurially hostile segment characteristics make it very difficult for the small player to target the segment effectively. Both highly fragmented customer bases and high-end customer dependence on channels make it relatively more difficult for the entrepreneurial marketer to reach her target customers. Of course, the Internet makes it easier to reach fragmented customer bases because geography no longer plays a role, but even on the Internet, if the base is too fragmented, the cost of customer acquisition may rise to unprofitable levels.

For corporate intrapraneurs, those who work in large corporations pursuing new ventures, Hay, Verdin, and Williamson also report the product market segment types that were hostile and fertile for corporate ventures. The results are summarized in Figure 2-2.[3]

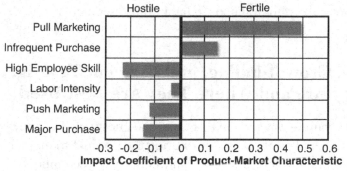

Source: Hay, Verdin, and Williamson, "Successful New Ventures: Lessons for Entrepreneurs and Investors." *Long Range Planning* 26 (5), 1993, 31-41

Figure 2-2 The impact of product and market characteristics on the survival of corporate ventures

The only segment characteristic common to higher likelihood of survival for both corporate and independent ventures is *infrequent purchase.* Segments in which a customer is more likely to be receptive to new information are evidently fertile, regardless of the assets that the new venture brings to them. Segments that require high employee skill are also hostile to both independent and corporate entrepreneurs. Evidently, high employee skill is a barrier to entry of established competitors, regardless of whether the new entry is corporate or independent.

The other characteristics differentiate those segments that corporate resources can impact. *Pull marketing* requires resources for mass marketing and may also leverage the reputation of a corporate parent.

Corporate subsidiaries seem to be at a disadvantage when infrastructure to support *push marketing* is required by the segment. Perhaps long periods of experience are necessary to set up effective networks. This experience with the push marketing infrastructure can be an effective barrier to entry.

Even though these results can help an entrepreneur or corporate subsidiary to choose a more receptive product/market to enter, keep in mind that all of the positive and negative characteristics are only effective on the average. Certainly, not every entrepreneurial venture that attacks segments with the fertile characteristics will be successful. The results just show that the entrepreneur or corporate subsidiary will be more likely not to fail or to fail in those segments.

Dry Tests, Crowdfunding, and Concept Testing: What They Are and Where They Are Best Used

The most accurate way for you to answer the question, "Do I have the right offering and positioning?" is to bring the product to market. If many customers buy your offering—and better yet, recommend it to others—you have achieved your marketing objectives. However, spending the money to get to this point, the marketing "Hail Mary pass," is not a wise use of resources. We recommend using adaptive testing to try options before committing to one. This ensures that you are committing scarce resources in the best way possible. Adaptive testing can be used in all aspects of marketing and marketing tactics. There are many ways and approaches to testing, and we share methods and examples of the most efficient and effective tests.

Getting Customers to Part with Money: The Real Tests of Value

Although screening may help you choose which opportunities to pursue, continued testing helps navigate toward success in the market. The best way to reduce the risk of the market not buying your product is to sell the product in advance of production. A *dry test* is one in which an order is asked for and typically a credit card number is obtained for a new product or service. Once the order is obtained, the buyer is then told that the product won't be ready for a while, and the credit card is not charged. The buyer is then typically offered some premium to thank them for their confidence. Typically, it is a charter discount on the new product when it is available.

For products that will be sold or promoted with the Internet as a primary marketing tool, you may perform a dry test directly on the Internet. In fact, depending on your ethics, it is very feasible to "dummy up" online ads and/or product descriptions, and *actually ask for the order online.* When respondents start the order process, you then can explain to them that the product is in development and that you were testing marketplace reaction. You could then send them some kind of a gift as a token of thanks and apology and put their name on a list of those who will get the first chance to buy the product when it's ready. This dry test, as direct marketers call it, is the most valid way of getting real consumer demand for a new product or service. The Internet is not the only place dry tests are used. Direct response marketers have been using dry tests for years. Depending on which media vehicles they use for advertising, they have to consider prematurely letting their competitors know their new product plans. Dry tests with direct mail are much easier to hide than dry tests in radio, TV, or print.

Crowdfunding is a relatively new innovation that the entrepreneurial marketer may use to conduct dry tests. Entrepreneurs may use platforms such as Kickstarter or Indiegogo to sell products in advance of production. The platform accepts the money in advance for the new products but will only release the funds to the venture after certain goals have been achieved. A successful crowdfunding initiative is an excellent way to reduce the risk of many ventures. Crowdfunding also may be used to test many aspects of the offering, positioning, and marketing and has emerged as one of the most cost-efficient means to perform valuable marketing research. In Chapters 4, 10 and 12, we discuss more about how crowdfunding can be used in marketing and finance.

Victoria's Secret Uses Their Stores as Test Beds for New Products and Brands

As discussed in Chapters 1 and 4, "Marketing-Driven Strategy to Make Extraordinary Money" and "Leverage Public Relations for Maximum Value," respectively, an important competitive advantage of Victoria's Secret (VS) is that they own their own stores. Not only are there ongoing strategic advantages of this, such as controlling the user experience in the store and the product's display, but another strategic advantage is that not all stores need to have the same product line. It is conceptually very easy to choose some representative stores and use them to get real consumer reaction to potential new lines or new display strategies for old lines. Recently, VS did a consumer segmentation study of current and potential customers. The study showed a need for a younger line for a more casual lifestyle. The VS brand Pink is aimed at filling this need. In each VS store that sells Pink (now all of them), there is a separate "Pink" room and environment. The Pink line was first introduced in only 10 stores chosen to be representative. The product-offering bundle was then modified to reflect the consumer feedback and the sales trends that these test stores exhibited. The line was then rolled out to 30 stores, modified again based on customer feedback, then rolled out to 100 stores, modified again, and then rolled out to all stores. Compared with dry testing or testing via crowdfunding with a small sample of consumers, this "real" test marketing is an extremely valid, reliable way of evaluating and launching a new product. Pink became a $500 million revenue product line in less than two years!

If a company that owns its own end-user distribution is not using the sites as possible test beds, the company may be wasting one big asset that can strategically keep them ahead of their competition. VS competition that sells through department stores will have a much riskier proposition trying to evaluate and roll out new product lines. They won't be able to use the very valid, reliable testing methodology that VS used. Given the large investment that is required to develop owned-store distribution, it makes sense to leverage this investment in all profitable ways. Testing new products and product lines is almost always a productive use of the company-owned distribution channels.

Testing Purchase Intention: The Concept Test

If you cannot realistically perform dry tests or secure orders via crowdfunding to determine whether customers will buy your product, then the next most valid information to obtain is *purchase intention*. Purchase intention is an indication of how likely the respondent would be to buy the product after he is exposed to the concept. The *concept test* is a valuable tool for the entrepreneurial marketer to test purchase intention. Concept testing checks whether the prospective purchaser and/or user of a new product-offering bundle understands the offering, feels that it answers a need, and would be willing to purchase and/or use it. The technique can also help to improve the product-offering bundle by understanding problems and/or improvement opportunities that are perceived by the potential consumers. Its primary purpose is to estimate customer and/or intermediary reactions to a product-offering bundle concept before committing substantial resources to it.

Concept testing forces the entrepreneur to expose the idea to the people who will have to receive perceived benefits from it and to make sure that these people indeed do perceive the benefits. If done well, concept testing and associated procedures can provide a number of important benefits to the entrepreneur:

- First, concept testing can identify likely product failures and limit the amount of resources spent on ideas that the market does not perceive as helpful.

- Second, concept testing can separate the good ideas from the poor ones and support resource allocation to those ideas that the market does want.

- Third, the concept-testing procedure can supply suggestions for improving the product-offering bundle to make it be perceived as more useful to the market participants.

- Fourth, as you will see in Chapter 3, "Entrepreneurial Pricing—An Often Misused Way to Garner Extraordinary Profits," concept testing can also be used to generate rough price-sales volume demand curves for new product-offering bundles. Well-designed and executed concept testing can provide estimates of how the demand for a product will change at alternative price levels.

Concept testing is best at estimating consumers' reactions to the product-offering bundle *before* they actually would use it; it is okay for estimating the trial of a new product or service, but obviously not very effective at estimating repeat purchase for goods that are bought more than once. The experience with the physical product or service bundle and whether it delivers on its implied promise will be the most important determinant of whether the customer purchases the product again. Thus, concept testing will be more useful for estimating trial rates for frequently purchased products and potential sales for consumer durable products as well as business-to-business durable products. However, even for durable products and business-to-business products, if the initial customers are not satisfied, then they will tell other potential customers that the product is bad if they are logistically able to do that. Word of mouth can be the biggest help and also the biggest hindrance for entrepreneurs, depending on whether the initial users are satisfied that the product meets their expectations. You should keep in mind that concept testing can only help estimate revenue *assuming that the product meets the customer expectations* when the customers actually use the product or service.

Given the preceding caveats, concept testing can be a productive addition to the entrepreneurial marketer's "bag of tricks." It can be done relatively quickly at a fairly low cost. It is also a flexible technique. A number of ideas can be handled in a single study, as well as the evaluation of different versions of the same basic product-offering bundle. From a cost-benefit viewpoint, concept testing is usually a great value. Not enough managers or entrepreneurs use concept testing in relation to its value. Hopefully, this chapter will help rectify the situation. The next section discusses some "nuts and bolts" of actually doing concept testing and then discusses what concept testing doesn't do—that is, some of its limitations.

How to Do Concept Testing—the "Nuts and Bolts"

If your positioning planning is complete as discussed in Chapter 1, then you have much of the information required to perform a concept test. You have a strong sense of the segment that represents the greatest potential perceived benefit for your product, and you know best how to differentiate your offering vis-à-vis competitive offerings. To use concept testing productively, the following issues are important:

1. What should be in the concept statement?
2. Who should be exposed to the concept?
3. What kind of information specifically should be collected from respondents?
4. What are the best modes of data collection?
5. How should the questions be asked?

The following sections answer each of the preceding questions in the order asked.

What Should Be in the Concept Statement?

The concept statement presents the product-offering bundle to the respondent for reaction. It should as closely and realistically as possible mimic how the respondent would be exposed to the product and its attributes when the product is actually introduced. Most concept statements look like product brochures, print ads, or web pages describing the product or service. The concept statement typically also includes where the respondent could expect to buy the product or service and all the benefits that are part of the positioning plan. The price of the product is also one of the attributes that should be an integral part of the concept statement. Figure 2-3 shows a concept statement for one product from a new novelty diaper line that has university and sports team logos on them. To be realistic, the concept test should be done in each of the possible target market segments with the specific logo for that segment as part of the concept description. One of the possible market segments was alumni of the University of Pennsylvania. The concept is slightly disguised to protect confidentiality.

Figure 2-3 Logo diaper concept statement (slightly disguised)

Product Concept: Futurewear is a line of designer diapers that feature university and professional sports team logos. One of the diapers has the University of Pennsylvania "Penn Quaker" logo, both on the tape and bottom ("tush") of the diaper. This diaper is made of premium materials and is functionally equivalent to a good disposable diaper. It is a fun, novelty item, which will typically be purchased as a gift (for example, baby shower, Christmas) rather than as an everyday item by parents. The diapers will be white, will be packaged in a very nice gift box of 19 that also has the Penn Quaker logo, and will be priced at $11.95. The diaper will be available at most stores that have other University of Pennsylvania logo merchandise, as well as online stores that sell baby merchandise. What a nice, fun, way to help a loyal Penn alumnus start his or her child showing their support of Penn! The perfect gift for anyone who is a Penn supporter!

Who Should Be Exposed to the Concept?

If your segmentation planning is complete (see Chapter 1), then it is obvious that you should expose the decision-making members and decision influencers of the target segments to the concept. In concept testing, it usually pays to be inclusive with possible target segments. If you are doubtful about a target segment, it makes sense to concept test some members to help decide whether to include the segment in your plans. The cost of concept testing is typically small compared to the foregone profits of missing a possible segment.

For business-to-business products and some complex and/or expensive consumer products, the entrepreneurial marketer must be careful to interview all of the possible influencers of the purchase decision. For example, if the firm is considering introducing a new angiography product to hospitals, the entrepreneurial marketer should interview not only the physicians who would use the product, but also the hospital administrators who would need to approve the purchase, as well as nurses who might influence how the product is to be used. For high-involvement consumer purchases like appliances, computers, telecommunications equipment, and so on, there may be many possible decision influencers who need to be tested. For example, for computers and telecommunications equipment, many consumers turn to "experts" whose opinions they request before they make purchase decisions. It is very important for the entrepreneurial marketer to seek out and interview these experts.

If the entrepreneurial marketer does not know the decision process in her target markets well enough, before performing the concept testing, it makes sense to do some qualitative questioning of market participants to find out how these types of decisions are typically made. Questions such as "Would you consult anyone else before making a purchase decision?" or "Who else would have to approve this decision?" can be very enlightening.

Chapter 7, "Distribution/Channel Decisions to Solidify Sustainable Competitive Advantage," discusses concept testing being as important for channel members as it is for the end purchasers. However, concept testing with channel members *is no substitute* for getting systematic end-user reaction to a product. In his book, *The Silicon Valley Way*, Elton Sherwin Jr. describes a disguised, but real, company, The Palo Alto PC Company, which neglected to concept test the end purchaser and solely relied on the results from the distribution channels.[4] This company had been successfully designing and building small, good-looking, premium-priced notebook PCs and selling them through a strong network of distributors.

As Palo Alto PC began designing their fourth generation notebook, they did a cursory survey of their largest distributors. They assumed, and their distributors confirmed, that "customers want it even smaller."

The new Palo Alto PC was a hit with the media. Its innovative keyboard made it both small and cute. Unfortunately, few customers bought it. Sales plummeted. It turns out that executives wanted longer battery life, brighter screens, and thinner PCs—but not smaller keyboards.[5]

Distributors are very good at reacting to the aspects of the product that affect how well they will "push" them—the markup, the terms, the logistics, the end-user marketing program, and so on. They also can sometimes tell you what *they think* their customers will want. However, as this example points out, there is typically no substitute for getting end-user reaction to concepts.

What Kind of Information Specifically Should Be Collected from Respondents?

The most important element of concept testing is assessment of purchase intention. The best way to determine purchase intent is to present the respondent with the concept statement and ask her to rate her purchase intention. The usual scale that is used to rate purchase intention is the following:

| definitely would buy | probably would buy | might or might not buy | probably would not buy | definitely would not buy |

It is risky to interpret purchase intentions absolutely, especially any answer except "definitely would buy." The exposure of the concept will typically sensitize the respondent to the product concept and may bias them to tell the perceived source of the concept test what they feel the concept tester wants to hear. People want to "be nice." The purchase intent question also implicitly assumes that the respondent has been exposed to the product, has understood the attributes of the product, and is able to find the product available in the channel that the respondent would use to buy the product.

It is critical to ask purchase intent early (first) in the concept testing process in order to avoid bias introduced by questions about product attributes, preferences, or even demographic information. These questions may follow the purchase intention question and allow the entrepreneurial marketer to explore the underlying reasons, both positive and negative, for the respondent's purchase intention response.

What Are the Best Modes of Data Collection?

The entrepreneur wants to have the respondent exposed to the concept in a manner as close as possible to how they would be exposed in reality. There are limits and trade-offs of costs versus validity of the concept test results. If you would use a web page, print ad, or direct mail piece to introduce your product, it is not very expensive to "dummy up" some sample ads as part of the concept statement and then expose people to those ads. These kinds of concepts are most validly exposed through personal interviews with the respondent either at her home or at her place of work. Depending on the segmentation targets, it sometimes is cheaper and not less valid to use centralized locations like malls. Telephone interviews can be very cost effective for concepts that are easily understood over the phone and may be advertised on radio when they are introduced. Sometimes mailing, e-mailing, or creating an online version of the concept statement can be combined with telephone interviews. These combinations can be cost-effective and for many products and services do not lose much validity compared with in-person interviews.

It is usually cost-effective to contract with a local market research firm to actually field the concept test. They have much experience in getting with the right people and can help with the actual test design. However, if the firm tells you to do something that contradicts the major points in this chapter, then you should change suppliers. Depending on your time versus resource constraints, it may be possible to use students at nearby universities who are studying market research. If they use your product as a class project, it may take two or three months to get results. Commercial firms can turn around some concept tests in a few weeks. Best of all, online concept tests can yield results within hours or days of deployment.

How Should the Questions Be Asked?

Concept testing for entrepreneurial marketing situations typically involves either *monadic* testing (a person gets exposed to only one concept) or *paired comparison* testing (a person is exposed to a pair of concepts).

Monadic testing should be used when you seek a detailed, uncontaminated reaction to a concept. It is typically better to monadic test when direct competitors are hard to identify. Monadic tests also work better when there is little external search for alternatives prior to purchasing.

On the other hand, when there are direct competitors already in the market, it can be useful to also do a *paired comparison* evaluation of the new product versus others. If there's enough time, the paired comparison can be done after the monadic evaluation. The paired comparison purchase intent can be asked as, "Which would you prefer to purchase, Product A or Product B?" Here, also, a scale can be used, just as it was in the monadic purchase intent:

definitely prefer A | moderately prefer A | toss-up | moderately prefer B | definitely prefer B

As discussed previously, this comparison evaluation helps to ground revenue predictions in what you know about existing products. For example, if your new entrepreneurial product is preferred by 20% more people than existing Product A, you know that its potential is to sell even better than Product A. This is only a *potential*, however. The preceding caveats on any purchase intent measure are also salient here—for example, awareness, understanding the product benefits, and finding the product in distribution.

Best Practices and Uses for Concept Testing

Over the years, we have found many ways to improve the information gathered from concept testing and improve the accuracy of results.

Concept Screening

Getting reactions of potential purchase influencers can be helpful, not only after one product concept has been determined, but also to help *screen* candidate product ideas before much work or resources have been spent on them. For this screening application, *card sorting and evaluation* is sometimes cost effective. Simply give the respondent several product descriptions, each on a card or a separate sheet. The respondent can sort them into a rank order and can rate each idea on either a semantic (for example, excellent, good, fair, poor) or numeric scale.

Avoiding the "Nice Bias"

Concept testing may lead respondents to tell the marketer what she wants to hear in order to "be nice." To counteract the "be nice" bias, it's best to include somewhere in the concept test a comparison of the new product with some existing product it might replace. Equivalently, some respondents can respond to a concept that describes the existing product in the same form as the new product. The purchase intent scores on the existing product can then be a base from which to compare the intent scores on the new product. For example, if product A is an existing product and product B is the new product, both products would be described by a concept statement (as discussed later in the chapter), and purchase intent would be collected for both products. The fraction who "definitely would buy" can be compared for A and B. If B has 20% more intent to "definitely buy," then it is reasonable to assume that if consumers are aware of product B, understand its attributes, and can find it distributed, then B could reasonably sell 20% more than A. In fact, this leads us to one of the most valuable uses of concept testing: forecasting trials.

Forecasting Trial

Some researchers who have performed a number of concept tests and have seen the real-world consumer trial of the tested products have developed a formula for predicted trial from the concept test intent. They will take 70% of the "top box" (definitely would buy) purchase intent and add it to 20% of the second box (probably would buy) to estimate the fraction of the market that would buy subject to three reduction factors.

To counteract the other awareness and distribution limitations, you should multiply the fraction of the market that the concept test says would buy by at least three estimated reduction factors, all fractions less than one. The first factor, f1, is the fraction of the target population(s) that will be aware of the new product. This will depend on how successful the marketing plan is for the product. The second factor, f2, is whether those who are aware will understand and perceive the attributes and benefits of the product as well as those who were exposed to the concept in the concept test. This reduction factor, f2, also depends on the success of the marketing plan. Finally, the third factor, f3, reflects the odds that members of the target market(s) will be able to easily purchase the product where they would expect to find it. Multiplying the concept test purchase intent fraction by f1 × f2 × f3 will reduce the purchase intent number to one that is much more reasonable and more predictable of in-market performance.

Follow-Up Questioning

Other questions that might be asked can aid in both improving the actual product and the way it is described to potential consumers. These other questions should be asked *after* the purchase intent question. The purchase intent question is meant to measure the attraction of a concept after the potential customer has been exposed to the concept, not after the potential customer has been asked a lot of questions about the concept, which normally heightens their interest in the concept.

Questions about how well the potential consumer understood the concept and what they liked and didn't like about the product are usually helpful. The "likes and dislikes" can be useful in improving either the product or the way the product is communicated. The respondents should be able to "play back" the product's attributes and benefits, as they perceived them after having been exposed to the concept statement. The respondents could also answer questions about how interested they are in the product—extremely interested, somewhat interested, and so on. If lots of respondents are "extremely interested," but relatively few express high purchase intent, then perhaps the price used in the concept test was too high.

Depending on the product and its target market, other questions can be asked such as situations for which the respondent sees the product as useful or problems the product might solve. If the respondent can tell which products the new product might replace, this is also helpful. Answers to these questions can be valuable for improving the marketing materials for the product's introduction.

Price Testing

Some people put price response questions right into the concept test by asking *the same person* purchase intent questions *at different price levels in the same concept test*—for example, "How likely would you be to purchase the product if it were $140, $130, $120, or $100?" The respondent would give a separate response for each alternative price level. *This procedure is extremely biasing and should be avoided.* The respondent assumes that she is "negotiating" with the concept tester and gives biased results that are not usually indicative of how the respondent would actually react if she were exposed to the product at different price levels.

A better way to include price response in a concept test is to include *one price* as part of the product's description. *Each respondent* is exposed to only one price as a descriptor of the product. However, *each respondent* can be exposed to *different prices* than other respondents. As you'll see in Chapter 3, price is a psychological attribute and can have a big impact on how potential consumers perceive a product or service. This procedure ensures that the potential consumer only sees one price, the same way the person will see the product in the real market.

Using Crowdfunding for Concept Testing

Many times, the reactions of consumers to concepts are biased by their inability to really understand what would be offered. The Internet allows for certain concepts to be tested in a live manner, with direct validation or refutation of the basic concept. In the past few years, Kickstarter and Indiegogo have allowed entrepreneurs and companies to do this concept testing and get at price sensitivity as well.

Idealab had built a $1,500 3D printer called the Desktop Factory in 2004, and the company was sold to 3DSystems (a public company) within two years. In late 2012, it was clear that 3D printing trends were accelerating, but there was still no low-cost solution that could get to a mass market. Working with an engineer, they developed a concept for a $249 retail priced 3D printer, which would compete on features with the $1,500 MakerBot. In a few weeks, they started an Indiegogo campaign for the New Matter Mod-t (a takeoff on Ford's first mass market vehicle). Users could sign up to purchase the printer when it would come out the following spring. The first users were given a $249 price, with special packages to give 11 Mod-t's to a school for $2,490. Slightly later users saw a $299 price, and ultimately, as demand grew, the price was raised to $349, without any slowdown in volume. Everyone understood that the product was not yet in production, even though a video showed a very early prototype operating.

Once it was clear that users really did want a printer at this price point, a lot more money was put into engineering and building the product, and its associated design market website. The Indiegogo campaign not only generated thousands of orders and good information about pricing, it also attracted volume buyers. One of the nation's largest retailers called to see if they could order 20,000 units for Christmas sales. This further validated the concept and showed that enough units could be sold to justify better tooling that would lower the cost of the units even more than first anticipated.

Caveats for Concept Testing

Even though concept testing is typically very valuable in terms of cost/benefits for you, it has a number of limitations that you constantly must keep in mind:

1. As discussed previously, if the product or service does not deliver the benefits promised in the concept, the revenue predictions will never happen. The more costly, risky, and high involvement the product is, the more important is the experience of the innovator and early adopter users. If this experience is

worse than the benefits expectation of the concept test and the expectations of these "lead users" based upon the introductory sales and marketing material, then the product will be severely penalized.

2. Changes in the product between the concept test and the product's introduction will cause possible changes in consumer reactions.

3. Sometimes research and development (R&D) and production cannot execute the product exactly as promised in the concept test. This may lead to the same problems as discussed in #1.

4. If the concept has not been tested in a realistic way, respondents may overstate their preferences in order to "be nice" to the interviewer. It is human nature to tell someone what you think he would like to hear. Thus, respondents may say they like the product but not buy it when it actually comes on the market.

5. Concept testing can only predict initial purchase. It cannot predict how many people will use the product regularly or how many will repeat purchase it. For repetitively purchased products, high trial rate alone does not guarantee success.

Trakus: The Value of Concept Testing

Trakus, Inc., was founded by a Massachusetts Institute of Technology (MIT) MBA, Eric Spitz, and two high-tech MIT undergraduates. The company was originally named Retailing Insights to reflect their initial product concept. They were going to do Videocart right using the latest technology. Videocart was a computerized shopping cart that was developed and introduced in the early 1990s. The cart would know where it was in a store and let the shopper know about specials and other useful information that depended on the cart's location in the store. So if a shopper was in the cereal aisle, the screen on the cart would show the cereal specials for the day. The cart could also show advertisements for cereals when the cart was in the cereal aisle. To keep shoppers' attention, the cart had a number of useful consumer functions. These functions included locating items in the store, getting a number for the meat or deli line remotely and being paged when your number is ready, providing recipes and store location for all of the recipe's items, getting local news, and so on.

The original Videocart venture failed because of poor execution. The carts were not recharged or repaired on a timely basis. Thus, when a consumer went to take one, the odds were that the cart would not function well. Word of mouth among consumers and the early store sites became negative, so no new stores wanted to utilize the carts. From a public market value at one time over $300 million, Videocart, Inc., failed and declared bankruptcy in the mid-1990s.

Eric's team was going to do Videocart right using all the new technology. Instead of FM transmitters for location in the store, they had developed an indoor version of the GPS global positioning system to use. They would be able to identify the shopper's frequent shopper card or name and pull information from the Internet. Thus, the shopper could enter her shopping list at home and it would be available electronically at the store. The carts would be of value to store operators because they would get more customers to patronize their store. The retailers would also be able to sell promotion opportunities on the cart to the manufacturers just as they did in their weekly circulars. This was a significant profit opportunity for the retailers. To advertisers, the computerized shopping cart was the perfect opportunity to reach the consumer at the most important point—just as they were making their actual purchasing decision. The new Videocart was going to be much cheaper than the original because of the lower costs of new technology. On paper, the venture looked terrific. Eric obtained $50,000 seed money from an angel investor. The angel investor requested that before the team spend any money on product development, they concept test the idea to both of the customer groups that would need to buy off on the idea. These were the retailers who needed to subsidize putting the carts in the stores in return for promotional funds they would receive and the advertisers who were to pay for advertising on the carts.

The team developed a compelling description of the new generation Videocart, which included all of the benefits that either the retailer or manufacturer would obtain. They even had a neat simulation of how the system would work and what the cart's screen would look like that they put on their laptops. They then showed this to retailers and manufacturers, and at a given price, asked how likely they would be to buy their role on the carts. After asking the purchase intent question, they also asked a number of questions about what manufacturers and retailers liked and what they disliked about the cart concept. The answers the team received were not very encouraging. For retailers, the cart's previous bad reputation was a big barrier. Retailers were apprehensive to try another version of a product that had a terrible reputation. This implied that the team would have to establish extensive beta sites (at the venture's expense) to prove over a long term that the carts would work and would provide the benefits the team anticipated. Not only that, but retailers were also very frugal and were reticent to commit their own funds to investing even partially in the carts. The retailers were used to having manufacturers pay for most new innovations as a way of getting or improving their shelf space and in-store position.

For the manufacturers, they were only willing to pay for advertising on the carts if the carts would demonstrate that they actually had an incremental effect on the manufacturer's sales in the stores. Not only that, but manufacturers also required significant scale to justify their infrastructure to support the new advertising medium. That meant that Eric's team would have to be in a significant fraction of all of the U.S. supermarkets before the manufacturers would begin to commit significant advertising and promotion funds to the medium. It did not take much rough calculating to determine that the cash investment required to reach a break-even (if a break-even were at all possible) would be huge. The probability of convincing venture capital or angel sources to invest that kind of money was very low. Eric's team was discouraged for a couple of days by the results. However, they had most of their angel's seed money left and lots of technical skills in the areas of GPS location, communications, and digital signal processing. After the bad concept-testing results sunk in, the team had a brainstorming session where they generated and evaluated a number of product ideas that would leverage their distinctive competence as they viewed it.

The outcome of that brainstorming session took the team in a very different but much more profitable direction. Eric, a sports nut, conceptualized a product concept that the rest of the team said could be accomplished technically. They put little rugged transmitters on athletes (in their helmets or on their clothes) and put receiving antennas in a few places in the stadium. They could then determine in real time, digitally, where every athlete on a team is located, record it, process that data to generate new valuable statistics, and display the information virtually immediately. The information would include speed and acceleration of each player and real-time location of each player. If you know the weight of two players and their acceleration the instant they collide, you can easily calculate a "hit" gauge. This hit gauge would be a valuable addition to the broadcasting of football or hockey. The broadcaster could also analyze any plays by showing the digital picture of the replay and associated speed and acceleration statistics and processing the digital data to illustrate good or poor performance of some players. The digital, real-time data and information would also be perfect for "broadcasting" the games over the Internet.

The team concept tested this idea similarly to the way they had potential customers evaluate the Videocart. They developed a simulation of what the system might look like and presented it to members of potential market segments that might be interested in the system. They also changed their name to Trakus, Inc., to reflect their new orientation. The segmentation and decision process that would be used by each segment was much more complicated for the new Trakus sports product. There were teams, leagues, players associations, coaches (who could use the system for training), advertisers, agents, Internet sports companies, and so on who all could contribute to or influence Trakus' market reception and potential revenue. Before they exposed the concept to all of these market participants, they applied for patents on their ideas to give them some protection after they exposed them to the market.

In contrast to the lukewarm reception they received for Videocart, the Trakus concept "rolled the socks up and down" of almost all the people they interviewed. The biggest concern anyone expressed was whether the team could actually develop the product and have it work reliably. They didn't interview the sports league officials, however. They found out after going through development of the technology that the sports leagues would not let an outside firm make enough money from the technology to make the venture succeed.

Therefore, Trakus found another niche using their technology to track horses for electronic transmission to pari-mutuel betting parlors around the world. This technology uniquely lets betters "watch" a race digitally in real time and track the horse they have bet on. The existing video technology that Trakus was replacing could only show some of the horses, but not all at the same time.

If the Trakus team had not concept tested their original Videocart idea and had gone ahead to develop and implement that concept, it is not certain that they would have failed. However, given their concept-testing results, the odds of having a huge success were low. On the other hand, the concept-testing results were used the way they should have been used—to screen an idea before a lot of resources were spent on it. The concept testing caused the team to "go back to the drawing board" and generate other product ideas that could best leverage their unique skills and abilities.

The team deserves a lot of credit for interpreting the concept-testing results in a rational manner. Human nature goes against rational interpretation of valuable, but negative, information. When the team had organized itself and made its mission to "do Videocart right," it was difficult emotionally to receive and rationally process information that said that the market did not want a new Videocart nearly as much as the team thought they did. The U.S. culture seems to reinforce these emotional reactions to negative, but valuable, information. It is not seen as "macho" to decide to give up on an idea, admit you were wrong, and go on to make the best of what you have left. Especially in an entrepreneurial venture that is typically started with the product/ service idea as the main motivation for the team to get together, it is difficult to admit that the initial idea may not be as profitable as the team first thought.

Summary

Dry tests and crowdfunding allow the entrepreneurial marketer to test samples of customers to answer the most important question: Will they buy your offering? This testing is valuable because it answers this question before you spend the time and resources to develop, produce, and introduce it. However, when you cannot test in this manner, evaluating purchase intention is the next best thing. Concept testing really amounts to getting systematic direct reactions of market and channel participants to your product/service concept. Historically, concept testing has been able to predict product trial rates within a 20% range, about 80% of the time for frequently purchased packaged goods. For example, if the predicted trial was 50%, the product trial rate would be between 40% and 60% in eight out of ten cases. However, even today, most packaged goods firms do qualitative focused groups rather than systematic concept testing for their new product screening and evaluation. Entrepreneurial firms do not have the luxury of using less than the most cost-effective methods.

The details of exactly how and who should be concept tested are not nearly as important as *just doing it!* The most important thing is to get direct reaction, including some measure of purchase intent from members of your target markets. If you don't do that, you *significantly increase your odds of failure* for your new venture.

As an added bonus, concept testing can be combined with price testing to help maximize the profit contribution of the new product. The next chapter explores this topic.

Endnotes

1. Michael Hay, Paul Verdin, and Peter J. Williamson, "Successful New Ventures: Lessons for Entrepreneurs and Investors," *Long Range Planning* 26, no. 5 (1993): 31–41.

2. Ibid., 36.

3. Ibid., 38.

4. Elton B. Sherwin, Jr., *The Silicon Valley Way* (Rocklin, CA: Prima Publishing, 1998), 63.

5. Ibid.

3

Entrepreneurial Pricing: An Often-Misused Way to Garner Extraordinary Profits

Determining Price at Warby Parker

Neil Blumenthal, CEO and cofounder of Warby Parker, likes to tell the story of how his pricing was determined. When he was still an MBA student at Wharton, he presented his original pitch deck to Professor Jagmohan Raju, a pricing expert. The value proposition was very stylish, hip, prescription glasses sold over the Internet, with free try-ons of up to five different frames at home, delivered with excellent customer service, and donation by the company of one pair of glasses to a needy person for each pair purchased. The price in the pitch deck for all of this was $45 per pair of glasses. With his forecasted costs, the business would be solidly profitable with that price. Please keep in mind that similar glasses at your neighborhood optometrist would cost $300–$500 because of the dominant global market position held by Luxxotica for glasses.

Professor Raju told him a few things. First, the glasses would probably cost more to make and sell and deliver than they forecasted. Second, the glasses might be too inexpensive, causing people to question how good they could be at such a low price. Third, they could make a lot more money at higher prices. Finally, they should test alternative prices to see how they impact revenue and consumer perception.

Fortunately, the team listened to Professor Raju and tested alternative prices. The end result was that a $95 price was actually more attractive than a $45 price because $45 was not credible to many people. Professor Raju was also correct that their costs were actually higher than they forecasted, but the doubling of the pricing gave them plenty of room to remain solidly profitable. As of this writing, Warby Parker just announced that they have donated over a million pairs of glasses to needy people around the world. They also have raised more than $115 million in venture capital funding to fuel their rapid growth.

Our only additional recommendation would be that instead of the flat $95 price, they should have also tested odd prices, like 96.35. We would expect that such an "odd" price would be perceived as more credible and more related to costs, which might be viewed more favorably by consumers.

Pricing to Create and Capture Value

Pricing is typically the most difficult marketing decision for most firms. It is also probably the most important because it ultimately determines how much money a company can make. In today's world, you not only have to price products that have significant manufacturing costs, or services with large human elements in delivery, but also intellectual property that can be replicated for essentially zero cost on the Internet. Unfortunately, some managers think pricing is much too easy. They use comfortable, precise rules for pricing. These simple rules are usually one of two types: markup rules or competitive matching rules. Markup rules just take the product or service's costs and mark them up by a margin percentage. This margin percentage may be standard for the industry, related to what you are used to, or what you need to make your forecasted profit at the forecasted revenue for your venture. The competitive rules usually have the manager planning on pricing being just a bit lower than or matching the competition's prices. These "rules" make it easy to make the pricing decision without having to do much work or careful thinking. However, like many things in life, "no pain, no gain." The problem with these "rules" is that they may leave lots of money on the table.

The entrepreneurial marketer should strive to base pricing on the value of the offering. Dolan's Value-Pricing Thermometer[1] provides a valuable context for assessing price and the factors that impact price (see Figure 3-1).

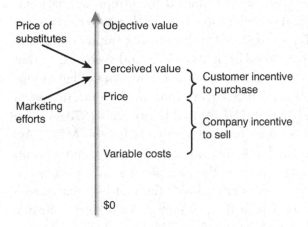

Figure 3-1 The Value-Pricing Thermometer

(Adapted from "Principles of Pricing," Robert J. Dolan, HBS 2009.)

In the figure, the *objective value*, also referred to as the true economic value (TEV), is a measure of the benefits that the offering delivers to the customer "relative to other products and regardless of whether the customer understands those benefits." However, perceived value, the value the customer understands the offering to deliver, is more important because in the marketplace, perception is reality. The entrepreneurial marketer can use all the elements of the marketing mix to enhance the perceived value, and the availability, price, and perceptions of competing products can detract from the relative perceived value. The closer the price is to the perceived value, the greater value you can capture from a sale. Yet marketers often resort to markup or competitive matching rules and, therefore, leave money on the table.

Managing pricing really is highly dependent on how well the entrepreneur manages the *perceived value* of her product bundle. This perceived value is affected or can be affected by every element of the firm's marketing mix. The price itself can be a big driver of how potential customers will perceive your product-offering bundle.

Price and Perceived Value

Sometimes, a price that is too low, particularly for a new product, can have a big impact on how valuably it will be perceived. Our next example crystallizes this phenomenon. When one of the authors was in graduate school, his professor had started an entrepreneurial company to manufacture and sell educational kit machines to help people understand how the binary logic and arithmetic of computers worked. The machines were composed of lights, wires, and switches, so that binary arithmetic and logic could be simulated by series of light bulbs being either on or off. The first kit machine in the entrepreneur's line was the red and blue MINIVAC 601, priced at $79.95. The entrepreneur had three target market segments for the MINIVAC 601—home hobbyists, high schools and colleges, and computer and technology companies (for training their employees on how computers worked). The product did very well with the first two market segments. Home hobbyists bought the product at consumer electronic stores and some higher-tech hobby shops. Many colleges and some upper socioeconomic high schools also bought the MINIVAC as an educational aid. However, no one in the third segment, the corporate sector, bought the product. The entrepreneur interviewed some target customers to try to find the problem. He found out very quickly. The typical description of the MINIVAC by the corporate types was: "Oh, that—it's just a toy!"

The entrepreneur was creative, and he listened carefully. He also understood marketing. His next product was the same basic kit—with the switches upgraded to higher tolerances and the machine color changed from blue and red to gunmetal gray. The name was changed to the MINIVAC 6010, and he increased the price from $79.95 to $479. The MINIVAC 6010 sold very well to the corporate segment at $479. The $79.95 price was too low for the corporate buyers to take the product seriously—at such a low price, it had to be a toy. The color and packaging of the original MINIVAC 601 amplified that perception. By changing the color, name, and packaging, and most importantly the price, the entrepreneur was able to change the perception in the corporate segment. The impact on his bottom line was just amazing! The price you put on your product offering, by itself, creates an important part of the perceptual position.

Getting Price Right Early—It's Hard to Raise Prices Later!

It is even more important to get the pricing done well early in the product's life because of human nature. If you lower a price over a product's lifetime, no one will complain (except possibly the customers who just bought it at a higher price). However, if you want to raise a price significantly because you realize the product's perceived value is much higher than you thought, it is very difficult. Human nature does not consider such price rises as "fair." If you can convince potential customers that your costs have gone up, that is usually perceived as a legitimate or fair justification for raising prices. Customers do not typically go through such fairness evaluations when they originally see a price for a new product or service. Human nature and fairness arguments take over only when prices are raised. Thus, it is even more important to have your initial price set at a very good level. In some cases, you can even leave it up to the customer—eBay and Priceline both do, and both are big moneymakers, as you see later in this chapter.

However, for many new products or services, it is usually the innovators who will take a risk on a new product or service. For taking this initial risk, the first customers want (and deserve) special pricing treatment. Sometimes they even deserve to get the product at no cost to try until they are convinced of its value. It is okay for the entrepreneur to give special pricing to these first innovative customers. However, the prices should be structured as *charter customer discounts* or *introductory discounts* from a *regular price* that is publicized as what will be normal after the introduction. This paradigm gives the entrepreneurial marketer much more room to determine marketplace reaction and adjust his actual selling prices by adjusting the introductory discount level and time period.

By having a regular price stated up front, the entrepreneur is free to charge up to that level without generating market perceptions of unfairness. There are some entrepreneurial marketers who have kept introductory prices for over a year after a product has been introduced.

Perceived Value in Use for Business-to-Business Products

A key way that an entrepreneur can market new products and services to businesses is to show the target business that they will be more profitable if they adopt the entrepreneur's new product or service. If the potential customers *perceive* that their business will be more profitable if your product or service is used, then they will likely buy it. The key word here is *perceive.* If the customer understands and believes that your product can make the production, service, or delivery process more efficient or more valuable to the customer's customers, then you can make a nice sale. In order to use this value-in-use positioning, you must understand how the potential customers will want to calculate the value-in-use of your new product. If there are certain measures that an industry uses to indicate efficiency or productivity, customers will probably feel more comfortable if they see the new entrepreneurial innovation with data on that measure.

How does all of this relate to pricing? According to Irwin Gross of the Institute for the Study of Business Markets at Pennsylvania State University:

> "Customer Value" is the hypothetical *price* for a supplier's *offering* at which a particular customer would be at overall economic *break-even* relative to the best *available alternative* to the customer for performing a set of functions.

> "Customer Perceived Value" is a customer's *perception* of his/her own "customer value."[2]

Although customer value, referred to by Dolan in Figure 3-1 as "objective value," can never be known precisely, it is a useful idealized construct, similar to a "perfect vacuum" or a "frictionless plane" in physics.[3]

The best pricing situation occurs when there is a perceived win-win situation. The buyer perceives that she will have higher "customer value" when adopting your offering, including the price of the new product. You in turn make much higher profit margins than normal because of her understanding of how to create perceived value better than her competition. In Figure 3-1, this would be pricing as close to "Perceived Value" as possible without exceeding it.

Your competition might not be as treacherous in many business-to-business situations as it might first appear. The concept of really going into depth to understand perceived customer value is not that common. According to Gross, who has studied business-to-business markets for over 20 years: "Customers spend more effort to know supplier's costs than suppliers spend to know customer's values." A really effective entrepreneurial marketer will spend her scarce time and resources to understand exactly how her target market participants develop perceptions of customer value and what methods are best for changing those values.

There are typical components that make up perceived customer value for new entrepreneurial product offerings. These can be grouped into product value, supplier value, and switching investments. According to Gross, the product value is the relative benefits delivered by the product itself, independent of the supplier; the supplier value is the relative benefits delivered by the supplier, independent of the product itself. The switching investment is the costs and risks involved with the transition from the current practice to the implementation of the new alternative.[4] All of these benefits, of course, are as *perceived* by decision makers in the target market. Gross has categorized components of attributes that affect perceived customer value, dividing them into attributes that impact perceptions of immediate customer value versus those that will impact expected customer value in the future. Table 3-1 outlines the attributes that can impact perceived customer value.

Table 3-1 Attributes Affecting Perceived Customer Value (Parentheses Indicate Negative Attributes)

	Immediate	Expected
Product	Product performance	New technology
	Durability	Product flexibility
	Serviceability	Follow-on products
	Downstream performance	(Long-run risks)
	(Current risks)	

	Immediate	Expected
Supplier	Supplier performance—delivery technology, sales, services, etc. (Promotional values, services)	Supplier relationship Technology access Security of supply Strategic (Supplier power)
Switching	New capital Training Transitional quality Communications	

A good entrepreneurial marketer will do whatever is necessary to make sure that his offering's perceived customer value is higher than his competition's. He will understand the components that are important to the members of the target market. He will then make sure his product offering and all of the marketing elements that support it are doing the best job possible in positively impacting the value perception. As reflected in Table 3-1, it is not just the product or service offering itself that needs to be impacted. It is the complete product, including much of the supporting services and impressions that the entrepreneurial venture leaves. The sales force, the marketing communications, the channels used, the product packaging, the product's name, the service package, and so on are all part of what can impact perceived customer value. For business-to-business markets, real entrepreneurial marketing can enable much higher prices than competition.

The SAS Institute, Inc.—Very Effective Management of Perceived Customer Value

The SAS Institute, Inc., has become the world's largest privately held software company by creatively and uniquely applying many of the concepts in this chapter. The Institute provides business analytics software and services to target markets in business, government, and education. The end result of this entrepreneurial marketing is a very unique software pricing strategy. All SAS Institute software products are licensed, not sold. According to their literature: "SAS Institute's pricing strategy is designed to foster Win/Win relationships with our customers, which lead to building productive long-term partnerships."[5] The Institute is not shy about the objectives of their pricing policy. "The strategy is to establish pricing consistent with the value received by SAS software customers, as they implement mission critical applications."[6]

The SAS Institute pricing model was unique among major software vendors. The other vendors typically sell a software purchase along with a maintenance contract. Their customers buy each new software release and have the option to pay ongoing fees for technical support. These other software vendors, typically public or with objectives of going public, want to maximize the short-term revenue they obtain with each sale. The suppliers of investments for software vendors in the financial markets do not necessarily let software firms price for value over time as SAS does.

The SAS Institute license model has the customer pay a first-year license fee and an annual fee to renew the license. According to SAS, the annual license model provides the customer with a number of valuable benefits:

1. Low cost of entry (typically less than fees paid for entering a purchase/maintenance model)
2. Rapid return on investment (ROI)
3. The most current release
4. Technical support
5. The most current documentation
6. All updates during the license period
7. Protected customer investments by ensuring that they always have the most up-to-date technology[7]

The customer is never locked in to more than a one-year commitment to SAS. The company must then be perceived by their customers as continually providing excellent technical support and ongoing enhancements to the software. If the customers do not perceive they are getting value from SAS, they can go elsewhere. The customers can also easily add or delete components of the SAS software as their needs change over time. SAS even comes out and says in their own literature that: "The strategy is to establish pricing consistent with the value received by SAS software customers as they implement mission critical applications."[8]

Let's compare SAS's pricing model to the typical enterprise software company. The typical company sells its software once, with a very big sales effort. They then charge annual ongoing maintenance fees of 15%–18% of the initial purchase price. These maintenance fees sometimes include updates and improvements to the software. Is this pricing consistent with the customer's perceived value? Not really. The customer should receive increasing value as the software becomes implemented and tailored to the customer's specific situation and as it is improved and updated over time. The perceived value to the customer of software will almost always be higher after a successful implementation than before it. If the implementation is unsuccessful, then the reverse situation would hold. Because of these risks, customers are not willing to pay as much up front for software as they would pay if they had continual successful experience to value. The amount the typical enterprise software company can charge up front is thus less than the discounted present value that the customer would pay over time under the SAS Institute rental plan.

SAS's job becomes keeping its customers continually delighted so that they will continue to pay the relatively large yearly license fees. SAS does that very well. They renew 98% of their customers annually! Thus 98% of their revenue is recurring. This is an astonishing statistic for any software company. They also have used their recurring revenue as a base for expansion. The latest public statistics available show revenue of over $3.0 billion for 2013, more than double that of eight years earlier. SAS also has enough gross margin to spend over 30% of revenue (*revenue, not profits!*) on research and development, to enable them to provide software improvements that continually delight their customers.[9]

The SAS customer-value orientation and their pricing model that captures more of that value than the competition is supported by a superb employee group that is, in turn, supported by marketing-oriented employee policies. SAS treats its employees in ways that foster excellent long-term performance and high loyalty. Some of the policies include 32-hour work weeks, onsite day care, unlimited sick leave, and a fully supported gym on the premises. In an extremely competitive market for software talent in the Raleigh Durham research triangle, SAS has a turnover rate lower than 5% compared with over 20% for many competitive software companies.

Why don't other software companies emulate the value-oriented pricing model of the SAS Institute? We can only speculate. One reason may be that too many U.S. companies (and their financial backers, including public shareholders) are too short-term oriented to pass up one-time purchase prices for a longer-term, but higher-value, rental revenue stream. The other reason may be lack of courage to look a customer in the eye and ask for a legitimate percent of the perceived value that your software is delivering. We note that the rise of web-based application service providers (ASPs) such as Salesforce.com have enabled value-based pricing. We hope that more entrepreneurial marketers will be encouraged by the SAS Institute example to not be afraid to set pricing policies to receive some of the perceived value they are creating.

Pricing of Intellectual Property

One of the most difficult things to price is something that has essentially no cost associated with another copy—that is, intellectual property. On the Internet, much of what is being sold is information, which has the property that once created (especially in electronic form), multiple copies can be re-created for no cost.

In physical goods, the price is often related to the cost of producing the item, including some amortization of the intellectual property (research and development) used to create the design, as well as the raw materials and processing cost to turn those materials into the item for sale. Gross margins of 60%–80% are not uncommon in high-tech industries, so that an Intel chip that sells for $300 may have a cost (including marketing, R&D, and production) of $50–$60.

With information, the marginal cost of providing news reports on Yahoo! is effectively zero. The gross margins on the product are often above 95%, with the small cost of goods being associated with maintaining the servers that hold and transmit the information. How, then, should one select the pricing?

One price that has often been successfully used on the Internet is *free*. Give away the intellectual property so that people will come to a website and see the advertising or take advantage of e-commerce opportunities. Most of the stock trading operations provide research reports and other products that way. E-Trade, DLJ Direct, and Wit Capital are all examples. They also price their actual services—for example, stock trading—as close to their real cost as possible, with only Schwab making a profit on the transaction costs.

Facebook, LinkedIn, Dropbox, Gmail, and other "virally marketed" services are all vehicles that provide a free service, which is purely communications or other nonphysical product, so that they can do advertising and marketing to the users. They can also upsell users to a premium version of the service, which is revenue producing. LinkedIn has done an especially good job of leveraging all of their users who have put profiles on the site for free, to sell access to those that can use LinkedIn's services for more specialized uses. In fact, LinkedIn has premium subscriptions that reflect the segments of their market: professional, job search, sales, and recruiting. Each premium offering matches enhanced features of LinkedIn with the networking objectives of each segment.[10] LinkedIn uses the power of the Internet to increase the perceived value for their clearly segmented market and to drive them from the free offering to a paid service.

There are other groups that can successfully charge for intellectual property, usually through some form of subscription pricing. The *Wall Street Journal* online is one of the most successful subscription-based services on the Internet, with a $28.99 per month price for people who do not also get the print edition, and a lower price for those who are already print subscribers. The *New York Times* charges $39.95 per year (or $6.95 per month) for access to their crossword puzzles online, getting a dedicated audience to whom they can also e-sell. Many traditional media publishers offer subscriptions to digital versions of their print media as well as additional editorial content, not available in the print version, all to increase the perceived value and revenue generation of their digital content.

What Else Can Impact Price Response?

Anything that can impact the perception of your product-offering bundle can impact the price that potential customers will be willing to pay. Very simply, if the customer does not believe that the value she perceives more than justifies the price, she will not purchase. We use the term *product-offering bundle* here as we do in other places in this book in the widest interpretation possible. It includes anything that the customer can perceive impacts the value they get from the whole experience of buying and using your product or service. The first time potential customers come in contact with your firm or product or service, they begin to get impressions that will affect their value perception of the offering bundle. If it was an advertisement, did it connote the right positioning? If it was an e-mail, did it come across consistent with a high-value positioning?

When a customer or potential customer calls in to your firm, is the phone answered in a manner consistent with a high-value perception? If potential customers get put on hold for very long, they will get bad perceptions about how fast your firm might react to any problems that need to be corrected. If the phone people are not polite, considerate, and genuinely helpful to the caller, the firm and its product's perception will suffer.

A 100+-year-old shipping company was concerned that they were losing business to competition and that their margins were continually being squeezed by what they thought was increased competitive price pressure on their routes. The firm retained a market research consultant who interviewed some of their customers and potential customers. The consultant found a number of problems that influenced how customers or potential customers perceived the firm and its product-offering bundle. One pervasive problem was that the firm's telephonic interface with customers was appalling compared with competition. If someone called into a regional shipping office to either ask about a price quotation or what the status of a shipment was, there were many instances when the phone just rang and rang and was never even answered! The increased price pressure the firm was facing was not brought about by competition, but more by the reaction of their potential customers to the perceived value decline in the product-offering bundle. The appalling telephone interface was just one example of the problems with customer treatment at the firm. Only after the customer sales and service operations of the firm were completely redesigned from the ground up, would the company possibly be able to command what it considered reasonable prices.

Other chapters show how all the elements of the marketing mix can affect perception that then affects price response. All of the channel management decisions affect how the end customer will perceive your product-offering bundle. The environment your product is in when the customer sees it can have a large impact on its perceived value. The same product will have a higher perceived value if the consumer sees it at Tiffany's rather than at Walmart. The dynamic management of distribution channels described in Chapter 7, "Distribution/Channel Decisions to Solidify Sustainable Competitive Advantage," has as its major objective to achieve high contribution margin and prices. Once a product has been sold at low-end channels, it typically cannot be sold at premium prices at the higher-end channels.

Customer-Determined Pricing

Another method for pricing at the perceived value to the customer is to let the customer set the price. This includes various auction methods, a large choice of pricing alternatives, and even riskier strategies of "pay what you think it was worth." The auction world has been completely transformed by eBay, which now helps generate sales of more than $82 billion of merchandise per year. Here, each customer believes they are getting a good deal, while the excitement of the auction often generates prices above what the same item is available for elsewhere—extra profits for the seller.

eBay has several methods for the customer to determine pricing: BuyItNow, auction, and half.com's offers. In the traditional auction, there is a seven-day period during which multiple bidders can make offers and see who the highest bidder is. The person with the highest bid when the auction closes wins—with eBay's software automatically bidding up to preset limits for customers who cannot be present in the final seconds. A set of software called sniping software has been developed to conceal bidding until the final seconds. But ultimately, it is the customer who determines the price of the items on offer. The seller can ensure some gross margin by having a reserve price, below which the item won't be sold. Sellers can also offer a "BuyItNow" price for those customers who cannot wait till the end of the auction. This is usually set to a price above that which previous auctions in similar items have sold, although if the seller has multiples of the same item, it may be set lower (more like a traditional store price). Finally, eBay acquired half.com, which offers books, CDs, and some other items at what was originally meant to be half of the price for new items. Because condition and seller reputation are both important to buyers, there is now a range of prices for popular items, so the buyer can choose to pay more or less for the same book, depending on condition, seller reputation, shipping date, and so forth.

In all the preceding cases, it is the customer who determines what he is willing to pay. This is much like the old days when one bargained with every merchant—before James Cash Penny posted fixed pricing in his stores. And it is much the same in many other countries in the world, where the listed price is just a starting point.

At Priceline, the customer selects the price, but not the specific merchandise. You can bid for a first-class hotel room in New York but may be given one in any of a large selection of hotels. Similarly, Priceline has deals with Delta and other airlines that allow them to sell airline tickets at whatever price they'd like. Customers bid for tickets between a city pair but cannot select the time of day or airline. Priceline determines if they can make money selling the user a ticket out of the inventory that the airlines have made available to Priceline at fixed prices. Here, the customer is determining price, but with time of day and airline chosen by the seller.

Often, the customer will have a different utility for money than the vendor. In this case, smart vendors will offer a range of prices that allow the customer to make the choice that is optimal for them, while increasing the profits to the vendor. Often this involves the capital/expense budget trade-off. Much of today's outsourcing of services falls into this category.

Evolution Robotics, for example, is offering their LaneHawk system, which combats supermarket losses with three different pricing plans. LaneHawk recognizes items that are on the bottom of shopping carts but not rung up on the register, either through innocent error or deliberate fraud. Some chains are willing to pay the full capital cost up front, in return for much lower monthly software maintenance costs. Others prefer to not pay any capital costs and just pay a monthly rental—in this case, Evolution's cost of funds is taken into account, and customers often give Evolution much higher total margin (over three years) than if they had borrowed the money and paid the capital costs. A third choice—sharing the savings from loss prevention—is also offered. Here again, customers are determining the price they will pay based on their own preferences, capital availability, and risk tolerance.

Although not all entrepreneurial ventures lend themselves to customer-determined pricing, when the products and services are new, and there is no established competition to overcome, it can often lead to much higher profits than the traditional price-testing methods. In addition, when the customers are determining the price themselves, something that is often a source of negative feelings (high prices) becomes the source of positive feelings because it is truly a customer choice for what to pay, which is empowering.

Revisiting Costs in Determining Price

So far, most of this chapter has discussed the importance of perceived value and value-based pricing and ensuring that you do not leave money on the table by underpricing by using a markup approach to pricing. However, costs play a critical role in evaluating the profitability of your offering. For example, if my widgets cost $1, and I sell them for $2, a "keystone" or doubling markup, why shouldn't I as an entrepreneurial marketer be happy? You shouldn't because you haven't asked the proper question. The right question is: *Of all the possible prices I can charge for my widgets, which price will maximize my profitability over my planning horizon?* If when I price my widgets for $2, I will sell 400,000 units per year, is that the best possible price in terms of total profitability from the widgets over the product's life? Selling 400,000 units at $2 per unit brings in revenue of $800,000. From that revenue, product costs of $1 per unit make costs equal to $1 × 400,000 equals $400,000 in product costs. This leaves $400,000 as gross margin or contribution to fixed costs and profit due to the widgets.

As an entrepreneurial marketer, you must ask, "What would happen to my units sold if I charged other prices than $2?" If a reasonable estimate can be made of units that would be sold at other alternative prices (the "elasticity of demand"), then the entrepreneur can easily find the price that does maximize profitability over the planning horizon. We will describe methods for getting estimates of demand at alternative prices later after we show how valuable they can be if they are integrated into the cost structure of the venture. Let's assume that our widgets would sell the amounts indicated in Table 3-2.

Table 3-2 Contribution and Revenue Consequences of Different Prices

Price per Unit	Units Sold	Revenue ($)	Cost @ $1/Unit	Contribution ($)
1.0	600,000	600,000	600,000	0
1.5	500,000	750,000	500,000	250,000
2.0 (original)	400,000	800,000	400,000	400,000
2.5	350,000	875,000	350,000	525,000
3.0 (highest revenue)	300,000	900,000	300,000	600,000
3.5 (highest profit)	250,000	875,000	250,000	625,000
4.0	200,000	800,000	200,000	600,000
5.0	100,000	500,000	100,000	400,000

The maximum revenue price is $3 per widget for revenue of $900,000, only $100,000 greater than the original price of $2. However, the contribution is $600,000, 2.4 times the profitability of the original $2 price! However, there is even a better price—the price of $3.50 per widget has a lower revenue of $875,000 but has a higher contribution of $625,000. This contribution is 2.5 times the contribution that would have occurred had the original price been used. This is an obviously simplified example, but not simplified in isolating how important the analysis of alternative prices is to most ventures. The impact of the initial pricing decision on the venture's ultimate profitability is typically huge. We'll show some real examples later of what this decision has meant to some firms as well as how to estimate the revenue at alternative price levels. However, first, it is now time to give the quick entrepreneurial marketer's guide to *cost accounting!*

The reason for bringing up cost accounting is that the profitability of pricing decisions depends solely on revenue and *variable costs*. Fixed costs are almost irrelevant to the decision on the best price to charge for the product or service. Why is this true? Because if fixed costs, by definition, don't change when the number of units sold changes, then they will be incurred *regardless of the alternative price that would be charged.* All of the "contribution" numbers in Table 3-2 should really be contribution to fixed costs and profit of the venture. The $1 cost assumed in the simple example should be only the variable costs to produce, sell, and deliver an incremental unit. Fixed costs that will be incurred regardless of the price will be subtracted from the contribution to estimate the profitability of the widget product. If any constant number were subtracted from each contribution row, the price that maximizes contribution and profit will not change. Thus, fixed costs do not affect the best price to charge for a product or service. There is only one exception to this rule. If the estimated contribution of the best price is *not enough to cover the fixed costs* associated with the product or service, then the product or service should *not be introduced.*

Methods for Determining Revenue at Alternative Price Levels

After reading the preceding section, you are probably saying to yourself, "Sure, it would be more profitable to price so as to get the most profit, but how can I get good estimates of the sales I would realize if I charged alternative prices?" There are a number of ways to do this that can be grouped into two categories—premarket and in-market testing.

Premarket Methods—Pricing and Concept Testing

Chapter 2, "Generating, Screening, and Developing Ideas," discussed the value of concept testing before a product or service is introduced, and it mentioned that you may use concept testing as an effective vehicle for estimating the relative differences in sales that would occur at alternative price levels. The basic idea is very simple.

Part of the concept description of the product or service is the price. If you want to concept test four alternative prices, then make every concept description have only one of the four pricing alternatives, with each respondent being exposed at a .25 probability to one of the alternatives. So every fourth concept test will have the same price. The estimates of number of units that would be bought at different price levels can be calculated in the same way as any other concept test. What is valuable to the entrepreneur is to analyze the resulting revenue implications from the alternative pricing policies.

Because any biases of the concept test would be constant over the four different prices, the relative differences in response of one price versus another will usually be quite valid. For example, if the concept test results indicate that 40% more widgets would be sold at a 20% lower price, that percentage difference will be the same regardless of what the base absolute sales of the widgets would be. Regardless of whether the actual sales of the widgets in market would be 1,000 units or 10,000 units at the base price, the estimate of 40% more units that would be sold at a 20% lower price should hold.

A Price-Concept Testing Example: ABLE Faucets

A small, non-U.S. manufacturer (whom we will call ABLE) of faucets for kitchen sinks had been selling one model of faucet through a major do-it-yourself retailer for two years—and just barely breaking even, when all of the costs associated with the faucet were taken into account.[11] ABLE wanted to see if they could convince the retailer to change the retail price from $98 to a higher price, enabling ABLE to raise the wholesale price to the retailer. As part of a larger study, a paired comparison concept test was administered in the retail store to customers who were about to buy a kitchen faucet. The customers were asked to choose which of two alternative faucets they would rather purchase and provided concept descriptions of each. The concept statements included a picture of the faucet and all of the descriptions of the product features and/or benefits that were on the respective faucet boxes. In the large do-it-yourself retailers, the box on the shelf was the major way in which the customer was able to evaluate alternative products prior to making a purchase. The box's perception on the shelf is very important in most mass merchandisers.

Each concept statement also had a price associated with it. Each customer who was tested received a concept test with one of four alternative prices for the ABLE faucet—$98, $127, $141, or $160. The other faucet they were given to evaluate was constant throughout the test. It was the major seller at the retailer with a price of $141. An example of part of the concept test survey is shown in Figure 3-2, where the ABLE faucet is B.

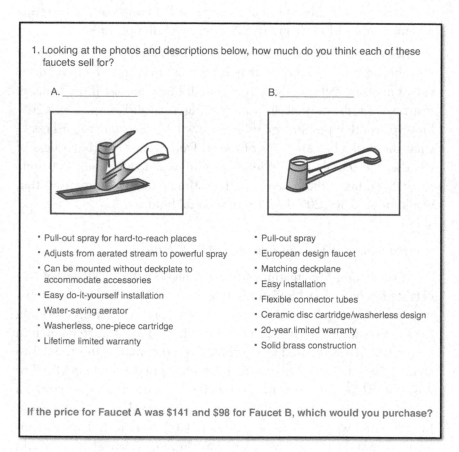

Figure 3-2 Portion of ABLE faucets concept test survey

Twenty-five percent of the people received the ABLE faucet concept description priced at $98, a different 25% received the ABLE concept priced at $127, and so on. The competitive faucet was always constant and priced at $141. The results of this part of the concept test are shown in Figure 3-3.

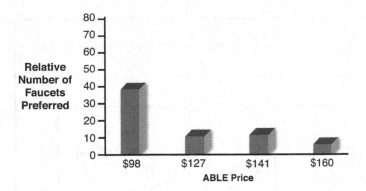

Figure 3-3 ABLE faucets concept test results

From the results, demand seems to go down significantly at prices over $98. It falls from 40 to 5, a drop of 85%. If this pricing option was the only alternative ABLE could pursue, it would not make sense to raise the faucet's price. However, some entrepreneurial marketers looked carefully at the ABLE box. They observed that the product description on the box was all stated as product *features* as opposed to product *benefits*. For example, flexible connector tubes probably don't mean very much to the typical faucet buyer. However, if the feature was translated into a benefit such as "flexible connector tubes to fit into tight spaces under the sink," it might have more value to a potential purchaser. How many potential purchasers would know the benefit associated with the feature "ceramic disc, washerless cartridge?" How much more valuable is "ceramic disc, washerless cartridge design eliminates leaks and ensures maximum control?"

Price Response Depends on Perceived Value: The Example Continues

To estimate the impact on price response of describing the product on the box with benefits versus features, another cell was added to the concept test described previously. Half of the respondents saw a benefits-oriented concept statement, while the other half saw the original feature-oriented copy from the box. The concept statement for the benefits-oriented box is shown in Figure 3-4.

1. Looking at the photos and descriptions below, how much do you think each of these faucets sell for?

A. _____   B. _____

- Pull-out spray for hard-to-reach places
- Adjusts from aerated stream to powerful spray
- Can be mounted without deckplate to accommodate accessories
- Easy do-it-yourself installation
- Water-saving aerator
- Washerless, one-piece cartridge
- Lifetime limited warranty

- Pull-out spray for multi-purpose use
- European design faucet
- Matching deckplane to cover sinkholes
- Easy step-by-step installation instructions
- Flexible connector tubes fit in tight spaces under sink
- Ceramic disc cartridge/washerless design eliminates leaks, ensures maximum control
- 20-year limited warranty
- Solid brass construction for long life

If the price for Faucet A was $141 and $98 for Faucet B, which would you purchase?

Figure 3-4 Benefits-oriented concept statement

The benefits-oriented box copy was also shown to different respondents at one of the same four alternative price levels. The concept test was not only able to estimate the response of the new box copy at the four alternative price levels, but also to compare the *benefits*-oriented copy versus the existing *features*-oriented copy for the box at the different price levels. This is because the control faucet was the same for all eight versions of the concept test—two copies times four different price levels. The results when the responses to all eight versions of the concept are compared are very interesting (see Figure 3-5).

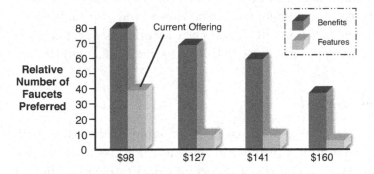

Figure 3-5 ABLE faucet demand estimates results

Keep in mind that the concept test biases, whatever they are, are not typically going to affect any one cell of the eight test cells versus any other. The results really add a lot of value and are a wonderful illustration of how important perception is to price response. They also illustrate how valuable it is to help the consumer understand product benefits that are associated with certain features. First, notice that *just by describing the product with benefit-oriented statements on its box, sales would double compared with the current box's feature-oriented statements.* Twice as many respondents chose the ABLE product versus its major competitor when it was described by relating the features to their consumer benefits. The benefits-oriented description added considerable perceived value to the customer. Approximately the same number of faucets would be sold at $160 (a 60% higher price) for the benefits-oriented box copy compared with the original features-oriented copy. Thus, just *changing the box copy to a benefits orientation added over 60% to the perceived consumer value of the same physical faucet!*

The other cells in Figure 3-2 are also quite valuable—both to ABLE and to the retailer. Notice that demand goes down much less severely for the benefits-oriented copy as the price goes up, compared with the existing features-oriented copy. When the retailer evaluated her costs and profit alternatives, the $141 price made the most sense if ABLE were to raise its wholesale price for the redesigned benefits-oriented box. At $141 with the redesigned box, the concept test shows a true win-win-win situation. ABLE gets to significantly raise its price to the retailer, and the retailer sells more units of ABLE's faucets. The consumer gets a faucet that they would value at $160 for $141. Everyone is happier. It doesn't always work this way, but when it does, it is extremely gratifying to true entrepreneurial marketers.

In-Market Methods

The in-market method is usually preferable because it is typically a very valid predictor of what revenue would be at alternative price levels. However, it is not always practical to charge different prices for the same product or service in the marketplace. You cannot charge different prices for what is perceived as the same product bundle if market participants will communicate with each other. If one market participant finds out that another participant bought what they perceived as the same product bundle at a better price, they will feel cheated. Even though rationally, they got enough perceived value from their purchase or they would not have made it, psychologically they feel cheated. If they feel that way, they can begin saying bad things about your product. Bad word of mouth is damaging to a new product or service that lives based on customer perceptions. If a potential customer hears bad things about a product from a respected source, it can undermine all the other marketing activities you do.

If the customer perceives the product bundle to be different, then the consumer will not necessarily be upset about hearing that someone else paid a different price. For example, airline seats or concert tickets will be priced differently depending on when the customer decides to buy them or exactly where they are located. You will learn more about yield management and other methods for charging different prices to different segments for different product bundles of the same physical product later in this chapter.

However, there are circumstances where it is highly unlikely for market participants to become upset. These are products or services that are purchased individually and usually not discussed very much among consumers, or products whose prices may be difficult to compare because they are customized to each potential customer. Many product/market combinations can be tested in-market. For example, if one of your primary marketing vehicles is personal sales and your product price is somewhat dependent on the potential customer's characteristics, it is relatively easy to do evaluation of market reaction to different price levels. The best way to do this is to have each of the salespeople involved in the test use different price levels for every nth potential customer on whom they call. For example, if there were three alternative price policies to test, then every potential customer would be exposed to one of the three different pricing policies, and each customer would have a one-third probability of being exposed to each policy. As long as it's pretty difficult for the potential customer to compare the pricing algorithm actually used by your salesperson, it will be difficult to compare prices across different potential customers. Thus, even if two customers do talk who have been exposed to different pricing algorithms, they will not be able to find out that they actually were quoted different pricing options. For example, if the pricing of software is developed based on a fixed charge for organizational training, another charge for installation, and another set of charges per "seat" or installed computer terminal, then it becomes difficult for two firms of different needs to compare prices.

The Internet as the Perfect In-Market Price-Testing Vehicle and a Reasonable Concept Price-Testing Vehicle

Concept testing with different recipients receiving different prices can easily be done on the Internet. A company had developed a new storage medium for portable computers—the Disk on Key (DOK). DOK is a USB device that has flash memory and can be an external storage device. The same physical DOK device can also be programmed to perform functions that make it easier to leverage working on more than one computer. Confidentiality prohibits us from giving more details. The problem of pricing the different versions of the DOK were made to order for concept testing at different price levels. A web survey was done on samples recruited to be in the various target markets for different potential versions of the DOK. The respondents were shown a picture of the device, a description of the device and its benefits (depending on how or whether it was programmed), and given a price as part of the description. Each respondent was exposed to one price for each concept. One quarter of the respondents were exposed to a $59 price, one quarter to $95,

$195, and $295, respectively. They were then asked a few questions, the main one being how likely they would be to purchase the product.

Figures 3-6 and 3-7 show purchase intent versus price results for two of the concepts. The first concept, the ABCDEF Key, was basically the unprogrammed, storage version of the key. Here, the purchase intent (70% of the top box plus 20% of the second box) goes down as the price goes up.

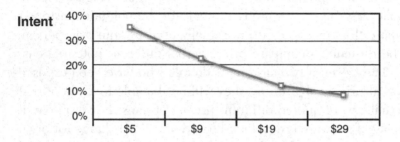

Figure 3-6 Concept testing: price versus purchase intent ABCDEF Key

Another concept was the same physical device (the EFGHI Key) but programmed to perform some functions. Again, the different respondents were exposed to the concept at one of the same four price levels. The concept description portrayed the features and benefits of the programmed device. The purchase intent response was much different for this version of the device. As Figure 3-7 shows, the purchase intent reached a maximum at the prices of $95 and $195 and was much lower at either $59 or $295. The qualitative feedback on the survey and further personal probing of respondents showed that at $59, the value proposition was not credible to some of the respondents: "How could something so valuable be so cheap?" On the other end of the spectrum, the $295 price was not as good as the perceived value for many of the respondents.

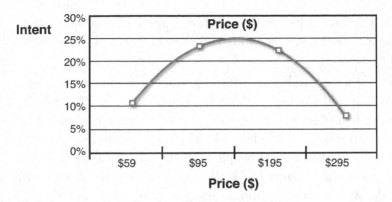

Figure 3-7 Concept testing: price versus purchase intent EFGHI Key

Please keep in mind that this concept testing was done before any DOKs were introduced and when this firm thought competition would not be coming for a reasonable time. The firm used this methodology for two very important and valuable functions. First, they were able to price the versions that they decided to introduce at appropriate levels, given the consumer value perception of the different versions. Second, they were able to prioritize their development resources to bring out the product versions that would be most profitable. This web-based concept testing cost under $30,000 to perform. The value of the activity was easily in the millions. Entrepreneurial firms of all sizes need to do more of this kind of research.

Because purchasing is done individually on the Internet, and each person can be exposed to a different, customized website, the Internet can be an extremely effective and valid in-market price-testing device. Immediate feedback, large sample sizes, and live customer reactions make it much more efficient and valid than focus groups or limited city tests. Idealab will often test banner ads and pricing by using 1,000–5,000 banners to drive viewers to specific pages on a site, keeping cookies to track their behavior, and then examining the follow-through once they have reached a site.

With utility.com, a provider of deregulated electric power in a number of states across the United States, the pricing and messages were honed through a series of tests. The VP of marketing first stated that he thought they needed to offer 15% off in order to get customers to switch from their existing suppliers. Perhaps, he said, we could get away with only 10% off if they chose "green" (environmentally clean) power. There were a number of skeptics that led to the company using a test.

After testing a number of different banners to get the best colors, animation, and messages, utility.com tested offers of 5%–15% off, each leading to a page that offered 0%–5% additional if you signed up right away (summarized in Table 3-3). The results were nonintuitive. The offers that drew the most people to the site were 7% off and 11% off. They were significantly higher draws than 15% off or 10% off. Once at the site, the best additional offers were 0%, 1%, and 3% off.

Table 3-3 Experimental Offerings Tested

Offer at Site	Offer to Get to Site										
	5%	6%	7%	8%	9%	10%	11%	12%	13%	14%	15%
0%	x	x	x	x	x	x	x	x	x	x	x
1%	x	x	x	x	x	x	x	x	x	x	x
2%											
3%	x	x	x	x	x	x	x	x	x	x	x
4%											
5%											

The best combined action came from a 7% offer to get visitors to the site, where they were offered 3% off for immediate sign-up—a total of 10% off. Green versus nongreen power had only a very small effect and is now offered as an option on the sign-up pages. Without the testing, the company would have used the "instinct" of 15%, with both higher cost and lower effectiveness.

The cost for the test was under $5,000 because off-peak banner advertising can be purchased inexpensively, and it only took several thousand tests to make it work.

Why were these counterintuitive results achieved? Some qualitative interviews were done with the people who were on the site. The numbers 10% and 15% didn't seem like they were related to costs or very carefully thought out, whereas 7% and 11% were perceived as related to the costs of providing the electricity by most of the potential customers. They perceived those discounts as fairer than even numbers. This phenomenon is actually generalizable to most new product/service situations where the product doesn't have an easily comparable competitive product/service. The generalization for these situations is:

Always price new, unique products at odd numbers, not even hundreds or thousands.

For example, many consultants will price jobs for $40,000 or $50,000. What they should do is price them for say $51,565. This will be perceived as more well-thought-out and related to some kind of costs, when it really is the consultant's estimate of what he thinks his client is willing to pay.

Victoria's Secret Can Use Its Many Stores for In-Market Experimentation

The Internet is not the only vehicle for profitable in-market price experimentation. Another advantage of the L Brands and Victoria's Secret "own store" strategy is that there is an opportunity to do price testing with different stores having different prices for the same item. Originally, VS did their price testing by doing their tests among different stores in the same region. In these tests, different stores in the same region would have different prices for the same items. This method should conceptually be pretty valid because stores in the same region should be comparable on consumer and competitive characteristics that would affect price response. However, VS found that they got into some legal issues in some regions for having different prices in their stores. Also, as discussed previously, there is a possibility of negative consumer reaction from finding out that your friend paid a different price for an item than you did. There is also a public relations risk if a newspaper or TV news reporter wrote a story on the different prices.

VS then moved to a less valid, but more doable testing method— varying prices across regions and then comparing the sales effects by store across regions. This method has caused no problems and is done a lot because the insights into the revenue price relationship VS obtains are very valuable. Here again, the experimental results may not be as precise as VS would like, but they give them the broad magnitudes of how their products respond to price changes. This is another example of being "vaguely right rather than precisely wrong." VS's price decisions are more profitable using their price tests than they would be if they didn't do them and used some arbitrary, precise formulas for calculating their prices.

Summary

This chapter began by showing how common cost-based or competitive-based pricing rules may be "precisely wrong." We showed that a "vaguely right" approach is to attempt to charge the price (or prices) that maximizes your profit return over your planning horizon. It also is important to get the initial price at a good level because it is much more difficult to raise prices over time than it is to lower them. Next, we described methods for in-market and premarket (concept testing) for determining the potential relationship between alternative prices and the sales revenue that those prices would produce. The Internet is the perfect in-market price-testing vehicle for many products.

We then showed a number of examples of how the price you can and should charge is intertwined with all the rest of the elements of the marketing mix. The marketing mix and the product-offering bundle all affect the perceived value for the potential customer. This perceived value in turn affects the price the consumer is willing to pay. For a consumer product, we demonstrated how a change in the product description on its box would double the sales of the product. The new box described valuable consumer benefits as opposed to the older box that described product features. We showed how perceived value in use affects the price response of business-to-business products. We showed how the SAS Institute's unique marketing mix and pricing structure captures and creates more perceived customer value than competitive software customers. Examples of eBay and Priceline helped to clarify how it is often possible, and even desirable, to have the customers themselves determine the price dynamically. This can lead to higher gross margin and more satisfied customers. Finally, we concluded the chapter by sharing several examples of concept testing and in-market testing to improve prices.

Endnotes

1. Robert J. Dolan, J.T. Gourville. *Principles of Pricing.* (Boston: Harvard Business School Publishing, 2009.)

2. Irwin Gross, Presentation at the Wharton School, March 1999.

3. Ibid.

4. Ibid.

5. SAS Institute white paper, "SAS Institute Business Model," 1998, Cary, NC, p. 3.

6. Ibid., 4.

7. Ibid., 4.

8. Ibid., 4.

9. SAS press release, January 2014.

10. *LinkedIn Premium.* (2014, November 1). Retrieved from LinkedIn: https://www.linkedin.com/premium/.

11. This is a disguised real example from the author's experience. The data has also been slightly altered. None of the conclusions would change because of the disguising. The disguising is to protect confidentialities.

Section Two
Demand-Generation and Sales—
Lead Your Customers to
Your Offering

Marketing strategy, positioning, and targeting establish the goals and objectives that the entrepreneurial marketer should achieve through a crafted collection of marketing activities. Marketing activities must serve their purpose in a cost-effective manner that attracts the largest number of customers and ultimately leads them to purchase. This is the basic premise of demand-generation and sales.

Through your actions and choices, you must efficiently reach the most valuable market segments, make them aware of your offering, educate them about your offering and its benefits, engage them in a trial and evaluation of your offering, and cultivate their interest to lead to a purchase. This may happen within a single website visit or over an extended period of time and may involve many touchpoints from your company and channel partners. These activities represent the marketing mix and may be integrated into a marketing plan comprising public relations, promotion, viral marketing, advertising, distribution, and sales. This section addresses each element of the marketing mix to help you develop and execute an effective marketing and sales plan.

A fundamental premise of entrepreneurial marketing is to direct your scarce resources to the most effective marketing activities that yield the greatest results and secure paying customers for a long period of time. Customer lifetime value (CLV) is the total revenue contributed to your venture by a customer over the length of their relationship with your venture. CLV is dependent upon three factors:

- Customer acquisition cost (CAC), the total cost to secure that customer
- Annual profits a customer generates for your venture
- Number of years the customer is likely to purchase from your venture

In its most simplistic form, we can express the CLV in the following equation:

$$CLV = m \times L - CAC$$

where m is the contribution margin generated from a customer in a year (or other time period),

L is the expected purchasing life of a customer (measured in the time period represented by m), and

CAC is the customer acquisition cost.[1]

In actuality, the equation and analysis become dramatically more complex as we factor in other variables, such as retention and churn rates (rates at which customers continue or end, respectively, their purchasing relationship); referral; up-sell and cross-sell opportunities (which can both lower CAC for new customers and increase contribution margin for existing customers); and present value (which discounts value of future purchases). However, CAC in relation to the incremental profitability of the customers attracted is at the heart of evaluating your demand-generation and marketing effectiveness.

Each marketing activity has an associated cost and moves customers closer toward purchase and beginning to contribute to their CLV. CAC includes the costs associated with reaching all prospects and potential customers, yet yielding a single customer. The entrepreneurial marketer must consider each marketing activity in terms of its ability to reach customers with the highest CLV at the lowest CAC to capture the greatest value for your venture.

The most effective way to develop a comprehensive marketing plan is to map the adoption process for your customer, understanding the movement of information, influence, goods and services, benefits and value, and, of course, money, on the way to the customer actually making a purchase. Each marketing activity should have a positive effect, moving your customer closer to purchase.

Each element of the marketing mix has specific objectives and outcomes; however, taken as a whole, they lead your prospective customers through a process of adoption that may include many phases (see Figure S2-1). At each phase, the prospective customer determines whether your product has enough perceived value to them to proceed to the next phase. As you develop your marketing activities, you must understand where in the adoption process the customer is and craft each activity to drive the best prospects to the next phase.

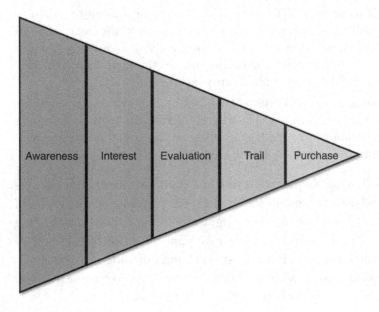

Figure 32-1 Consumer adoption process

To create effective marketing activities, you must understand your target customer, understand that customer's experience at the current phase of adoption, and communicate your value in such a way to allow the customer to assess whether to proceed. Develop personas or profiles of your customer segment(s) to bring them to life. Turn the psychographic and demographic information normally associated with market segmentation into a reflection of the activities, desires, and behaviors that the customers experience. Strong personas allow you to understand how your marketing tactics will engage and motivate your customers through each stage of the adoption process.

Finally, to create a successful marketing plan, the entrepreneurial marketer must ensure that every marketing tactic has a clear sense of:

- **Audience**—The target profile of prospects that you want to reach with your activity

- **Objective**—The goal that will allow the right prospects and customers to move on to the next phase and the wrong ones to seek alternatives

- **Call-to-action**—The specific action that the right customers will take to engage with you and move to the next phase of adoption, whether it be call a number, visit a website, redeem a coupon, or another action that moves them closer to realizing value for themselves and your venture

- **Measurable outcome**—The metric that will determine the success or failure of the marketing activity in terms of numbers of customers engaging, executing the call-to-action, and contribution of the activity to the CAC

The following chapters describe and demonstrate effective development and use of elements in the marketing mix to generate demand and lead to sales. There is no one right way to implement a marketing activity, and each should be undertaken and evaluated for effectiveness, making changes to improve success and outcomes for your business. You also learn ways to evaluate effectiveness to ensure that you make the best use of each marketing dollar spent.

Endnote

1. Thomas J. Steenburgh and Jill Avery, "Marketing Analysis Toolkit: Customer Lifetime Value Analysis," *Harvard Business School Background Note* (August 2011).

4

Leverage Public Relations for Maximum Value

PayMyBills.com—Battling Competition with Public Relations

PayMyBills.com began as a project at the Wharton School and was entered into the annual Wharton Business Plan Competition. As the judging proceeded, and the plan made it into the final eight, a leading Internet firm decided to fund it as a full-fledged business. The cofounders were brought out to Idealab's Pasadena headquarters and told that they had 60 days in which to launch the company and the business. The business plan competition provided the opportunity to get some buzz about the company. Because it was covered by major media, articles appeared in the *New York Times, Philadelphia Magazine,* and other publications. This helped the company in its initial hiring and fundraising.

The founders moved to Idealab in May 1998. Ten days later, they had hired ten people, mainly through a job fair and contacts on the Internet who had heard of them through the articles and the *Industry Standard Internet* online newsletter. Three weeks later, Idealab used the buzz to raise more than $4 million for the company at a much more favorable valuation than would have been possible without the public relations (PR). The Alexander Ogilvy agency, which has a long relationship with Idealab, was hired to get a fast-track product launch. They created an interview schedule for trade press, business press, and radio that focused on a product launch date of July 19 (slipped from an original July 4 target). Meetings were held with the *Wall*

Street Journal, LA Times, PC Magazine, and others, for a focused print at the launch.

In addition, spot radio advertising was purchased in several cities, including advertising on the *Howard Stern Show* for the first two weeks after launch. All of this orchestration led to a number of interviews, lots of customers, and acknowledgment as the leading player in this new field. This notwithstanding that the two competitors, PayTrust and CyberBills, had been in existence much longer but had not quite launched and were staying in stealth mode. By taking the aggressive route to PR and product launch, PayMyBills.com tilted the playing field and gained 50,000 customers in less than a year. It then merged with PayTrust, and the combination was later sold to a major firm in the financial services space.

Aspire to Be a "Winner"

Before people can buy your product or use your service, they have to know it exists and how to get to it. Even more important, they should feel that they are going with a winner if there is a choice among products in the category. Proper use of public relations and publicity can provide this "winner" feeling far faster and at much lower cost than a big national advertising campaign—one that an entrepreneurial company may not be able to afford.

The key to public relations is creating a "strategic communication process that builds mutually beneficial relationships between organizations and their publics."[1] That mutually beneficial relationship establishes your venture's positioning while offering interest and value to the public. Although you may pay an agency to create and execute a PR strategy, the cost-effectiveness of PR lies in the marketer's ability to generate interest among the press to encourage them to write and talk about you and your venture in print, on radio and television, and on the Internet—without paying them.

In the Internet world, the key driver to quickly gaining leadership in a new category is the creation of "buzz"—the feeling that you are the winner. Facebook, Instagram, Yahoo!, Microsoft, Google, and others have all been beneficiaries of this. Gaining the mindshare of a user—so that she routinely downloads your app or tries your web page before a competitor's—quickly translates into market share. As Ann Winblad, general partner of Hummer Winblad Associates and an extremely successful venture capitalist, has said, "It's the cheerleader approach, where you tell the world that we're the winner even before the game has started, which is successful in the Internet space."

ePinions, for example, secured a high profile story in the *New York Times Sunday Magazine* long before their site launched. The article made it seem as if the management team was experienced— the best and the brightest—and that they were certain to be the leader in shared opinions. The fact that About.com had thousands of users and millions of page views doing the same thing did not stop ePinions from making its claims. The perception of leadership quickly became the reality, allowing ePinions to be sold to Shopping.com after the crash at a reasonable price. When Google first released its Chrome browser, competing products were already successful in the marketplace, such as Mozilla Firefox, Apple Safari, Microsoft Internet Explorer, and others—some of which were technically superior. But a concentrated PR campaign, coupled with guerilla marketing tactics that you learn about in Chapter 5, "Promotion and Viral Marketing to Maximize Sustainable Profitability," got tremendous coverage in the trade press—which declared Chrome as the browser to beat. And Chrome soon gained overwhelming market share to make the perception a reality.

Gaining the Perception of Leadership

How can you achieve this perceptual edge? First, you must understand how most users make their decision about which app to download, which website to visit, or which product to buy. Generally, they ask someone they trust—an information gatekeeper in their organization or personal life—or they read a trusted source in a social media post, newsletter, trade, or general publication. Thus, the key to gaining the perceptual edge is to influence the influencers, or gatekeepers. And where do the gatekeepers get their knowledge? From a smaller set of influencers whom they trust. It is like a pool, where a stone thrown in the center creates waves that ripple outward, growing ever larger in diameter, until they reach the shore. You need to reach the following groups:

- **Gurus**—Key industry insiders
- **Influencers**—Key trade and business press; industry analysts
- **Decision makers**—Key bellwether buyers; those who can say yes
- **Naysayers**—People who can say no along the way
- **Mass buyers**—The masses who mainly follow what they perceive as the winning trend

In every industry, a few insiders are considered the industry experts or gurus. They are generally the ones quoted in *Business Week,* the *New York Times, Forbes, Fortune,* and the *Wall Street Journal* when key industry events occur. In the past, they mainly published high-priced newsletters and ran invitation-only conferences for CEOs of industry companies. In the personal computer industry during the 1980s and '90s, Ben Rosen, Stewart Alsop, Esther Dyson, and Richard Shaffer filled this role. At the middle of the new decade, Chris Anderson has taken over the TED Conference (TED stands for Technology, Entertainment, Design) from Richard Saul Wurman, Walt Mossberg and Kara Swisher have the Re/Code conferences and newsletters, AOL has TechCrunch Disrupt, David Kirkpatrick has the Techonomy conference, and Jason Calacanis has the Launch series. Reaching these players—and being covered in their newsletters, in their blogs, on their Twitter feeds, or appearing at their conferences—creates some immediate buzz, both with key industry buyers and partners and with key venture capitalists who can fund your entrepreneurial venture.

In today's new media world, social media has taken an important role in this information spread. The best public relations groups try to reach out to the key tweeters, instagrammers, and bloggers on a topic, knowing that their comments will be read and, more important, shared and "liked" by other influencers and press. Selective leaking to the influential blogs may be as important as bringing in the trade press. At a recent <Code> conference, the media list included three pages of print journalists and one page of bloggers. Bloggers will get the word out far more quickly (often in hours) than the more thoughtful edited journalists. The follower mechanism inherent in Twitter, Facebook, Instagram, and other social media spreads the word quickly. These can be searched easily and are indexed on Google and Bing.

New companies today use crowdfunding sites like Kickstarter and Indiegogo to gain both awareness and some funding. Electric Objects launched with a Kickstarter campaign and has kept thousands of interested buyers informed every week about the development progress. This openness has helped not only in preparing the press for their eventual launch, but also in getting the venture capital community lining up to invest. Similarly, no new cell phone product is introduced without having been seen on TechCrunch (5.1 million Twitter followers), Gizmodo (1.39 million followers), or Engadget (1.35 million followers), three key blogs for leading-edge tech products. And Product Hunt's 74,700 followers include influential venture capitalists and others who are looking for what's new.

The telecommunications, semiconductor, database software, and applications software sectors all have additional gurus, letters, and conferences. And the same holds true for biotech, energy, and every other field we have examined. At the core of the industry are a handful of influencers, who spread the word about new ideas, products, and services, along with their opinions. These opinions are usually strong indicators of success or failure in the first year after launch.

After the gurus come the influencers—editors and writers at the key mass trade and business publications in the field, most of which are now web-based rather than in large print publications. In the computer world, the Ziff Davis publications (for example, *eWeek* and *PC Magazine*) and the IDG *InfoWorld* and *Computerworld* newspapers have the broadest reach among decision makers. You must be sensitive to the lead times of each publication to maximize the coincident coverage of your story. That is, if you want to launch a new product in May, you need to meet with the longer lead weeklies two to three weeks before the news should hit, and with today's daily e-mail zines (online magazines), the day before the news should hit. Of course, in today's leaky web world, keeping a story embargoed for more than a few days is only managed by the likes of Apple, who effectively manages release of information.

For products with a consumer focus, the key mass media columnists can provide tremendous boost in product launch. Walt Mossberg, formerly personal technology columnist for the *Wall Street Journal,* and now at RE/Code and CNBC, can make or break a product with an early review. He receives hundreds of requests each week and has policies for filtering that good public relations agencies understand. He demands and usually gets to be the first to publish about your product. He likes to have them significantly in advance so that he can actually work with them and provide feedback. When Franklin Electronic Publications and Starfish Software were launching REX, Mossberg was brought in almost a year prior to launch—under appropriate embargo agreements. His input on the early betas was invaluable in making a better product. His review at the launch was a key factor in early product sales and in helping the visibility of a product that had very little advertising dollar spending.

Bloomberg Business Week, Forbes, and *Fortune* have a number of respected journalists who post on their sites and are widely read. It is necessary to view these influencers not just as targets for getting a message out, but as highly knowledgeable users who can help to improve the design and feature set of a product or service. Clearly, in today's world, it is not only the print press, but television, radio, and the Internet that must also be attended to. It was, after all, the Internet's Matt Drudge who broke the Lewinsky story rather than *Newsweek,* which held it while awaiting further confirmations.

With the plethora of cable channels has come an opportunity for companies to provide short (30-second to 2-minute) video news releases (VNR), which are often picked up by local news or specialized cable services. The impact of such a piece shown on television, often with a voice-over by the local news or science reporter, should not be underestimated. For most Kickstarter or Indiegogo campaigns, the video message is crucial. This video, or others on your company's website, will also be picked up and shown on cable or local news stations. Sproutling recently announced their next generation baby monitor, and the video on their website was used directly by Fox and other national news outlets, quickly driving traffic and orders, as well as the crucial awareness. When MetaCreations announced its Power Goo consumer image funware, the VNR was picked up by dozens of stations, and sales were noticeably increased. CNN's *Science Today* often does report on products of interest. Energy Innovations' new solar energy project had a CNN interview—and heavy web traffic in the weeks following it.

Reaching the decision makers is best done with focused direct marketing and with special events, which are described in Chapter 5. But the more general positive buzz you can get with a product, the less likely the naysayers are to voice negative, against-the-crowd opinions.

Spokespersons/Evangelists

One of the key tasks for a public relations effort is to help one (or at most two) people in the company create personal one-to-one relationships with the gurus. Most often, the CEO and chief technical person are the ones who should build and nurture these relationships, and they (or others) serve as evangelists for the product and company. This requires visiting the gurus on "press tours," getting them prerelease (beta) software or hardware, and providing oodles of technical support to ensure that any product usage goes smoothly and that your positioning and customer benefits are clearly communicated. You should understand that this is a two-way street; the guru can't be a guru without being in on the latest product entries, and everyone likes to know a secret or be in the know a little earlier than the next person. Often, if the relationship can be built early enough, the gurus can contribute to making the product more user friendly— and by having an emotional stake are more likely to help declare the product a winner.

The evangelists who meet with the press need to be personable, knowledgeable about the company and its products, and sensitive to what can and can't be said regarding fund-raising without triggering legal obligations (in the case of public companies) or concerns about "hype" (in private companies). It is important not to lie to the press or influencers—although spin is certainly acceptable and common. One of the biggest mistakes is talking in the "hoped for present" tense— that is, "Yes, the product can do xxxx," when it can't. It's also important to plan the pitch in a way that is respectful of the available time of the person being wooed. Some training in public speaking—of the type that Power Presentations of San Jose provides to entrepreneurs going on road shows—can be very helpful in correcting typical mistakes. The wrong body language, too much hesitation when responding to questions, and other problems can leave a mistaken impression on the guru. Remember, in most of these cases, first impressions last.

The overall company and product pitch should be planned for at least three lengths: the "elevator pitch," the 15-minute demo, and the 30 to 45-minute road show pitch. The elevator pitch is meant to be told in the time it takes to go a few floors next to someone in the elevator—typically 30 seconds to 2 minutes. It should engage the listener, providing something of interest to convince them that they should want to hear more. There are some iconic ways to do this, the most popular current one being, "We're going to be the Uber (or Amazon, or Facebook...) for [fill in the blank]." This is similar to pitching a Hollywood script idea as "Rocky but for women's lacrosse." However, be wary that analogies can divert attention from your product either because the audience is unfamiliar with the company or business mentioned in the analogy or the audience has a different understanding of those businesses than you do. Therefore, it is always best to focus your elevator pitch on your positioning in the most clear, compelling, and concise manner possible.

The 15-minute demo should be just that. No more than a minute or two to introduce the speaker and company—naming any credibility enhancers (advisory board members, directors, investors), followed by a demo that ideally allows for the person being briefed to get hands-on with the product. This is the amount of time that TechCrunch or other events allow companies for the pitch, so most evangelists should be ready to keep to that limit. Most of the gurus in high tech are gadget nuts at heart—they are the epitome of early adopters—even where, like Walt Mossberg—they try to put themselves in the mindset of the more average user. This puts the evangelist, whether she is CEO or CTO or just a plain marcom (marketing communications) person, in a position of preaching to people who want you to succeed. But they need to make the product vision their own so that they can preach it to others.

Finally, if there is lots of time available, prepare a slideshow (Microsoft PowerPoint or equivalent), which can be quickly tailored to the specific audience. This should include sections on company history, financing, product rollout plans, advertising plans, partnering deals (quite popular with Internet companies), and, of course, the product itself.

Linkage to Fund-raising

For those entrepreneurial ventures that are also raising money (almost all of them), the public relations efforts serve two purposes—helping the product to be perceived and perform as a winner and helping to fuel the fund-raising. With today's crowdfunding platforms (discussed in Chapter 12, "Marketing for Financing Activities"), the fund-raising is a PR event in and of itself. A successful Kickstarter campaign shows the venture community that the public will buy the product. For some products, the amount raised can dramatically lower the venture funding target and minimize dilution. The Pebble watch raised over $10 million in preorders for its first generation product, and the Ouya game console over $8.5 million with well-executed videos and PR around the campaigns. An additional set of influencers reach this community. There is a feedback effect of strong venture capital support on the core gurus and influencers. Sequoia Capital ("Sequoia") is one of the premier venture capital funds in the world. A Sequoia-funded venture has the credibility of one of the most successful partnerships behind it, and gurus take its investee company claims with somewhat less skepticism than those of an unknown company. Social media can contribute to the fund-raising efforts and credibility-building, with sites such as Producthunt.com, Angellist, FundersClub, Gust.com, and the techcrunch.com site getting early investor visitors to the sites.

Similarly, having the company mentioned at the top of the Re/Code daily e-mail may open doors that have been closed on Sand Hill Road (a location in Silicon Valley well-known for having many top-tier venture funds). Because most venture capitalists want to be seen as riding with a winner, the buzz proclaiming that a company is winning acts like perfume to the investor.

PR Agencies

There is always a lot of controversy about the value that a PR agency can bring to the table. Many small companies believe that they can get to the gurus and influencers themselves and that the often sizable cost of using an agency may not be worthwhile. Our experience is that, properly managed, PR fees gain you a tremendous multiple on your investment in them, as long as your expectations are properly established at the outset. The agency provides three basic functions:

- **Creative**—Helping to define the message
- **Execution**—Getting the message out
- **Rolodex**—Knowing who to go to and having the ability to get them to listen

Although there are dramatic quality differences among agencies with respect to how they perform the first two functions, it is the third that distinguishes the top few agencies from the next tiers. Many of the very top agencies (BrewPR, Outcast, The Horn Group, and many others) have become selective about taking on clients—in much the same way as successful DC lobbyists offer access to the right people as part of their value-added service.

Creating the positioning and its associated message in a form best suited to reach the various types of audiences is mainly a task for the company's top management. The agency can and should, however, guide the words and "spin" of the message so that it tells the story in a memorable, quick manner. Newmatter.com, Idealab's new 3D printer, adopted the slogan "Simple. Affordable. 3D Printing." All of management has gotten training in sticking to the message. One of the marks of great politicians is their ability to stay on the message—this is a lesson that should not be lost on entrepreneurs.

Once the press releases, press kit, and evaluation or demo software and hardware are created, the execution phase begins. The best agencies have good mailing lists of editors and other influencers. Each company must create their own contact lists and maintain them internally so that they can continue follow-up even if they switch agencies or bring the function in-house. Agencies often have direct access to *PR Newswire, Business Wire,* and so on to get a story out there quickly. Their Twitter streams are followed by key reporters. They are also more likely to know who has recently been assigned to which specific beats in the various periodicals and which stock market analysts are willing to see nonpublic companies.

Measuring the effectiveness of PR is something that should be done in as quantitative a manner as possible. A good clipping service can let you measure how many column inches of print and radio or TV airtime the PR efforts have generated. Having a spreadsheet with the posted ad rates of key periodicals allows you to translate column inches into the equivalent cost, if you had run those inches as paid advertising. Although not a perfect absolute number for value, it is quite useful if tracked over a period of time and gives at least some handle on the advertising alternative. When possible, a good lead-tracking system can be used to tell which mentions led to actual calls, website visits, or customer e-mails. At some companies, purchases are tracked all the way back to these types of leads—showing again the true value or the PR effort. This same practice translates well into the online domain. Many people use the number of followers added on Twitter or Instagram or the number of likes on a Facebook campaign as a first proxy for measurement.

As with most hiring, interviewing and reference checking are key in selecting the PR firm. It is imperative to check out the work they have done for similar customers. Call the CEO or marketing counterpart and ask how easy they were to work with. Be specific about the staff that will work on your account—some junior people will normally be assigned, but make sure the supervisor is someone you trust and will actually be on the account. Too often, the name partners at these firms are mainly out marketing, not performing the actual work—although they will argue that they're keeping the influencer relationships strong, from which your company benefits. Finally, PR firms often work on retainers, billing monthly fees to perform their services. As with every dollar spent on marketing, you must ensure that the firm consistently delivers value for the fees charged.

Timing Is Essential

The sequencing and timing of the PR effort is crucial to getting maximum bang for the marketing buck. Ideally you are creating a crescendo that begins with buzz about the company, moves on to create buzz about the specific product, gets industry gurus and key influencers talking off the record about the product, and culminates in a blizzard of press coverage led by the daily mass and trade press and followed up over each of the next two or three months with additional stories in monthly magazines, radio, and television.

As a counterpoint, if you are going to be that aggressive, you have to deliver. Boo.com, a luxury apparel site funded by Bernard Arnaut of LVMH, orchestrated the PR campaign and got the company buzz; however, repeated delays in launching the site (more than eight months late) caused people to be skeptical. When it was launched, it was so slow and painful to use, that the company developed a negative public image and never recovered. Remember, marketing should reflect the positioning, segmentation, and sustainable competitive differentiation of your offering, and most important, your product must deliver on that promise!

Crisis Management

One key use for public relations that goes beyond building awareness and engagement is in the area of crisis management. Every company runs into situations that threaten its reputation and well-being. When Intel's Pentium chip was found to have mistakes in its arithmetic computation engine, the initial publicity was horrendous. Intel was becoming the company that couldn't add two and two, a huge embarrassment. In such cases, public relations can help.

An effective PR effort at times of crisis can make sure the public knows how quickly and thoroughly the company is reacting to the crisis. It can help to provide credibility to the company actions. When a customer supposedly found a piece of a finger in Wendy's chili, the PR effort was quick and expansive. It showed how they were cooperating with police and health authorities, and why it was unlikely that this had happened through Wendy's fault. Once the perpetrator of this fraud was arrested, PR was used to show that the company was in the right, and store traffic went above prior levels.

In every case, two rules are clear: Communicate the truth and get out in front of bad news. No matter the crisis, lying about it will, in the long run, certainly make things worse. And it is best for you to manage your message rather than leaving it up to customers, the media, or competitors to spread the bad news for you, while you sit by in silence.

Summary

"On the Internet, no one knows you're a dog," says the famous *New Yorker* cartoon showing a dog at a keyboard. No one knows your company exists either, unless you take the proper steps to gain the perception and then deliver the reality of leadership. Working through the various circles of influencers and their often huge social media reach is the best way to quickly have that perception created. This perception of leadership will help not only in reinforcing your positioning and selling your product or service, but also in hiring and fund-raising for the entrepreneurial venture.

Endnote

1. Public Relations Defined. (2014, December 29). Retrieved from Public Relations Society of America: http://www.prsa.org/aboutprsa/publicrelationsdefined/#.VKAaAV4AA.

5

Promotion and Viral Marketing to Maximize Sustainable Profitability

The Coolest Cooler—One of Kickstarter's Most Successful Campaigns

Ryan Grepper's Coolest Cooler is one of the most successful Kickstarter campaigns ever, having raised more than $13,000,000. (Kickstarter's most successful campaign is the Pebble Time campaign discussed in Chapter 12, "Marketing for Financing Activities.")

However, the first time Ryan sought funding on Kickstarter, the campaign failed to raise the targeted $125,000. The lessons learned between the two campaigns are excellent examples of the principles in this book and especially the promotional methods outlined in this chapter.

Ryan attributes the success of his second attempt to three reasons:

- Supporters were more receptive to a summer "fun" product in August than in November, the timing of the initial campaign.
- The Kickstarter video, the key element of sharing the concept with potential supporters, more clearly demonstrated the product, communicated the benefits, and connected with the target audience.
- Ryan leveraged simple viral tools in the campaign to encourage supporters of the product to spread the word.

In hindsight, it appeared obvious to Ryan, but the first time he introduced the Coolest Cooler, it was November, and he had hopes of capturing the holiday market. However, coolers are more closely associated with summer activities, so the second campaign provided a more consistent context by launching during the summertime.

The Kickstarter video for the successful campaign presented a much clearer value proposition for the customer. The Coolest Cooler is all about fun—a "party in a box." Whereas the first video did an excellent job highlighting features, the revised video focused on how those features delivered benefits to the customer (increased the "fun"). The first video had great energy and used much of the same video footage as the second video. In the video for the successful campaign, the images of fun were delivered with a voice-over that focused on how the features enhanced fun rather than addressing problems of other coolers. Finally, the second video concluded with a clear "ask" that led to the third reason for its success, a viral component.

The final image of the successful video showed the Coolest logo, together with an image of the cooler and the message, "Please share this video now so we can make your Coolest!" With this simple message, Ryan engaged the early supporters of the Coolest Cooler as viral marketers for his product, spreading the word and sharing the effective marketing elements with a broader market looking for FUN. The end result? Ryan raised a record-breaking $13,285,226 of nondilutive capital from more than 60,000 customers who purchased the product before it was manufactured!

Methods for Promoting Products and Engaging Customers

There is no substitute for the actual trial of most products or services. Promotion gets your product itself in front of the customers, influencers, or press so that they can more easily try it or see it in action. If your public relations campaign has worked, they should be eager to get their hands on it, but even if it hasn't, pushing it into their hands or onto their phones, tablets, and screens can help not just at launch, but for years afterward. You can get products to the consumer in several ways, and this chapter discusses direct marketing promotions, viral marketing, event marketing, and other guerilla marketing techniques that entrepreneurial companies are more likely to use than long-established ones. These promotions can be tested and adapted to focus more resources on those that yield the best results—yet another example of adaptive testing and experimentation. In addition, product placement, where people see your product being used by a celebrity in a movie or television show, can be thought of as a cross between PR and promotion. Some of the methods to promote products are outlined in Table 5-1 and detailed in the sections that follow.

Table 5-1 Methods to Promote Products

Type	When to Use	Example
Giveaway	Low cost, viral product	Netscape
Try to buy	User needs experience to value product	Ameritrade
Credible exposure Product placement	Validate the hot product	Mini Cooper
Mass exposure Event marketing	Want large initial sales at one time	Windows 95 launch

Give It Away

In today's Internet world, giving away the product has become a long-term strategy, not just a short-term promotion that puts a free trial bottle of shampoo in your Sunday newspaper delivery. However, as an aunt of mine was fond of saying, "Just because it's free, doesn't mean it's cheap." Users have also become more savvy about accepting free apps or software and understanding what it may cost them to operate and maintain it. The Open Source software revolution has even spawned companies such as Cygnus Solutions, whose slogan is "Making free software affordable." When Apple opened up the App Store to developers, few thought that almost all of the apps would be free. Yet this is the model that the phone and tablet market has adopted.

Netscape popularized the Internet craze for giving away software in the mid-1990s by making its Navigator browser software freely downloadable for nonprofit users and downloadable for 90-day trials for other personal or corporate use. After they had achieved a very high market share, Microsoft got religion and made their Internet Explorer browser completely free—forcing Netscape to do the same for their browser. Once all the key competitors in the space had "free" as the price tag, it became almost impossible for anyone else to enter. Netscape then initiated an open source spin-off foundation, Mozilla, which eventually created the free Firefox browser that would supplant Netscape's own Navigator. Firefox rapidly became a major force in the browser wars and held sway (outside of Apple's Safari) until Google released Chrome—also for free, which has taken a major share of the browser market. Of course, although the browsers are free to the end users, they must find another way to create value for the companies. In this case, browsers make a lot of money for the providers by directing searches to providers (Google, Bing, and Ask, among others) who pay a small fee for each search. This allows the Mozilla Foundation to fund its continued development.

The Netscape strategy actually had two parts to it, with virality being a key goal. The first was to encourage usage among the college and university students who had high-speed access to the Internet within their dorms and schools. The word of mouth generated by this group spread rapidly to their professors, who, as consultants to industry and sources for the press, were able to certify that Netscape was the winner. At the time Netscape was launched, Spry, Quarterdeck, and Spyglass all had licensed versions of the software from the University of Illinois NCSA (National Center for Supercomputing Activities), where the original Mosaic browser (the precursor to Netscape Navigator) had been developed. Netscape had also realized that if they captured the space on the user's desktop, they could turn that into later revenue (monetize the users, in today's Internet terminology), by selling advertising and other items on their home page, which most browsers pointed to when the program was started. During their first year, they sold search buttons to companies such as Yahoo! for $5 million each. This translated into more than $100 million in advertising-related revenue in the early years—and the user base would drive the corporations to believe that Netscape's winning position translated to their Internet servers, for which Netscape could charge large sums.

With any advertising-supported medium, be it network television, controlled circulation magazines, or Internet searching, the true customer lifetime value (CLV) of a user (viewer, reader) must be estimated to determine how much one can spend attracting them. If the CLV is substantially larger than the cost, free can be made to work. Google changed the game in e-mail with its beta of Gmail, offering first 100MB, then 1GB, and now 15GB of free storage, more than ten times that of the competitors at the time. Gmail is now a huge player in e-mail, with ads being shown and searches coming from mail more than paying for the costs of providing the service.

Giveaways are not limited to free software. There are now two free morning newspapers in New York (*AM* and *Metro*) that are given away to people entering the subway—a captive readership market. The *Washington Post* has also started a free morning paper to get new "users" into the habit of reading a paper. Their hope is that this leads to purchases of the flagship *Washington Post* as well. The key to these giveaway products is the ability to generate revenue through another means, whether it be advertising or paid versions of related products.

Free Trials Versus Free Forever Versus Freemium

Making it easy for a user to try a product or service is a key factor in creating demand. If a user takes advantage of a free trial and gets hooked, he is quite likely to be amenable to paying for the value received later on. You must take care to ensure the user realizes the true value and doesn't perceive the product as one that should be free. *Many brokerage-only firms give you your first few trades free.* On the Internet, this leads to a number of hybrid models, where limited usage is free, while unlimited or professional versions cost money, or in the case of apps, where in-app purchases can dominate. Fred Wilson, a leading New York venture capitalist, called this the "Freemium" model, and it now dominates in the Software as a Service (SaaS) and app worlds.

Most of the consumer games on smartphones and tablets have monetized their users through in-app purchases. *Angry Birds* was generating hundreds of millions of dollars per year from users who wanted a little boost in their ability to kill the birds, pigs, and so forth.

Candy Crush similarly enticed users into increasing their ability to win with small purchases. But the free versions are what drew people in. The rule of thumb is that 2%–5% of the users will buy, but they'll buy a whole lot—creating big profits for companies that have almost zero cost of distribution.

Free trials are especially common with software and are designed to overcome the perceived cost of switching to a new product. If several software products perform similar functions, users will stick with the first one they learn. It is important to get them to install and use your new service, come to your website, and so on. They need to play with the user interface and learn your offering's benefits so that they can make the purchase or switch decision.

Not only software can be served up free. Most newspapers and magazines offer several weeks or months of free trials, delivering their product to your door so you can read it and then subscribe. This approach is not new. For years, book clubs, record clubs, and many other direct mail promotions (for example, Gevalia coffee) have given you the product and tools to use it (such as a free coffeemaker with Gevalia), in the hope of gaining a long-term customer.

Key Metrics for Free Trials to Pay

The key metrics to consider when doing any business are the CAC (customer acquisition cost) and CLV (customer lifetime value), discussed previously in the "Demand Generation and Sales—Lead Your Customers to Your Offering" section introduction. Free trials (or paid trials, for that matter) are worth it when the CAC is below CLV by enough to make money. When AOL gave out CDs to almost every household in America for ten free hours online, they knew that a 1% conversion rate from free to paid led to a very high (42-month) average lifetime value of over $400. So 100 $0.75 CDs ($75.00) led to very high value.

So it is today in the app world. There, we use the additional metric ARPU (average revenue per user), which can be either daily ARPU, monthly ARPU, or annual ARPU. If it costs $1.00 to get your app downloaded, and the daily ARPU for your downloaded game is $.05, then 20 days of play gets you back your cost (assuming very little variable costs)—and if you can keep your users engaged for 45 days, they have a CLV of $2.25 against the $1.00 cost.

The best thing about doing this in the app world is that Apple or Google does all the billing and collection (for a 30% fee), and your venture doesn't have to create this expensive infrastructure, further lowering the costs of creating a business.

Viral Marketing

The rise of the Internet has given rise to even faster and cheaper forms of promotion—and the term *viral marketing*. The phrase *viral marketing* was coined by the venture firm Draper Fisher Jurvetson, investors in Hotmail (originally HoTMaiL, to indicate that it was an e-mail service based on HTML). Hotmail was founded in 1996 and sold to Microsoft for $400 million a little more than one year later. Hotmail was a free e-mail service that added the text, "P.S. Get your free email at Hotmail," to the bottom of every e-mail sent through its service. This signature was linked to Hotmail's home page. Although contentious at the time because of its blatant advertising nature, this signature allowed every recipient of a Hotmail-processed e-mail to learn about and become a user of Hotmail. What made Hotmail so powerful was its inherently viral nature. Hotmail grew to more than 30 million users within three years and created one of the most significant marketing concepts of the time.

In a viral situation, each user tells her friends to download the app or visit a website because it will enable them to communicate, share experiences, or work together. Thus each new user "infects" many of her friends with the product, and the company offering the product may achieve exponential growth. Messaging apps have led in this category because they require the sender and recipient to each have the app. The recent sale of WhatsApp to Facebook for $19 billion, after gaining 500 million users, is just the latest in this trend.

Many companies and industries have followed the viral mode of promotion, including the entire field of social networking. Facebook, Twitter, LinkedIn, and Pinterest have grown into powerhouse companies because each user of these and other similar services is expected to get their friends to join. It is the large, extended network of "friends of friends" that make these services valuable to each member. Over the past several years, hundreds of millions of venture capital dollars have been invested in these social networks, even before they have proven business models that generated revenue, much less profits. The largest ones, such as Facebook, have more than 1 billion registered users, all secured from a small core of initial users who invited their friends and acquaintances to join. In the case of LinkedIn, there was an early competition to have the most connections. The business models for most of the social networks came after they grew to scale. For LinkedIn, which is meant as a professional (work-related) social network, the money is in job hunting and recruitment. For Facebook, it's as an advertising platform, with e-commerce close behind. Customers who come to a website from a Pinterest link are far more likely to buy than those who get there from banner ad links.

One of the key metrics for any company using viral marketing is the viral coefficient. This is the number of new users who sign on (or download the app) for each additional user. If I send a new Instagram photo to five people who are not on, and 2.5 (average) download the app, Instagram would have a 2.5 viral coefficient. This creates exponential spreading of an app or a meme (or product campaign). Although anything above zero means growth, numbers above three indicate potential explosive growth and can be conducive to raising investment capital for these companies. As with many of the marketing tactics we discuss, the viral coefficient provides a measurable way to assess the success of adaptive experiments. In this case, we can allocate greater resources to activities that improve the viral coefficient.

Most messaging-based sites or applications have a natural virality because each recipient of a message needs to visit a website or download an app to receive the message. The best-known early use of this technique was ICQ ("I seek you"), which made instant messaging available on the Internet. It was also the technology for AOL Instant Messenger (AIM). Instant messaging had been one of the most attractive features on AOL—it permits a user to see if a friend is simultaneously online, and if so, to pop up a message on the friend's screen and get a response in real time. ICQ required web users to download a moderately large piece of software, which took several minutes on normal modems, and to register their e-mail and alias information with ICQ. Within a year, they had over a million users and have since grown to several hundred million users. As AOL moved onto the Internet, they purchased Mirabilis, ICQ's Israeli parent, for almost $300 million, and continued to operate it—all this before ICQ had figured out how to monetize their users. Instagram moved sharing of pictures to the same level, and Vines has done the same for sharing of short videos.

Although not a social network per se, Dropbox has used viral marketing to increase its user base by offering incentives for referrals. Initially, Dropbox provided 250MB of free space to both the user and a friend referred by the user. Now each referral earns a user 500MB up to a total of 32GB of free Dropbox storage space. In 2012, Dropbox launched an incredibly successful promotional campaign targeting universities, the Great Space Race. This viral campaign created a competition among institutions of higher learning. Each member of the community earned points by referring other members of the community to sign up for Dropbox. Points in turn earned storage space on the service. National University of Singapore won the Great Space Race with more than 45,000 points earned by 20,532 participants.[1]

Outside of the messaging and software spaces, many consumer product companies use "member get a member" type promotions. These offer a discount coupon to both the current member and any friend who signs up and purchases using that special code. At Fab.com, the offer was $5 off your next purchase and $5 off your friend's first purchase. Other than limits to prevent fraudulent abuse, these techniques are a reliable way to get customers. And because you receive the invitation from a hopefully trusted friend, it has higher redemption than just getting a random e-mail offer from the company. Diapers.com used a similar offer to encourage delighted current customers to bring their friends to the site. For their first five years, before they were acquired by Amazon, diapers.com was getting over 35% of their customers by referrals from existing customers.

Using Social Media for Viral Marketing

Social networks are built on the value of trust, and the perception of trust is a valuable marketing concept. According to a recent study by Ogilvy, TNS, and Google, word of mouth was the number one influencer, cited by 74% of the participants.[2] Now that there are such large social networks, marketers use them to create the viral marketing loop for goods and services. This has spawned a social media management industry. A brand can create a social media campaign that offers prizes or recognition for the best photo of the product's use, as posted on the brand's Instagram feed. Many brands have tied Super Bowl advertising campaigns to likes on their Facebook pages, hoping to dramatically increase awareness of a new brand.

Because consumers trust their friends more than the brands that are advertising, getting user-generated positive remarks about your product is very powerful. Old Spice was one of the first brands to make a big splash on Twitter. They had Isaiah Mustafah, the star of their hugely successful *Smell Like a Man* television commercial, respond to consumer tweets in real time. This generated over a million responses from users.

Viral marketing can also help charity campaigns. In the spring and summer of 2014, the ALS foundation raised millions of dollars through the Ice Bucket Challenge. People, starting with Boston sports figures, poured buckets of ice water over their heads, and posted videos (on YouTube, Facebook, Twitter) that then challenged some specific friends to do the same or donate to ALS. As the videos spread, the campaign became viral and led to television personalities, movie stars, sports heroes, and thousands of just plain folks doing it—and donating cash as well as getting splashed. Although things such as the Jerry Lewis Muscular Dystrophy Telethon have always had the ability to reach lots of people, these viral campaigns can explode in a few days to millions of followers. The Ice Bucket Challenge raised more than $120 million in just a few months!

When Do Giveaways Work?

Clearly, not every product or service is suitable for the "free" strategy. The four key elements needed to make it an efficient way to build customers are as follows:

- Low product cost
- Low switching cost

- Easy distribution
- High customer lifetime value (CLV) relative to customer acquisition cost (CAC)

Any software product, by its nature, has low cost of goods. Most of today's software is downloadable, with online documentation. Even if there are physical media, the marginal cost of reproduction is at worst the cost of a CD-ROM (under $1.00 in volume), and at best the cost of maintaining FTP or web servers from which potential users can download the software and documentation. With cloud-based processing power from Amazon or Microsoft, the cost of maintaining servers for downloads is extremely low. And the cost of delivering Software as a Service (SaaS), such as Salesforce or Gmail, has gotten to be an extremely low expense relative to the revenue one can get from even a small percentage of users.

Free trials have long been used in other media, even where cost is high, as long as the customers are well qualified. Bombardier will even give you a free trial ride on a corporate jet in order to convince you of the Flexjet program's benefits. To qualify for this trial, however, you have to do more than send an e-mail.

A key factor in deciding whether or not viral marketing can work is the cost to the user of switching to the new product or service. In the Internet world, this can be equated to the amount of time (or number of forms) a user must spend to set up his new account, software, and so on. For example, there are a large number of portfolio management sites, which keep you updated on your stock holdings. For someone with two or three stocks, the setup is usually fast—but for users with extensive holdings, who may be the best customer targets, this can often take a half hour or more. This often leads to the good driving out the best; that is, the first reasonable solution a user adopts may be good enough to keep them from switching to a better, or even much better, solution. Just as we discussed the value of being "vaguely right" in Chapter 3, "Entrepreneurial Pricing—An Often Misused Way to Garner Extraordinary Profits," "good enough" may be the winner in the market.

You can help this problem by automating the switch or minimizing the user work necessary to perform such a switch. Almost all of the social networks have tools to search your existing Outlook contacts and import them. Most of the portfolio management tools can accept an exported file in Quicken or Microsoft Money format. Making the OOBE (Out of Box Experience) as simple as possible is a key element in a promotion's success.

The critical thing is to constantly measure the metrics of every stage of the consumer adoption process. What fraction of users who see your product downloads the app? What fraction opens it for first use? What fraction uses it more than once? What fraction converts to some paid model? And what is the CLV for users? At Twitter, there is a group dedicated to continuous improvement on the metrics at each stage of this process, and more and more, companies are adapting their marketing strategies to take advantage of the marketing activities that yield the best results.

Event Marketing

Everyone loves a parade. The excitement of an event can create good feelings about a product or service and lead to a time-focused set of articles and press interviews that generate the all-important buzz about the new idea. Even a small company can generate a large amount of hoopla through a well-planned event—often enough to sound like a much larger company to the customers and competitors. The goal of event marketing is to have the press use editorial ink and space to promote a product, rather than paid advertising. And the press can not only write about the features and functions of the product, but also about the level of excitement surrounding the launch— which will often convince skeptical users to try it.

Apple and Pixar are *the* masters of the event marketing world. Several times each year Apple runs the World Wide Developers Conferences (WWDC) and MacWorld conferences. Essentially all of Apple's key product announcements are made at these events, which get large press coverage and are webcast to Apple enthusiasts worldwide. The iPod, iTunes, and even the U2 special edition were shown at this venue. Apple is so focused on these events that they have taken extraordinary measures to keep leaks from happening, even suing the bloggers who previewed the latest operating system releases. By controlling when the promotion and release occurs, Apple can maximize the impact. Having the CEO himself do the first public demonstrations also underscores the importance of each new release.

In the most recent example, the iPhone 6 and 6Plus launch, Apple sold $6.5 billion of product in the first weekend of shipping! The amount of free press, TV, and so on that they received would have cost tens if not hundreds of millions of dollars.

Although product PR can be gained from event marketing, so can general corporate image. The current trend of paying for the naming of football stadiums (AT&T Park) and postseason games (the IBM Aloha Bowl) is meant to associate the corporate name with certain images. This enhances the company image in many ways—as supporters of the community and supporters of sports. For smaller companies, local and charitable event sponsorships are good options to accomplish similar goals. Even companies adopting sections of highways and helping to keep them clean, provides image and branding. The key to these promotional activities is ensuring that they reinforce your positioning.

Industry conferences offer some of the best opportunities for event marketing. The key influencers and press representatives are usually present, as are many potential customers, distributors, and agents (not to mention competitors). Getting noticed above the clutter of exhibit booths and trade press ads may not be easy. Events can be as small and simple as the press conference, where company spokespeople announce a new product and invite the press to listen, or as elaborate as the big evening parties and entertainment events. Charityfolks.com provides an online method for companies to tie product launches and auctions together with a wide variety of charities, all of which can increase visibility.

MetaCreations Corp. (now Viewpoint) was a small computer graphics software company with some interesting new products. It was searching for a method of getting lots of press attention at Comdex—once the country's largest trade show—with only a small amount of money in the bank. John Wilczak, the CEO, decided to hold a large party (500 key people from the industry) at a location like the Hard Rock Café or House of Blues. He created the Digital Media Players Party, which would let several companies, including MetaCreations, showcase their newest technologies by having demo stations around the nightclub. The cost for throwing the party was a little over $250,000 that the company didn't have. Wilczak called on some of the biggest players in the industry—Kodak, Adobe, and so on—and sold them on being "sponsors" of the party. As sponsors, they would pay a fraction of the cost ($25–$50,000), and get an allocation of invitations and demo stations.

When the invitations went out, they read "MetaCreations Corporation (in big letters) invites you to the Digital Media Players Party, sponsored by Adobe, Kodak, and so on (in small letters)." This party was held at three to five major conferences a year for the next several years. MetaCreations managed it and got most of the PR credit, with a net cost to the company of zero dollars. In addition to being able to be identified with the big guns of the industry and to get the new products in front of the press and influencer community, the fact that it was seen as the entity throwing the party caused most of the customers to assume it was a much larger company than its sales would have indicated. This increase in customer confidence definitely helped the sales effort.

Consumer Events

Not all event marketing needs to be directed at the influencers. There can be great benefit from events focused on end consumers. The midnight launch has become a staple, not just for computer software (the Windows launches), but for *Harry Potter* books, movies (*Lord of the Rings, The Matrix*), and other new goods. The Xbox 360 launch, where Bill Gates gave out the first Xbox, generated millions of dollars of press for the company's launch.

Beer companies have certainly used summer events at beaches and student gathering places to promote their products, along with the positive messages promoting designated drivers. And the Oscar Mayer Weinermobile, which travels to fairs and other events, adds a promotional touch to a very mundane product.

Product Placement

If you can show the most influential people in the world using your product, consumers should follow suit—hence, the dramatic rise in product placement, where a prominently logoed or identifiable product is used in a movie, television show, or other highly visible application. At a time when television shows are recorded on DVRs and commercials are skipped by millions, having the product woven into the actual storyline of a series ensures at least some face time. With some recent movies, this can go quite far. *The Italian Job,* a caper movie, featured the Mini Cooper automobile to such a great extent that many felt there would be a backlash. But in fact, the film helped awareness and added a "coolness" factor that propelled sales for more than a year.

Richard Roeper, speaking about the Disney movie *Herbie: Fully Loaded,* said "This is a product placement movie gone wild. There's a commercial contained within every frame." Promotions appear for NASCAR, Tropicana, Volkswagen, ESPN, Goodyear (Lindsay Lohan wears a Goodyear baseball cap for 15 onscreen minutes). Of course, NASCAR itself is a master of logos because fans can't actually see the drivers when the cars are racing around the track. Ross Johnson, writing in the *New York Times,* points out that even the Broadway musical *Sweet Charity* got Neil Simon's permission to mention Gran Centenario tequila in return for financial remuneration.

There are agencies that specialize in getting your product written into a script or used as a giveaway. Franklin Electronic Publications, for example, offered their electronic dictionaries as a prize on *Wheel of Fortune,* a natural place. They also provide them as prizes in the National Spelling Bee. Nokia and Motorola often vie for whose phone will be the one shown in a movie or TV series, and Apple has a policy of lending Macs to any TV program that will show an office to be an all Mac office. If one were inferring computer popularity from television shows, Macs would be used in over 50% of the corporate world, quite a lot higher than their single digit percentage.

Even video games are not immune to product placement. A number of recent deals have been struck to place consumer product logos in the backgrounds of popular video games such as *Grand Theft Auto.* The hope is that the gamers, who are not watching network television, will get sufficient exposure to affect their buying habits. All of these examples provide another opportunity to reinforce product positioning and increase perceived value.

Winning the Tchotchke Wars

Getting your company's name, logo, and message into the mindspace of as many people for as long as possible is a major goal of any public relations effort. One way of doing this is with *tchotchkes* (the Yiddish word for a small freebie)—T-shirts, key chains, coffee mugs, and so on. These are given away at trade shows, fairs, public events, and so on. After a typical computer industry trade show, I come home loaded with half a dozen T-shirts, a few key chains, some mouse pads, Post-it note pads, a logoed Swiss Army knife (not easy with airport security), and more.

The key factors for a successful tchotchke are *longevity, visibility*, and *cleverness*. Longevity is the length of time the tchotchke is likely to remain in the receiver's possession so that it can keep making impressions. Visibility is the number of other people who are likely to actually see it and how many times they'll see it. Those tchotchkes that make use of clever text and images are more memorable and therefore have a higher impact. Each item should be chosen to maximize these factors for the specific target audience.

Articles of clothing are one of the most common classes of tchotchke. Hats, T-shirts, and better shirts (such as polo shirts) get your message out to only a few people at a time and are more effective when given to your own employees. They are likely to wear them proudly and, if asked about the company mentioned on the shirt, to provide real information. The people working a trade show should be given hats and shirts so that they are advertising the company not just at the trade show booth, but throughout their stay in the trade show location. Splunk, a successful high-tech data visualization company, makes use of various T-shirt slogans that appeal to the company's high-tech customers, who may wear them as proudly as employees. A slogan "put that in your | and splunk it," is a clever play on words that may only be understood and appreciated by developers (*Hint:* The character "|" is a pipe). One of the authors was wearing this particular Splunk shirt recently in Mexico, when a stranger on the beach came up and introduced himself as a fellow "geek," indicating that he understood the slogan, knew the company, and even praised the products. However, be forewarned that customers who get these items might give them to the kids, diluting the multiplier value of the gift, although there still is goodwill created with the prospect or customer.

For long-term mindshare, phone chargers can keep a company's name, logo, URL, and 800-number continually in front of current or potential customers at times when they most appreciate the value of your tchotchke. And they have all the contact information at their fingertips, quite literally. In a similar vein, pads of various types—for example, Post-it notes, cubes with the logo on the side and top, binders that hold 8 1/2-by-11-inch pads, coffee coasters and so on—often last for a long time on the desk and within the sight lines of the prospect. By contrast, pens and pencils, even with the company's name, phone, and URL, are often kept in a pocket or purse, and hence do not get the number of exposures that a desk item would. If the prospect is a coffee or tea drinker, a large coffee mug or travel mug will also lend itself to staying visible on the desk for long periods of time.

There are always new items being touted as the cool new thing— water bottles in various shapes, fanny packs, Frisbees, and so on. The recent wave of tchotchkes includes speed chargers for cell phones, charging cables, and USB thumb drives. Most of these have the same drawback that clothing does: They are not often kept around the office, where they can affect the decision and speed the ability of the prospect to get in contact with the company. And their cost is often high relative to their value.

On the other hand, using a tchotchke to get a more detailed prospect form, either on the Internet, over the phone, or at a trade show, is a time-honored tradition. "Fill this out and get a free . . ." still works better than a plea without the bribe. Again, items with longevity such as a small flashlight, a key chain that would be used and seen quite often, or a telephone rest, are better than the classic T-shirt or hat.

Summary

Creative methods to get your product into the hands of or in front of your intended purchaser or user burgeon every day. You should not just attempt to repeat the methods described in this chapter. The entrepreneurial breakthroughs will occur when you become the first to use a new method or trick. Although many of the tried-and-true techniques remain valuable, the public does become inured to some of the methods. Your job is to develop a number of possible promotion and marketing options, evaluate their potential cost and lifetime margin impact, and choose those with the highest returns on the marketing dollars. As with advertising, when there is a lot of uncertainty, testing before widespread rollout can point you to the most efficacious methods at any particular time. The entrepreneurial marketer needs to always keep in mind that any promotion must be consistent with the firm's positioning.

Endnotes

1. *Dropbox Great Space Race*. (2014). Retrieved from Dropbox: https://www.dropbox.com/spacerace.

2. Ogilvy, TNS, Google. (2014, June). *When the Path to Purchase Becomes the Path to Purpose*. Retrieved from https://docs.google.com/viewer?url=http%3A%2F%2Fthink.storage.googleapis.com%2Fdocs%2Fthe-path-to-purpose_articles.pdf.

6

Advertising to Build Awareness and Reinforce Messaging

Synygy Generated Productive Ad Options for Low Cost

Adaptive experimentation in advertising can provide large returns for modest investments. Synygy, Inc., is an entrepreneurial company that does administration of complex incentive compensation plans. The company improved its advertising dramatically by testing alternative ads and choosing the best performer, rather than developing and committing to a single campaign. Synygy had an advertising agency that they used in the traditional way. The advertising that the agency came up with was run for a period of six months in print media that their target audience—senior sales force managers and administrators—would read. The objective of the advertising was to bring good leads for their sales force to follow up. Figure 6-1 shows an ad that was typical of the ads the agency ran.

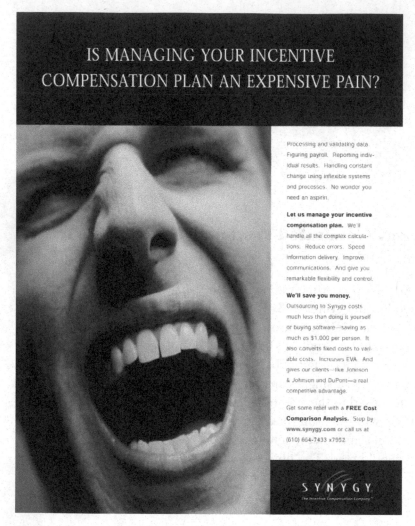

Figure 6-1 The typical ad they ran

This ad campaign brought in from two to five leads per week either over the phone or to the company's website. One of the company's employees (a graphic artist) approached Mark Stiffler, the founder and CEO, with a mock-up of a very different print ad. Mark directed the employee to make it into a print quality ad and tested the ad by running it once in place of the old ad. The new ad is shown in Figure 6-2.

Figure 6-2 The employee-generated print ad

The ad was much better than the old ad—it was obvious by monitoring the inquiries generated that it was orders of magnitude more productive. Synygy began using the new ad exclusively, both in their print media and their direct mail brochures. In the first six months the new campaign was running, inquiries were averaging 67 per week! With no change in media budget or media plan, the new campaign was at least 15 times more productive than the old campaign! It was certainly worth the nominal investment by Synygy to test the employee ad! The quality of the new "Tom" ad is probably not wonderful from an artistic point of view. However, *advertising for entrepreneurial companies is not an art form; it's a way to generate inquiries and sales.*

Moving to More Effective Advertising

Advertising is probably the most misused (and misunderstood) marketing instrument by entrepreneurial ventures of all sizes. Many entrepreneurs and other managers believe that advertising is too difficult to evaluate on a cost-benefit basis. Entrepreneurs often adopt approaches to advertising that large, packaged goods companies use. These advertising approaches have a number of "rules" that help a firm or its advertising agencies to make some advertising management decisions. Examples of some of these "rules" include the following:

1. The incremental revenue produced by advertising is not worthwhile to measure, so don't even try.

2. If an area or market segment has x% of revenues, it should get x% of the advertising exposures—its "fair share."

3. If you want to achieve a market share of x%, you must maintain an advertising budget that is greater than x% of the amount spent by all the competitors in the category.

4. You should pulse advertising expenditures into periodic flights, which will cut through all of the competitive clutter.

5. You need at least three advertising exposures on a consumer to have an effect. Any less than three has no impact.

6. Advertising takes a long time to work, and its long-term effect is difficult to measure—but is there.

7. If you believe TV advertising works, then more TV advertising is obviously better than less.

These "rules" become mental models that many firms use as rules of thumb to make their advertising decision making easier. Many companies have repeated these and other similar rules so often that they have become analogous to a religion. Many advertising decisions are thus made on faith.

Entrepreneurs can't run their businesses on faith. They must allocate scarce capital resources to maximize the value that the venture creates for customers and captures for the venture. Advertising is only one alternative use of scarce resources. Other marketing elements like public relations, promotion, and the sales force compete for resources with other uses such as working capital, new production equipment, and so on. These marketing elements contribute to the customer acquisition cost (CAC) and, therefore, have a direct impact on profitability. This chapter shows that it *is* possible to evaluate the potential incremental return versus cost for advertising. These returns can then be compared with other uses of scarce capital resources to enable the entrepreneur to make the most productive use of her available resources and minimize CAC. However, as we will show, these methods for estimating returns may be imprecise, but they are the best that can be done under the circumstances. We will show that it is better to be "vaguely right" rather than using rules such as the preceding ones, which are "precisely wrong."

To emphasize how misunderstood advertising is, even by the large "sophisticated" firms, we first share research that analyzes the incremental sales effectiveness of TV advertising. We then describe methodologies that entrepreneurs can use to make decisions on advertising so as to be able to at least roughly analyze advertising's return and compare it with other uses for the scarce resources.

The seismic shift to digital advertising is a key arrow in the modern advertiser's quiver. Digital advertising is highly measurable and cost effective; it includes search engine marketing, online display ads, as well as social media and e-mail ads. This shift to digital advertising, estimated to be almost $60 billion in the United States in 2014,[1] can be used to an entrepreneurial venture's advantage today.

Even Large Firms Waste a Lot of Their Advertising Expenditures

Two well-researched articles provide convincing evidence that even the largest TV advertisers can significantly improve the productivity of their TV advertising.[2, 3] The first study, sponsored by all the major packaged goods marketers, analyzed almost 400 in-market, split-cable, year-long TV advertising tests using the Behaviorscan system, a service of Information Resources, Inc. That study then was replicated twice over a 20-year period.[4, 5]

Behaviorscan is a household purchasing panel comprising approximately 3,000 demographically representative households from each of six geographically dispersed markets. All supermarket purchases are recorded via scanners and linked to individual household identification to measure precise purchasing behavior.

In addition, households receive all of their television transmissions via cable technology, and advertising can be directed to or removed from individual households on a targeted basis. This capability has allowed the execution of numerous carefully controlled advertising experiments. Media weights, media plan configuration, and many other advertising variables have been experimentally tested using this technology.

The tests that were analyzed were those in which some panelists received a different level of TV advertising than others for a year. These tests give very valid estimates of the incremental revenue impact of the tested campaigns. The study showed that only 33% of TV advertising for established brands was showing a statistically significant incremental sales response to this TV advertising. On the other hand, when TV ads worked, they produced big volume effects (a mean increase of 18% in sales), the effects lasted for a period of over two years, and they emerged surprisingly fast (within six months in most cases). The difference between the ads that worked and those that didn't was mostly idiosyncratically related to the copy that the campaigns used. There were more frequently run smaller brands ads that worked, while ads that promoted the status quo did not work as well as ads that tried to change something or impart "news." "What you say" was much more important than "how much you say it." The key takeaway for the entrepreneurial marketer is to focus on the positioning and messaging to ensure that it resonates with your target market.

These 400 in-market tests also cast much doubt on each of the "rules" in this chapter's introduction. All of these "rules" were not supported by the incremental sales response to TV advertising shown in the tests.

How Entrepreneurs Can Improve the Productivity of Their Advertising

The key advertising decisions are typically categorized as budget (how much should I spend?), media planning (where and when should I place the advertising?), and copy (what should I say?). Many books have been written on how best to make these decisions. However, you will probably not have the luxury of trying all the different theories (most of which have not been shown to be fully validated to help entrepreneurs make more productive advertising decisions). Instead, you must do the best with what you have—little money and little time. In that spirit, the following methods and concepts should be helpful.

Typically, the entrepreneurial business gets an idea for an advertising and/or promotion campaign from someone (the owner, an employee, an agency, a customer, a friend, or an advisor). The "campaign" is typically a combination of media, copy, and budget. Examples might be—"Let's e-mail an ad with a discount to promote trial of our new app," "Let's run ads on the radio to announce our new line of auto accessories," or "Let's put out circulars with our menu and a coupon for a free drink to the new office building that just got finished." Conceptually, what is needed is a way to evaluate whether the campaign will generate enough incremental revenue so that the incremental margin contributed by that new revenue will more than cover the advertising and or promotion expense. As long as this return is better than other uses for the campaign funds (including other possible different campaigns), the campaign should be continued.

The big problems are evaluating the incremental return of the campaign and generating campaigns that are even better. The following section first discusses methods for improving campaigns and then describes concepts and methods for evaluating incremental returns.

Improving Campaigns

Obviously, whatever can be done to make campaigns more productive is beneficial to the marketing process. There are a number of steps that the entrepreneur can take to improve the campaigns as they are being developed.

First and most important, you must make sure that every campaign you use is *supportive* and *consistent* with your *positioning* strategy. At every opportunity, you should be asking, "Is this campaign targeted at the right market segment and will it improve our customers' perception of our sustainable competitive advantage over competitive offerings?"

As long as the campaigns are consistent with the strategy, then it's your job to have the *most widely varied copies* generated and evaluated. Profitable copy generation can be compared to a lottery. The differences in incremental revenues between alternative copies and creative strategies can be large. Some campaigns can really add large amounts of incremental sales, while other campaigns (with similar budgets) will do nothing or might even hurt sales. *Conceptually, you should generate a number of very different campaigns, evaluate the potential incremental revenue impact of each of them, and run only the best one—as long as the best one is incrementally profitable and pays for its opportunity costs (including being more productive than the current campaign).*

However, in reality, it's just not that simple. Managing the advertising process involves a real balancing act for the marketer. A number of advertising management decisions are interrelated and should be determined simultaneously. These decisions include: How many different campaigns should I have generated? How much should I spend for the alternative campaigns? Should I retain an advertising agency? Who else should be tapped to generate new campaign alternatives? Each of these decisions depends on the answers to the other decisions. If you manage a huge organization with lots of time and resources, it is possible to think about an "optimally" profitable answer to these decisions. For the rest of us entrepreneurs, the best we can do is a "vaguely right" approach to the process. What follows is a discussion of the directional trade-offs that exist between the alternatives.

More campaigns should be created as:

- The cost of generating the campaigns is lower.
- The cost of evaluating each campaign is lower.
- The validity of the campaign evaluation method is higher.
- The reliability of the campaign evaluation method is higher.

- The variability of the sales impacts of the different campaigns that would be generated is higher.

As you saw in the Synygy example at the beginning of this chapter, what the entrepreneur is trying to do is only run with the most effective campaign. The more variability there is among the campaigns generated and evaluated, the more likely the best or most effective campaign will be more effective in increasing sales. However, if you chose the campaign that isn't really going to be the best, you will not do as well—thus the reasoning for being concerned about the reliability and validity of the evaluation technique. Also the more costly the evaluation or generation of campaigns is, it's obvious that the profitability of the process goes down faster as you generate and evaluate more campaign options.

More should be spent on evaluating campaign options:

- The more valid and/or reliable the evaluation methods
- The more variability in sales success the entrepreneur believes will occur among the campaign options that will be generated
- The lower the costs of generating and evaluating each campaign option

Obviously, if it is inexpensive to generate and evaluate each campaign option, it is likely to have a big impact on revenue from one campaign to the other, and the evaluation is likely to differentiate the best campaign, then it pays to generate and evaluate a lot of different campaign options.

For the typical entrepreneur, the biggest leverage can come from increasing the variability of the campaign options she evaluates. Increasing the variability of the creators of the campaign option does this. The more different the people and their approaches that create the campaign options, the more likely is it that the best of those options will have more revenue impact. How do you get more varied campaign option creators? Encourage option ideas from everyone who possibly can help in the creative process. Your employees and customers know the business and sometimes can generate very productive ideas. Also many times for the entrepreneur, friends and relatives with whom you discuss your venture can also be a source of creativity.

This reasoning goes against the "standard" way advertising is handled by the entrepreneur. Many entrepreneurs will hire an advertising agency and give them the job of creating and placing their advertising campaign. The agency will do its own creative development and media planning. After the agency has completed its work, they make a presentation to "sell" their campaign idea to the entrepreneur. You either accept their recommendations or send the agency back to try again. This approach has been shown to generate campaigns that are not very different from each other in sales impact.

It is much more effective to *separate* the *creative* and *media* functions of advertising agencies. Our logic would imply that more than one creative agency should submit proposed campaigns to be evaluated and paid for their time. The best campaign among those evaluated would be the one that is broadly executed. If for some reason you have trouble getting more than one creative agency to work for you, another option is to ask for separate, independent, creative teams from one advertising agency to each develop alternative campaigns to evaluate—and then run with the campaign that is evaluated as most likely to increase sales the most.

It is not necessary to have advertising developed only by traditional advertising agencies. Other sources would include freelance people who work part-time for ad agencies, advertising and marketing students at local universities, and art students at local art schools. The conception that artistic production quality for advertising has to be excellent in order for the advertising to be "great" is not borne out by the existing research. The definition of "great advertising" is where a marketer and the typical advertising professional will differ. The consumer who sees or hears advertising is typically not sophisticated enough (nor cares enough) to be influenced by very subtle artistic touches in advertising. Professionals judge most advertising competitions and awards (such as the Cleo awards). Their judging criteria do not include the sales impact of the advertising. Most of the money that is spent to make advertising (especially television) artistically beautiful (and it's often a lot of money) is of very questionable productivity.

If you are typical of most entrepreneurs, you are now asking yourself, "How can I afford to spend all this money generating and testing alternative campaigns, most of which I'll never even run?" The answer is very simple—you will make more money doing that than with "normal" ways of generating and evaluating advertising. A great advertising campaign that is really effective at increasing sales may be contributing five or ten times as much incremental revenue as a typical campaign. It's worth it to spend money to try to find the exceptionally productive campaigns.

For example, MetaCreations Corp. used radio advertising on Howard Stern's radio program to ask listeners to go to their website or call an 800 number to order a new software program for manipulating computer images. They let Howard Stern have poetic license to do whatever he wanted to advertise the product. In fact, the advertising cost was cheaper if Howard was free to extemporize his commercials.

This campaign generated more than *ten times* the incremental revenue versus the campaign cost. It was evaluated on a daily basis because it was simple to watch the big increases in calls and website visits every time the "commercial" ran on Howard's show. The campaign was orders of magnitude more effective than any other campaigns the company had run. We next hypothesize that Hindustan Lever missed productivity improvement possibilities in the way they handled the successful rollout of Lifebuoy.

The Hindustan Lever (HLL) Missed Experimentation Opportunity

As discussed in Chapter 1, "Marketing-Driven Strategy to Make Extraordinary Money," we hypothesize that HLL missed an opportunity for increased marketing productivity when they repositioned, retargeted, and relaunched Lifebuoy as a health soap to combat germs that cause diarrhea and other diseases. Though they were extremely innovative in their positioning, targeting, and distribution channels, the way they handled the rural communications plan was very traditional. They basically worked with one agency, Ogilvy and Mather, and screened some options to roll out one option that everyone was happy with. The logic we developed previously would urge them to have developed a number of different communications executions using different creative sources and then tested them as part of the early rollout.

Let's look at some of the criteria we discuss for recommending that more campaigns are generated and tested. More should be developed if the cost of generating them is low. In this case, either another ad agency could develop executions based upon the research done by HLL, or other "out of the box" creators could try their luck. Government workers who have been interacting with villagers may have some excellent ideas, or the villagers themselves might also be able to generate effective communications vehicles. Given this was to be a low-cost, personally delivered communication, the cost of actually developing and producing the new options would have to be quite small—especially in relation to the possible increases in revenue that more effective campaigns might generate.

The next three criteria say more campaigns should be developed if the cost of the evaluation is lower and the reliability and validity of the evaluation are higher. In the HLL case, they could randomize villages and test alternative campaigns in randomly selected villages from a set of villages matched on relevant criteria—such as current Lifebuoy revenue and competitive strength. In terms of evaluation, it would not be hard to get the sales from each of the independent sales/distributors they have in each village. They could compare sales before and after the campaigns across all the villages in each campaign treatment. Because we are measuring sales here in randomly selected villages where the only difference is the campaign used for communicating, there is a high amount of face validity. Given that there are thousands of villages that were visited by these marketing communication teams, it would be easy to isolate samples of 200–500 villages for each treatment. This would make the evaluation extremely reliable because of the large sample size. This is typically easy to do on the Internet, and in this case, because of the massive numbers of similar rural villages and relatively low implementation costs, this experimentation is very feasible in an offline manner.

Lastly, the preceding suggestion for multiple campaign generation would only make sense if there was room to believe that there was the possibility of higher sales that would result from different communications campaigns. Here, the company people and people from the field would be best at estimating the possibility. We find it hard to believe that the potential benefit of a campaign that might be evaluated as better than the current one wouldn't more than pay for the small incremental costs of the additional campaign generation and testing. Given that the villagers had not seen any marketing communications, there could be some different, innovative campaign that would really excite the villagers and the independent salespeople.

We can only hypothesize why HLL didn't try alternative campaigns as they rolled out the initiative. Probably the biggest reason is that they always did their communications the same way—even for innovative programs. As a big company, many times it is difficult to change the procedures without creating significant political problems. The current agency is not going to like having competition.

This example shows how globally progressive and innovative firms can also benefit from being more entrepreneurial and less traditional in how they manage their advertising and communication.

Victoria's Secret's Advertising and Testing Strategy

Victoria's Secret manages its advertising not only in relation to sales but also in relation to their pricing.

Direct mail and the Internet are big portions of VS advertising spending. They measure the incremental sales due to these media, and they are justified by the incremental profit they produce. VS's Internet site has been profitable from day one because the entire infrastructure was there to fulfill the Internet sales. It was an online extension of the existing direct mail catalog. TV advertising has been more challenging to manage.

Victoria's Secret has done a number of regional and local TV advertising tests in which some stores are in areas exposed to the advertising and others are not. They have typically not observed enough short-term incremental sales to justify a payout on the TV advertising expenditures. However, they have also measured a correlation of increases in TV advertising and their ability to increase the unit retail price. They have found that the TV advertising helps to make their customers less price responsive. The TV advertising changes and improves people's perceptions of who VS is, and it also is crucial for doing new product and product line launches. Even though there are probably opportunities for VS to fine-tune its TV media, budget, and creative content, the management is spending its time more on new products and line expansion because it feels it can add more value to the company with those activities.

Evaluating Campaigns—"Vaguely Right" Versus "Precisely Wrong"

The preceding examples illustrate the value of evaluating campaigns to choose those that yield better results. We should emphasize here that the procedures to help with these evaluations are not as precise as evaluating some other uses for capital. However, they are the best that the entrepreneurial marketer can do in the typical circumstances in which she finds herself. This situation calls for being "vaguely right" versus being "precisely wrong." The traditional advertising "rules" described earlier in the chapter are examples of the "precisely wrong" way to approach advertising or promotion decisions. These rules are easy to apply and can be calculated very precisely, but they have been shown not to generate campaigns that are incrementally profitable. We next show some ways to handle campaign evaluation.

For many entrepreneurial businesses, the incremental impact of campaigns is obvious if you are intelligently watching the daily revenues and either consciously or subconsciously relating daily revenues to the current advertising and promotion campaign. If the business is direct to the customer, you can also ask customers coming in or calling in if the advertising or promotion was involved in their decision to purchase. If the business is web-based, you may judge effectiveness of ads directly from analytics of the campaign. You have to estimate one number to compare with the actual achieved revenue. That number is "what revenue would have been without the advertising or promotion campaign." This number can be "vaguely" estimated by using combinations of differences in revenue in prior periods and differences in revenues from the area getting the campaign, versus the same time periods in other areas that were not subject to the campaign. If the data is available, the best comparison to use for evaluating a campaign is the difference between revenues per week during the campaign versus before the campaign started compared with the same numbers for areas in which the campaign was not used over the same time periods.

For example, if a campaign ran during May only in Cleveland, and sales per week increased by 25% in May compared with the prior three months, the first estimate you might make would be that the campaign increased sales by 25%. However, the next thing to look at would be: How did a comparable area without the campaign do in May? You could use the rest of the United States as a comparison or a market you judge to be similar, perhaps Detroit or Pittsburgh. If Detroit was up 5% in May, Pittsburgh was up 7%, and the rest of the United States was up 3%, you could reasonably estimate that the campaign might have increased revenues by about 20% more than they would have been had the campaign not run. The big assumption you are making when using such an estimating procedure is that no *other causes were responsible for the difference between the area with the campaign and the other areas.* For example, was something else also going on in Cleveland that might have caused the sales increases—such as competitive activities, weather, public relations activities, and so on? The same questions need to be asked about the areas used for comparisons—the "pseudo" controls for this "pseudoexperiment." This kind of estimating and analysis is called *pseudoexperimentation* because there is not random assignment of the campaign to one area versus another. Without random assignment, you can never be sure that there wasn't some other reason than the campaign that was affecting the revenues.

It has always been amazing to see how many firms, both large and small, don't take the simple necessary steps even to attempt to analyze the impact of campaigns. If they don't keep the data, they can't do any evaluation. If you don't do any evaluation, then you can't improve the campaigns or discontinue the ones that aren't working. Businesses should keep track of exactly what is occurring daily in each campaign and put it in the same place electronically as the revenue numbers.

A National Retailer's Campaign Evaluation

As an example, a national retailer of consumer electronics thought it was keeping track of its advertising and promotion programs. The way the data was stored could best be described as "market status reporting."[6] The data was there for managers to find out what they did in each market each day of the week. However, because the data was structured in the computer system, it was impossible to do any kind of analysis of the incremental impact of the advertising or promotion programs that the firm ran. An example of how the data looked as it was stored is shown in Figure 6-3.[7]

ELEMENT	ADVERTISING SCHEDULE		PLAN PD	5	PAGE	
ACCOUNT ABILITY	ADV DIRECTOR		MEETING	PLANNING	VERSION 12/06/89	
MARKET						

WEEK NO 1	SUNDAY 8/20/89	MONDAY 8/21/89	TUESDAY 8/22/89	WEDNESDAY 8/23/89	THURSDAY 8/24/89	FRIDAY 8/25/89	SATURDAY 8/26/89	WEEK 1
HOLIDAY								
EVENT TY	/----SUPER SALE----/					/--1-DAY SALE--/		
LY	/----BACK TO SCHOOL ROP----/	/------ENDLESS SUMMER ROP/TAB-----/						
ACTIVITY TY	AM (6X18) 6000	RADIO (100 PTS.) 3000	PM/	(6X18) C			AM (6X18) 7500	
	TV 195 PTS. 8000	TV	TV					
TOT EXP TY	14000	3000	0	0	0	0	7500	24500
LY	8700	0	0	0	0	19644	0	28344
SALES* TY	50	56	43	46	30	42	58	325
LY	40	56	32	47	25	60	84	344
BGT								
HPF								
A/S TY								0.0754

WEEK NO 2	SUNDAY 8/27/89	MONDAY 8/28/89	TUESDAY 8/29/89	WEDNESDAY 8/30/89	THURSDAY 8/31/89	FRIDAY 9/01/89	SATURDAY 9/02/89	WEEK 2
HOLIDAY								
EVENT TY	/----END OF MONTH CLEARANCE SALE----/			/----LABOR DAY ROP----/				
LY	/----ENDLESS SUMMER----/			/----LABOR DAY ROP W/RADIO----/				
ACTIVITY TY	AM (6X18) 9500		RADIO (200 PTS.) 6000	(6X18) C		AM/PM (6X18) 5605		
TOT EXP TY	9500	0	6000	0	0	5605	0	21105
LY	6700	0	0	0	5200	10200	0	22100
SALES* TY	44	38	43	48	35	43	83	334
LY	54	53	46	55	42	47	72	369
BGT								
HPF								
A/S TY								0.0632

*In '000 $

Figure 6-3 The historical data as stored

After the situation was analyzed, the data was restructured into a spreadsheet that looked like Table 6-1.

Table 6-1 The Data Restructured for Analysis[8]

Day Number	Day of Week	Sales ($)	TV ($)	Print ($)	Radio ($)
1	Sunday	50,000	8,000	6,000	0
2	Monday	56,000	0	0	3,000
3	Tuesday	43,000	0	0	0
4	Wednesday	46,000	0	0	0
5	Thursday	30,000	0	0	0
6	Friday	42,000	0	0	0
7	Saturday	58,000	0	7,500	0
8	Sunday	44,000	0	0	0
9	Monday	38,000	0	9,500	0
10	Tuesday	43,000	0	0	6,000
11	Wednesday	48,000	0	0	0
12	Thursday	35,000	0	0	0
13	Friday	43,000	0	5,605	0
14	Saturday	83,000	0	0	0

Using pretty standard regression analysis, we were able to estimate the incremental sales impacts of the firm's advertising using Microsoft Excel, which is widely available and inexpensive. If doing statistical analysis is difficult for you, any statistics graduate student at a nearby university could help you out at very nominal costs. They actually *like* to do these kinds of analyses!

The regression model related each day's total sales to print, radio, and TV advertising during that day and each of the prior seven days, as well as sales during the same day last year, and the number of stores in operation that day. The analysis was able to show the impact of one dollar spent in a Sunday newspaper insert on incremental sales for each day of the following week (see Figure 6-4).

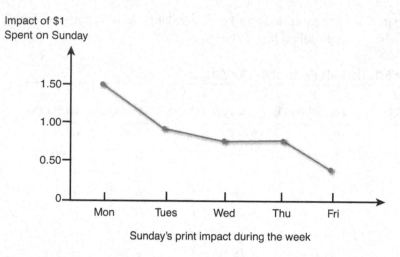

Figure 6-4 Sunday's ad impact on Monday through Friday

The analysis was able to estimate the average incremental revenue per $1 spent in all of the media options analyzed (see Table 6-2).

Table 6-2 Estimated Incremental Sales Associated with $1 of Advertising

TV Sunday	12.07**
Radio during week	5.91*
TV during week	5.27**
Print Sunday	5.06**
Print during week	Nonsignificant
Radio Saturday	Nonsignificant
Print Saturday	Nonsignificant

*$p < 0.10$
**$p < 0.01$

The relative impact of the various media and days of the week was helpful to the firm in scheduling their next campaigns. They used more TV on Sunday and cut back on other print. They did more weekday radio and less weekend radio.

The preceding example utilized naturally occurring experiments to determine the incremental revenue impact of an advertising campaign after the campaigns had run. The statistical analysis used a multiple of last year's sales in each store as an estimate of what might have occurred had the advertising campaign not been run. A better approach to campaign evaluation is using planned experiments instead of naturally occurring experiments.

"Vaguely Right" Entrepreneurial Marketing Experimentation

The basic idea behind planned experiments is simple. You want to try a campaign on a subsegment or subsegments of the market and be able to estimate what the revenue would have been had the campaign not been run by comparing the areas in which the campaign ran with those in which it didn't. To be as confident as possible that your valuation of the campaign is as "vaguely right" as possible, there are five ideal characteristics that an experiment should have. As an entrepreneur, you will not be able to execute perfect experiments, but they don't have to be. The experiments only need to help you go with the campaigns that work best and not spend money on campaigns that are unproductive. The five characteristics you should shoot for in designing market tests or experiments are the following:

1. The assignment of which areas or subjects will get the campaign or the control (nothing different) should be random. Flipping a coin or throwing dice are fine ways to fulfill this requirement.

2. Nothing else could have caused the results observed except for the campaign you are testing.

3. The results can be logically projected to the firm's real marketing situation in which the campaign would be used.

4. The experimental campaign must precede the sales effects it is supposed to cause.

5. There must be a comparison group that did not receive the campaign or received a different campaign.

The most important characteristic is number one—random assignment. If this does not happen, there is a persistent danger that those exposed to the campaign may in some ways be different from those not exposed.

Evaluation Before Is More Valuable than After

You should realize at this point that if the evaluation of the incremental revenue attributable to the campaign is not sufficient to justify its opportunity costs, then the campaign should not have been run. The funds for that campaign would have been better used in other ways. If you can find ways to evaluate campaigns *before* they are executed in the whole market, then you can only execute campaigns that will justify their expenditures. The *planned experiments* described previously are a very good way to evaluate campaigns using a *sample* of the market instead of the whole market *before* the campaign will be executed for the entire market. You need to balance costs of the evaluation before the campaign is widely executed versus the value of only executing those campaigns that are likely to be productive. This balancing act can be difficult for large consumer packaged goods firms, but for the typical entrepreneur, it is relatively easy. You just have to think about evaluating the campaigns in a reasonable way before they are widely executed.

For any one-to-one marketing vehicles, such as the Internet, direct mail, or telesales, it is feasible to test campaigns on selected samples and only broadly execute those that return more than their opportunity costs. On the Internet, it is easy to test a campaign based on a specific number of impressions. For direct mail, you may test a campaign on every nth name on a list before sending the advertisement to the whole list. For broader reach media such as radio, TV, magazines, or newspapers, more ingenuity is needed. If the firm has operations in more than one metropolitan area, then it can test campaigns in some areas, using some other areas as controls. What is important in these experiments is to match the areas based on forecasted revenues for the test period and to *randomly* decide which areas are the test and which are the control. Flipping a coin or rolling dice to make the choice is perfectly appropriate. The use of chance makes it much more likely that the differences in revenues that are seen in each market are really due to the advertising campaign versus some other reason that caused a person to choose one market versus another. An example of how matched market experiments helped Franklin Electronic Publications, Inc., to evaluate alternative media and campaigns prior to national rollout is shown in the box.

Franklin's Ad Experiment Design

The following are excerpts from a presentation that describes Franklin Electronic Publications' advertising test of three alternative campaigns before a choice would be made of which, if any, was to be run. The three campaigns were spot television, cable television, and radio.

Franklin BOOKMAN Advertising Test

- **Purpose:** To evaluate the impact of advertising on retail movement of Franklin product, especially Franklin BOOK-MAN.

- **Methodology:** A controlled test will be conducted to evaluate the following:

  1. **$4MM Spot TV plan.** If successful, this plan would be implemented in approximately 30% of the U.S., representing a combination of high-impact retail markets and more highly developed Franklin markets, as measured by warranty card returns. It is believed that these markets would yield a 95 reach and a 7+ frequency in the advertised markets. See theoretical plan.

  2. **$4MM Cable TV plan.** If successful, this plan would be implemented nationally. Implementation of this plan would yield a 60 reach and a 6.6 frequency in the advertised markets. See theoretical plan.

  3. **$3MM Radio plan.** If successful, this plan would be implemented nationally. Implementation of this plan would run approximately 100 announcements per week.

The Franklin marketing manager had done a careful job of developing payback criteria.

- **Measures of Success**

  In order to be deemed a success, the adjusted unit volume increase within the test markets would need to rise sufficiently to pay back the advertising investment. Based upon current volume, this would translate to an increase of approximately 200,000 units or an 11% increase in volume on an annualized basis. Volume increases would be measured across all Franklin volume—not just BOOKMAN.

- **Evaluative Criteria in Reading Test Results**

Adjustments must be made to data in test versus control to reflect the following:

- Seasonality.
- Market strength.
- Only portion of entire media plan implemented.
- Translation of national theoretical plan especially in cable markets: buying specs issued to deliver overall reach and frequency and not number of spots. Desired Daypart Mix would include a greater degree of prime and weekend than could be purchased on local cable basis.

- **Payback Criteria by Market**

Sacramento ($4MM Cable):

200,000 annual units × .72% US / 1.32 Index × .60 half the schedule × .60

(seasonality index for April/May) / 12 months per year × 2 (May/June)

Volume increase over two months in Sacramento would have to be 54 units over control.

Portland ($4MM Spot):

200,000 annual units × .84% US / 1.28 Index × .60 half the schedule × .60

(seasonality index for April/May) / 12 months per year × 2 (May/June) / .85

Adjustment for spot-only control.

Volume increase over two months in Portland would have to be 77 units over control.

Bakersfield ($3MM):

150,000 annual units × .25% US / 1.45 Index × .60 half the schedule × .60

(seasonality index for April/May) / 12 months per year × 2 (May/June)

Volume increase over two months in Bakersfield would have to be 13 units over control. The test design was structured with the three test areas and a control area.

The test results showed that the spot TV campaign increased sales 66% higher than the control, better than the productivity of the cable or radio options.

However, because the number of reporting stores was small and sales per week were small, there was a higher variability than the company anticipated in the sales estimated from the tests. There was still a big probability that the spot TV campaign could have been no better than the control. There was not enough upside for the company to risk its resources on such a risky payoff.

Media Planning

If the discussion of campaign creativity and evaluation were not enough to get your entrepreneurial juices flowing, then the next discussion of choosing media should do it. Just as there are big opportunities for increasing revenue with nonstandard campaigns, there are also big opportunities for increasing revenue by choosing the most productive among a wide variety of creative media options. The key in media planning is finding the media option that has the most likelihood of generating incremental revenue per dollar spent. We call this "bang per buck" analysis. There are a number of factors that should be considered in generating and evaluating media options. We have been able to distill experience and research over the past 30 years to develop a methodology that can guide the entrepreneur toward "vaguely right" choices.

Again, here the product positioning strategy (the market segmentation and product differentiation discussed in Chapter 1) and the firm needs to *drive the process*. The entrepreneurial marketer must eliminate any options that are inconsistent with the firm's basic strategy. The media chosen can be an excellent way of implementing a segmentation strategy. One of the reasons for Tandem's East's success is the availability of targeted media that reach their target customers cost effectively. Aside from reaching the targeted segment(s) cost, the media options chosen should also be able to convey the firm's advertising message in an effective manner. For example, even though the audience of *Hustler* or *Playboy* magazine may be very appropriate targets for life insurance products, they would probably not be good environments for the typical life insurance ad. The male reading these magazines is probably not thinking very long term or is not very receptive to arguments against current pleasure.

The media chosen need to be evaluated not only on who will likely see or hear your ad, but on how potentially effective the option will be in motivating people who will hear or see the ad. Thus, the media options chosen will be directly related to the campaign that will be used. Some campaign options will be more effective in some media options than others. Again, this is not a simple problem. We have developed a relatively simple ranking and evaluation procedure to get right at the basic trade-offs that are essential for evaluating the relative "bang per buck" of the available options. The methodology considers the relative value of reaching different target market segments, the probabilities of members of each segment actually seeing or hearing the ads, and the appropriateness of the media vehicles as motivators of people who are actually exposed to the ads in them.

Sample Template for Media Evaluation

The first step in evaluating media options is to divide the market into segments that will have different value to you. This is not as simple as it seems because you will need to estimate how those segments break out the audience of the media options you are considering. Most media audience ratings are typically only broken out by age and/or sex and sometimes other demographic variables. There is a balance between finding segmentation that is relevant to your venture and segmentation that has media audiences available. Sometimes the segments used for the media planning purposes can be as simple as "my target group" and all others. You can then estimate media audiences in the target group for all the options you are considering.

For our sample, we assume that the entrepreneur has divided his target into three segments: younger males with high income, younger females with high income, and all other adults, as illustrated in Table 6-3. The next step is to estimate the population of each segment—column A in the table. Column B in the table answers the question: "How valuable to me is reaching a person in one segment versus another?" This is an important judgment that will depend on the advertising's objectives, the potential of the segments, and so on. It is a per capita estimate that only has to be done on a relative basis. The numbers in column B could be just as easily 100, 40, and 10 instead of 10, 4, and 1. What is important is the relative judgment of how valuable reaching a person in one segment is versus reaching a person in another. Column C is just the multiplication of column A times column B to obtain a segment relative potential.

Table 6-3 Media Evaluation Data

Sample Segments	A Segment Population	B Segment Weight = Potential per Person in Segment (Relative)	C = A × B Segment Potential
25–49 Males with income > $35K	2,000,000	10	20,000,000
25–49 Females with income > $35K	2,000,000	4	8,000,000
All others	10,000,000	1	10,000,000

Table 6-4 describes some of the required numbers and estimates needed for each of the media options that are being evaluated. For our sample, we evaluate four vehicles: one Internet advertising option, a radio ad, a taxi ad on the back of the front seat of a set of taxis, and an ad in a newspaper. It is *very important* to generate *many* options to evaluate, even if you have to make rough, "vaguely right" judgments about some of the numbers needed for the evaluation. Creative media options can not only help you sell more stuff—they can also position you as different from your competition.

Table 6-4 More Media Evaluation Data

Sample Media Vehicle Options	D Cost/Insertion	E Probability of Ad Exposure Given Audience Membership	F Media Weight = Relative Value of Ad Exposure (Judgment or Experimentation)
Google AdWords campaign (Internet A)	$100 per week	.6	1.0
Radio 30-second spot classic rock station—drive time (Radio A)	$150 per week	.6	1.5
Taxi seat banners for one week (Taxi A)	$50 per week	.8	1.0
City newspaper ad 1/4 page financial section (Newspaper A)	$800 per ad	.3	1.5

Column D in Table 6-4 is just the costs per insertion for each option. The next column, E, is an estimate of the probability that someone who is counted as "in the audience" of the media will actually be exposed to the ad you would run. This estimate depends on how the "audience" number is determined for each media vehicle. It is absolutely true that your advertising can only work if the potential consumer is exposed to it. Just being in the media vehicles' audience and not seeing your ad does not help. For example, if a person reads the newspaper but does not see your ad in the financial section, this does no good for your business. Column E estimates the fraction of audience members who will actually be exposed to your ad.

The last column (F) is probably the most *difficult* number to estimate for each media vehicle, but also the most *important*. It answers the question: How much do I care to have a good potential customer be exposed to my ad in one media vehicle versus another? This number really only needs to be estimated on a relative basis. The best way to think about this estimate is to arbitrarily assign a one-dollar value to one media option (A). For the other options, you then answer the question, "If it costs one dollar for me to have a good prospect be exposed to my ad in media vehicle A, *how much more or less* than one dollar would I be willing to spend *to have my ad seen instead* in each of the other options?" In the example in Table 6-4, the radio and newspaper ads are estimated as roughly 50% more valuable *per person actually exposed* than the other two media options.

Table 6-5 shows the fraction of each segment that is counted as being "in the audience" of each of the media options being evaluated. The audience numbers come from the syndicated research that is used to estimate who watches, reads, or listens and for how long. The definition that is used by each media option to define "being in its audience" is very important to understand. For example, for TV, the definition of audience is typically having the TV set in the audience member's household tuned to the channel on which your ad appears. Whether the audience member actually watches your ad is a whole other story, which is handled by column E in Table 6-4. In Table 6-5, for example, 25% of the high-income, younger males are estimated to be in the audience of the financial section of the newspaper, but column E of Table 6-4 says that only 30% of those audience members actually see the one-quarter page ad we plan.

Table 6-5 What Fraction of Each Segment Is Counted as in the Audience of Each Media Vehicle Option?

Media Vehicle	G Segment 1. High-Income Younger Males	H Segment 2. High-Income Younger Females	I Segment 3. All Others
Internet A	.04	.02	.01
Radio A	.08	.06	.05
Taxi A	.03	.02	.005
Newspaper A	.25	.15	.10

The next step in the evaluation is to multiply the total segment potential in column C by the audiences in Table 6-5. The mechanics of this computation is shown in Table 6-6. For each media option, column M is the total audience of each media weighted by the importance of that segment to the firm.

Table 6-6 Relative Amount of Segment Potential in Media Audiences

Segment	J= G × 20,000,000 High-Income Younger Males	K = H × 8,000,000 High-Income Younger Females	l = I × 10,000,000 All Others	M = J + K + L Total
Internet A	.04 × 20M = 800,000	.02 × 8M = 160,000	.01 × 10M = 100,000	1,060,000
Radio A	1,600,000	480,000	500,000	2,580,000
Taxi A	600,000	160,000	50,000	810,000
Newspaper A	5,000,000	1,200,000	1,000,000	7,200,000

The following equation puts all this together by combining the media audience potential, ad exposure probabilities, and the relative media values into the *"bang."* This "bang" is divided by the costs per insertion of the media to get a relative *"bang per buck."* In our example, Radio A is most productive, followed within about 17% by Taxi A. The other two options are deemed less than half as potentially productive as Radio A and Taxi A.

Total Potential in Media Audience × Individual Ad Exposure Prob. × Relative Media Value divided by Media Insertion Costs = a Relative "Bang per Buck"

$$\text{Bang per Buck} = \frac{M x E x F}{D}$$

Internet A	=	636,000/$100	=	6,360
Radio A	=	2,322,000/$150	=	15,480
Taxi A	=	648,000/$ 50	=	12,960
Newspaper A	=	3,240,000/$800	=	4,050

The preceding template for media planning should be used to screen options: to run in the marketplace and evaluate, or test in a test market and evaluate. The Franklin Electronic Publications in-market media test described earlier is a good example.

The entrepreneur should continually be evaluating the incremental revenue performance of his advertising options as they are used in the market. Over time, the incremental revenue contribution may begin to decline because of diminishing returns. When this happens, it may be time to try some new options. This phenomenon will eventually happen even to search engine marketing, but in the meantime, it should be considered as a very plausible alternative for many entrepreneurial companies.

The Digital Marketing Revolution—Evaluating and Maximizing Its "Bang Per Buck"[9]

The recurring theme in this chapter, and throughout the book, is the importance of reinforcing your positioning through all elements of the marketing mix. This is equally true with digital advertising and traditional advertising. In fact, one of the great advantages of digital marketing is the ability to focus your ad spend much more specifically to market segments. The value of more focused advertising is reflected in two key trends, the growth of digital ad spend and the growth of mobile ad spend.

Digital advertising has grown dramatically as a percentage of overall ad spend. In fact, eMarketer predicts that digital advertising will become the number-one ad channel in 2018, surpassing television advertising, reaching 37.5% of total ad spend in the United States (see Figure 6-5). The growth of digital ad spend is reflected globally as well, especially in regions like the Middle East and Africa, Latin America, and Central and Eastern Europe. These regions have less Internet penetration and will grow digital ad spend at a higher rate as more consumers move online.[10]

The second, and perhaps more significant, trend is the growth of mobile advertising. As users have moved from their desktops and laptops to smartphones, tablets, and other mobile devices, advertisers have followed them at a rapid rate. Currently, mobile advertising represents 25% of digital advertising; however, mobile is expected to dominate digital advertising, exceeding 70% of digital ad spend by 2018.[11]

US Total Media Ad Spending, by Media, 2013-2018 billions						
	2013	2014	2015	2016	2017	2018
TV	$66.35	$68.54	$70.59	$73.77	$75.98	$78.64
Digital	$43.11	$50.73	$58.61	$67.09	$74.77	$82.95
—Mobile	$10.67	$19.15	$28.72	$40.50	$49.81	$57.78
Print	$32.44	$31.70	$31.17	$30.89	$30.79	$30.86
—Newspapers*	$17.31	$16.61	$16.12	$15.79	$15.63	$15.63
—Magazines*	$15.13	$15.09	$15.05	$15.10	$15.15	$15.23
Radio**	$15.21	$15.06	$15.13	$15.18	$15.21	$15.25
Outdoor	$6.96	$7.17	$7.39	$7.58	$7.73	$7.85
Directories*	$5.30	$4.90	$4.56	$4.25	$4.08	$3.95
Total	$169.35	$178.09	$187.45	$198.76	$208.56	$219.51

Note: *print only; **excludes off-air radio & digital
Source: eMarketer, March 2015

186534   www.eMarketer.com

Figure 6-5 U.S. total media ad spending, by media, 2013–2018

The ability to precisely target market segments, to learn about your customers via readily observable online behaviors, to engage with your customer, and to test campaigns cost effectively all have contributed to the rapid growth of digital and mobile ad spend. The following section describes the types of digital advertising, provides ways to improve the returns on your digital advertising spend, and provides important considerations about emerging trends in digital marketing.

Display Ads

The earliest ads on the Internet were display ads, often appearing as banner ads at the tops of web pages. As the Internet has evolved, so, too, have display ads. They may include text, images, audio, video, and may be interactive. Regardless of the form or format of display ads, it is critical that the entrepreneurial marketer reinforce positioning with the content of display ads. Given the short attention span of online users, display ads must grab the attention of the user, engage them, and lead them to take action, which usually entails clicking the ad to link to a website for further engagement.

Although the content of display ads is one contributor to effectiveness, placement of the ad is equally important. The websites, pages, screens, and context in which the ad appears all may influence campaign effectiveness. This dizzying array of options may be overwhelming. However, as discussed earlier in this chapter, adaptive experimentation is the best way to navigate your way to the most effective choices. A simple strategy of A/B testing alternative ads, placement, and other elements can quickly help the marketer refine an ad campaign. In Chapter 3, "Entrepreneurial Pricing: An Often-Misused Way to Garner Extraordinary Profits," we discussed using product concept testing to assess price sensitivity by offering two variations of a concept test to two different participant groups. By changing only the price in the two concepts, you can determine your users are price sensitive. Similarly, when testing variations of displays ads, it is critical to change only a single variable at a time in A/B testing to ensure that you can identify the reasons for varying results.

Display ads are sold based on the CPM, the cost per thousand impressions, or the number of times an ad may be viewed by users. As with traditional advertising, your objective is to have not only a large number of views, but also a high percentage of relevant views, in which your content is of interest to the viewer, and the context in which they view the ad is also relevant. Thus, the CPM pricing available may be tiered based on a premium associated with more focused targeting of ads (see Figure 6-6). While CPM still dominates the pricing models for display ads, those that sell display ads can offer higher value measures of customer engagement, such as the click-through rate (CTR). Customers that click on an ad to investigate your offerings more fully may be one step closer to purchase. This value is reflected in the higher cost associated with ads that have higher CTR. The additional cost may be more than offset by more effective capture of an interested customer, and perhaps greater revenue generation.

US Online Display Ad CPM, by Inventory Tier, 2010-2017			
	Indirect	**Midtier**	**Premium**	**Average CPM**
2010	$0.80	$3.00	$9.00	$1.70
2011	$0.90	$2.90	$9.50	$1.70
2012	$1.00	$2.90	$9.90	$1.80
2013	$1.10	$2.80	$10.40	$1.90
2014	$1.20	$2.80	$10.90	$2.00
2015	$1.30	$2.70	$11.50	$2.20
2016	$1.50	$2.70	$12.10	$2.30
2017	$1.60	$2.60	$12.70	$2.50

Note: excludes mobile display ad impressions; average CPM calculated
using weighted average for online display ad impression share
Source: Credit Suisse, "Web 2.012," Feb 21, 2012

137412   www.eMarketer.com

Figure 6-6 U.S. online display ad CPM, by inventory tier, 2010–2017

The rapid growth of mobile advertising has led to a resurgence of display advertising, and beginning in 2015, display advertising will become the greatest percentage of digital advertising spend. Prior to that time, digital advertising was dominated by one of the most significant innovations in advertising, search.[12]

Search Engine Optimization

Search engine marketing allows the marketer to pay for appearing high on the list of sponsored search results for a particular keyword that the search engine user searches for. Although Google did not invent the concept of search engine marketing, it has been and remains the innovator and dominant player in the market. Google, and other search engine marketing companies like Yahoo! and Bing (from Microsoft), sell placements in search results order in an auction format. The highest bidder gets the highest spot, the second highest gets the second spot, and so on. The payment to the search engine is the CTR, an amount per click-through to your site from the search engine.

Compared with other large advertising media, this "pay for performance" method is very unique. The only other large media that is comparable is the sometimes use of "per inquiry" schemes in radio and television. When a TV or radio station, network, or cable system has excess capacity, they will sometimes make "per inquiry (P.I.)" deals with direct marketers who pay for leads (typically phone calls or website visits) resulting from the advertising. These P.I. deals are looked upon as a last ditch, desperation tactic by the radio and TV media and viewed as better than not selling the time slot at all. Typically the revenue from P.I. deals to radio and TV is much lower than the standard price per spot. On the other hand, search engine marketing is predicated on paying for performance and potentially very valuable to many advertisers.

Search engine marketing works differently depending on whether you are a direct to consumer or B2B marketer. Figure 6-7 shows the logistics of what happens in each situation.

Business to Consumer:

| Consumer types keyword in search engine box | → | He/she clicks on one of the first listings | → | Link takes consumer to listings's Web site | → | Web site "landing page" begins the selling processes | → | Owner of listing is billed for the click ("Pay Per Click") |

Business to Business:

| Consumer types keyword in search engine box | → | He/she clicks on one of the first listings | → | Link takes consumer to listings's Web site | → | "Landing page" attempts to gather information about potential customer | → | "Lead" gets passed to appropriate Sales Rep. | → | Sales Rep contacts "hot" lead | → | Owner of listing is billed for the click ("Pay Per Click") |

Figure 6-7 Paid search—how does it work?
Source: Yosi Heber Communication, 2004

Search engine marketing is the perfect complement to many of the concepts emphasized in this book. It is made for continuous adaptive experimentation and evaluation based upon marginal revenue versus marginal costs. Many successful companies of all sizes generate new profit by intelligently applying search engine marketing utilizing the concepts in this book.

Search engine marketing is creating a seismic shift in how advertising is productively implemented. The reasons for its success and its even bigger potential for use by entrepreneurial entities have been elegantly portrayed by Yosi Heber in his "Heber's Advertising Relevance Matrix" (see Figure 6-8).

Figure 6-8 shows clearly how search engine marketing has broken through as a new medium that has attributes that are unique and very valuable to many marketers. It reaches only potential customers to whom the message is relevant because the customers are searching about the issue. The consumers are spending their time to solve a problem, and the advertiser is in position to provide perceived help to the consumers.

Heber's Advertising Relevance Matrix

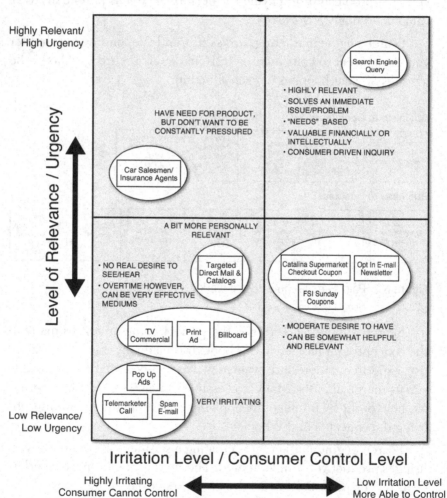

Figure 6-8 Heber's advertising relevance matrix

Source: Yosi Heber Communication, 2004

The other big advantage of search engine marketing is that the consumers feel much more in control than any other advertising medium. They do not feel irritated by the advertising exposure. On the contrary, they are in many cases searching for a solution to a problem that the advertiser can solve. Yosi, who until mid-2005 was the chief marketing officer of Entertainment Publications, Inc. (a subsidiary of IAC/Interactive Corp.), and is now president of Oxford Hill Partners, outlined a number of benefits that he had seen from using search engine marketing, as follows:

- It helps efficiently acquire new consumers and customers.
- It is measurable.
- It is relatively low cost.
- It has a generally proven ROI.
- It is very low risk—you typically pay for performance—per "click," and you can pay as you go and stop if the returns aren't there.
- For B2B situations, it can make the sales force more efficient by providing "warm" leads versus cold calls.

In terms of the previous template for media evaluation, the target segment that is reached is extremely precise and, thus, their segment weight will typically be high compared with other more traditional media. How much more valuable is a potential customer who has a high income and is searching for the problem you can solve on the Internet, than a typical high-income person who is not searching?

The other element of the media evaluation template that search engine marketing impacts is the relative value of an ad exposure. How much more value is there in exposing a target consumer to an ad while they are searching for the product or service you are selling than when they are exposed in an unrelated setting? The neat thing about search engine marketing is that the marketer doesn't have to do any elaborate experimentation or judgmental estimation—they can get the estimated revenue per $1 spent on search engine marketing on an ongoing basis as they use the medium.

Evaluating the Return on Search Engine Marketing

How does a marketer evaluate the productivity of search engine marketing? As we recommend for all marketing resource deployment decisions and in particular other media and advertising evaluations, we need to get as close as possible to evaluating the incremental revenue to compare with the incremental costs of buying the search words and the incremental costs of fulfilling the incremental revenue that is generated. The first step is to have an estimate of the value of a new customer over that customer's lifetime.

For typical direct-to-consumer situations, for each search word and position, you then need to monitor the number of customers converted as a fraction of the click-through population (the "clicks to customer" percentage). Then you divide this percentage by the cost per click to get the number of customers per dollar. Multiplying the number of customers per dollar times the value of the customer gets a Return on Marketing (ROM) number to compare with other search words and other alternative marketing expenditures. For example, if you bid and pay $.10 per click, 5% of those who click become customers, and the value of a customer is $10; then for each click, you will get .05 customers times $10 = $.50. So $.50 in value for $.10 spent =.50/.10 = 5.0, or a 500% return for the advertising investment. The key numbers in this analysis are the value per new customer and the clicks to customer percentage.

For typical B2B situations, the preceding analysis works with one exception. The "clicks per customer" percentage is obtained by multiplying together two component fractions—the percentage of clicks that become qualified sales leads (the "clicks to leads percentage") and the percentage of qualified leads that become customers after the sales force calls on them (the "leads to customer" percentage).

Obviously, the previous calculation can be made more precise if you keep track of the revenue patterns of the specific customers that come from each search word. Some words may attract customers who buy more than other customers. Also the copy you use in your sponsored search ad may have a big impact on response—either customers or leads or both. If it can be done cost efficiently, it usually makes sense to develop information systems to capture the specific revenue response from each word and ad combination. In many cases, the learning that comes from the data will easily pay for the costs of collecting the data. It is almost always beneficial to plan for this analysis and data collection when initially designing and building your website.

Methods for Improving Productivity of Search Engine Marketing

The basic message for improving ROM for search engine marketing is very simple: Test, Test, Test!

Because the cost of testing is so low and the variability of performance is so high, it almost always pays to test a lot of different search words, different search engines, different headlines, ad copy, and various promotional offers that might be involved on your website. However, keep in mind that you should change only one variable at a time to gain an accurate assessment of the impact. If we take the concepts from this chapter's previous section on improving campaigns, they fit search engine marketing like a glove.

More campaigns should be evaluated as:

- The cost of generating the copy is lower (the sponsored search ads are typically just a few lines of copy, which can be easily changed without any professional assistance).

- The cost of evaluating each campaign is lower (the cost is negligible if the information systems are already in place).

- The validity of the campaign evaluation method is higher (revenue due to each campaign option can be isolated—as valid as can be imagined).

- The reliability of the campaign evaluation method is higher (the larger the sample size of clicks on each word and copy option, the larger the validity (repeatability) of the evaluation).

- The variability of the sales impacts of the different campaigns that would be generated is higher (in some tests that one of the authors did, he found revenue differences of 15 and 20 to 1 just depending on the ad copy used in the sponsored search ad for the same group of search words).

For the preceding reasons, it is almost always beneficial to generate varied options from different creative sources for the sponsored ads. Until you test a bunch of options that can't improve on the best current option, you should continue an aggressive program of testing, generating new options, testing, learning, generating new options, testing, and so on.

SoLoMo, Personalization, and Other Emerging Digital Advertising Concepts

Digital advertising in all its forms is quickly evolving, and a thorough treatment of all of the emerging trends is beyond the scope of this book. However, there are several concepts that contribute to the success of digital advertising and serve to increase its effectiveness.

John Doerr, a prominent venture capitalist with Kleiner Perkins Caufield Byers, is credited with coining the term *SoLoMo*, which brings together three key concepts of digital advertising: social, local, mobile. Doerr saw these as the major trends in the opportunities presented by social networks like Facebook, local commerce like Groupon, and mobile platforms like the Apple iPhone and Android. For the entrepreneurial marketer, these three concepts provide a means to improve the return on advertising and increase engagement with customers for one very simple reason: Social, local, and mobile make ads more relevant to the user.

Facebook did not start as an advertising platform, but rather a means for friends to share information, media, and personal information. What started as a directory of students at a college has emerged as an enormous platform of living, breathing market segmentation! Facebook reflects common interests, experiences, and behaviors— the very definition of market segment we shared in Chapter 1. As a result, Facebook provides an outstanding advertising platform, allowing greater focus and targeting by advertisers. Although Google dominates search and search engine marketing, Facebook has leveraged its massive user base, social focus, and mobile leadership (more on that later) to become the second largest ad publisher. In fact, four of the five fastest growing ad publishers are social media companies Twitter, Yelp, Facebook, and LinkedIn (see Figure 6-9).

Net US Digital Ad Revenue Growth, by Company, 2013-2016
% change

	2013	2014	2015	2016
Twitter	95.5%	82.9%	50.9%	40.3%
Yelp	66.1%	60.1%	42.7%	32.3%
Facebook	50.5%	50.6%	24.1%	19.2%
LinkedIn	39.5%	27.6%	23.6%	20.3%
Amazon	38.7%	43.0%	23.4%	21.9%
Microsoft	17.1%	16.0%	22.0%	24.0%
AOL	6.5%	14.1%	11.3%	10.9%
Google	13.6%	13.7%	10.0%	7.0%
Yahoo	0.2%	-0.5%	2.5%	4.1%
IAC	8.7%	-11.5%	1.8%	4.5%
Total digital	**17.1%**	**17.7%**	**15.5%**	**14.5%**

Note: includes advertising that appears on desktop and laptop computers as well as mobile phones and tablets, and includes all the various formats of advertising on those platforms; net ad revenues after companies pay traffic acquisition costs (TAC)
Source: company reports; eMarketer, Sep 2014

178415   www.**eMarketer**.com

Figure 6-9 Net U.S. digital ad revenue growth, by company, 2013–2016

Although the Internet has enabled companies to expand their reach beyond their own geography, it has also enabled marketers to leverage one of the most important influencers on ad effectiveness: localization.

The Apple iPhone was introduced in 2007, and just seven years later, two thirds of every mobile phone user in the United States uses a smartphone. By 2018, two thirds of the U.S. population will use a smartphone. This technology wave has put a powerful, Internet-connected computer in the hands of consumers. Not only does this demonstrate the adoption of mobile, but it provides the opportunity to reach the user with digital advertising wherever they are and to customize that advertising to geography. Nokia ran a mobile ad campaign that leveraged localization of mobile phones with Dominos Pizza in India and McDonalds in Finland. By providing information in the ad about directions to the nearest location, advertisers were able to generate three to ten times the response rate to the ads. This power of localization has added a new dimension to advertising and allows even small businesses with local focus to capitalize on digital advertising.

The importance of creative execution and copy for mobile is underscored by Carolyn Everson, VP for Global Marketing Solutions at Facebook. In answering a question from *Business Week* on what makes a mobile ad work, she said, "We have a saying we use quite a lot with clients: 'You need to think about thumb-stopping creative.'"[13] *Business Week* then asked, "So what stops thumbs?" Carolyn replied, "No.1 is the creative. If you think about what works in any medium—print, TV, etc.—the creative is of utmost importance." The adaptive experimentation methods we recommend in this chapter will help ventures significantly improve the performance of their advertising by generating creative content that works better.

Summary

Advertising and the ability to pay to generate awareness and engage with customers is a large and complex task. To simplify matters, begin with a strong positioning that defines your target customer segments and clearly differentiates your offering from competitors. Develop copy that reflects this positioning and is created by widely different sources, and test the copy effectiveness. Plan your advertising to test and allocate your media spend on the most effective campaigns. Leverage the tools and concepts that are both established and emerging in digital marketing, and most important, adapt your advertising in response to the results of your adaptive testing as well as to changes in the marketplace.

Endnotes

1. eMarketer. US Digital Ad Spending, by Format, 2014-2019 (2014). www.eMarketer.com.

2. L. Lodish, M. Abraham, S. Kalmenson, J. Livelsberer, B. Richards, and M.E. Stevens, "How TV Advertising Works: A Meta Analysis of

389 Real-World Split-Cable TV Advertising Experiments," *Journal of Marketing Research* 32 (May 1995): 125–139.

3. L. Lodish, M. Abraham, J. Livelsberger, B. Richardson, and M.E. Stevenson, "A Summary of Fifty-Five In-Market Experimental Estimates of the Long-Term Effect of TV Advertising," Part 2, *Marketing Science*, 14, no. 3 (1995): G133–120.

4. "An Analysis of Real World TV Advertising Tests: A 15 Year Update," (with Y. Hu and Krieger), *Journal of Advertising Research* 47, no. 3 (September 2007): 341–353.

5. "An Update of Real-World TV Advertising Tests," (with Ye Hu, Abba M. Krieger, and Babak Hayati), *Journal of Advertising Research* 49, no. 3 (June 2009): 201–206.

6. J.D.C. Little, "Decisions Support Systems for Marketing Managers," *Journal of Marketing* 43 (Summer 1979): 9–26.

7. C.B. Bhattacharya and L. M. Lodish, "An Advertising Evaluation System for Retailers," *Journal of Retailing and Consumer Services* 1, no. 2 (1994): 90–100.

8. Ibid.

9. This section draws heavily from personal correspondence and speeches given by Yosi Heber in late 2004.

10. McCarthy, A. (2014, October 22). Worldwide Ad Spending: Q3 2014 Forecast and Comparative Estimates. Retrieved from eMarketer.

11. McCarthy, A. (2014, October 20). US Ad Spending: Q3 2014 Forecast and Comparative Estimates. Retrieved from eMarketer.

12. Ibid.

13. Ira Boudway, "Expert Outlook: Facebook's Carolyn Everson," *Bloomberg Business Week* (November 6, 2014).

7

Distribution/Channel Decisions to Solidify Sustainable Competitive Advantage

Anki—Emerging from Stealth Mode with Help from Apple

In June 2013, Tim Cook took the stage at the Apple World Wide Developers Conference and introduced Boris Sofman, CEO of Anki (http://youtu.be/QnsR-kZUx6o). Boris demoed Anki DRIVE, the company's first product, which became one of the top-selling products in U.S.-based Apple stores during the holiday season. A robotics and artificial intelligence company that had been operating in stealth mode, Anki launched on one of the world's largest and most visible stages. As you saw in Chapter 4, "Leverage Public Relations for Maximum Value," Anki could not have paid to gain such tremendous exposure. Rather, the company earned the right to launch in such grand fashion by delivering a compelling, sustainable advantage not only to its end users, but also to its lead distributor, one of the most influential brands and companies in the world.

Too often, we look to distribution channels as just another way to expand the reach of our offering to the market and to sell more products or services. The most effective way to approach distribution channels is to view your channel partner as a customer that requires the same positioning, segmentation, and differentiation that we have described in this book. You must earn your channel relationships by delivering product-offering bundles that are perceived by the distribution partners as better than your competition.

Distribution channels are the means by which you reach customers when they are ready to buy. Effective channel strategies can serve many objectives that help to unlock the value of your offering. In addition to expanding your reach into the market, channels can build awareness, reinforce your segmentation and differentiation, provide opportunities for customers to evaluate and try your offering, and even enhance the value proposition to customers.

In the Anki example, Apple provided Anki with a showcase to create awareness among a large group of technically savvy Apple developers—many of who had probably played with slot cars as young children. By providing distribution in the Apple stores, Anki also gained access to a large, targeted customer base during the peak holiday season. Anki's mere presence in the Apple stores enhanced its image as having cool, well-designed, high-technology products. The Anki DRIVE product requires later-generation Apple devices, including the iPhone, iPad, and iPod Touch. Availability in the Apple stores increased the probability of reaching the segment that already owned, or soon would own, the necessary devices.

How did Anki earn such preferred access to both the media attention and physical product distribution afforded by Apple? In short, Anki has all of the elements of being a winner for Apple (see Chapter 4). The Anki DRIVE product offering reinforced Apple's design-centric brand, delivered a compelling customer experience, and provided an opportunity for Apple to increase traffic and sales in its stores and products. Anki provided a value proposition consistent with Apple's positioning in the smartphone and consumer electronics industry.

This example embodies many of the key principles of distribution discussed in this chapter, including reinforcement of positioning, functions of distribution, direct and indirect channels, types of intermediaries, and earning your channel partners.

Making Distribution Decisions

Distribution encompasses all of the activities that need to be performed to get your product-offering bundle to the customers and users who will buy and benefit from it. The product-offering bundle includes not only your product or service, but all of the ancillary parts that help to mold the perception of the end customer. How the product is packaged, how the product is placed on the shelf, what the clerk says and knows about the product, the price paid by the end user, how the customer is treated when she has a problem or a question before or after purchase, and how easy it is for the end customer to evaluate alternative product offerings are all examples of ancillary parts of the product-offering bundle. The choice of which intermediaries are involved between your company and your customers and how these intermediaries are managed has a big impact on the product-offering bundle.

The distribution decisions now are much more complex than they were even 10 or 15 years ago. The alternative ways for the different parts of the product-offering bundle to be distributed have been increasing at a very rapid rate. However, one thing remains consistent: Effective distribution requires choice of channels and intermediaries that reinforce your positioning.

This chapter shares ways to generate new, creative, and productive distribution options. We describe a number of options that entrepreneurial firms have been able to use effectively. We also show methods for evaluating the options in terms of their impact on the perceived product-offering bundle to the entrepreneur's target segment(s). Figure 7-1 puts the macro logic of distribution channel decisions covered in this chapter in perspective.

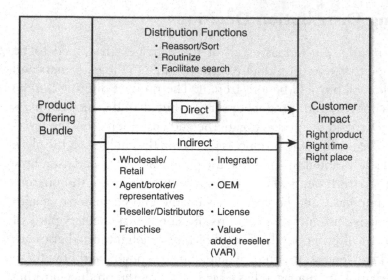

Figure 7-1 Entrepreneurial distribution channel decisions

To help you make some good distribution decisions, we first look at the required functions any distribution system must perform as well as the types of distribution partners with whom you may work. We then look at additional options that need to be considered as part of the effect of the distribution channel decisions on the perceived product-offering bundle.

Required Functions of Any Distribution System

Effective distribution delivers the right *product or service* to the end customer at the right *place* at the right *time* in the right *quantities*. Distribution choices also should reinforce your positioning by reaching greater numbers of your target market segment as well as highlighting your differentiation vis-à-vis competitive offerings. Whether you choose a direct or indirect distribution method (discussed in the later section "Other Aspects of Distribution System Design—Direct Versus Indirect"), distribution must increase the perceived value of your offering to the customer as well as capture greater value and profits for your company.

Intermediaries may be able to perform some of the required functions more efficiently and/or more profitably than your firm. Pitt, Berthon, and Berthon outline three basic functions that intermediaries can perform to improve the productivity of a distribution channel:[1]

1. Reassortment/sorting
2. Routinizing transactions
3. Facilitating search

Reassortment/sorting refers to all of the typical intermediary activities that need to happen for physical or digital distribution from a producer who likes to supply relatively large quantities of a relatively small assortment to an end consumer who will typically want relatively small quantities of a large assortment of product-offering bundles. These activities may include arranging the products, sorting them into groups that are relevant to consumers, aggregating goods from different suppliers, "breaking bulk" by providing the right smaller quantities to the end customer, and putting together new packages of goods or services from different suppliers.

Routinizing transactions arc activities that standardize products and services and automate transactions so that bargaining is not needed for each small transaction; it makes it easier for the end customer to compare alternative offerings. The authors point out some instances in which resupply of products is completely automated so that orders are entered and products replenished when inventories reach a certain minimum level.[2]

Facilitating search is the classic aid by intermediaries to make it easier for sellers to find buyers and to make it easier for buyers to find their best alternative product or service to purchase. The traditional retailer puts products from different suppliers on the same shelf so that the consumer can make a less uncertain purchase than she would if she didn't have the alternative products right in front of her. In general, intermediaries can reduce uncertainty for both buyers and sellers. A good intermediary can help an entrepreneur do a better job of understanding and responding to customer needs and can simultaneously help consumers to be sure that their purchases will indeed satisfy their needs.

Internet technologies have reshaped each of these functions, often disrupting existing industries and distribution channels by improving each of these functions and, therefore, improving the overall customer experience and access to products. Technology may also allow companies to capture greater value than existing distribution channels by eliminating intermediaries or unnecessary costs of distribution. However, you must consider the cost-benefit of channel choices as part of your overall marketing strategy. The following example demonstrates this concept in the music industry.

Evaluating Distribution Options, a Disintermediation Example

Technology has transformed the music industry over the last two decades as the product-offering bundle of music has moved from traditional fixed media CDs and live concerts to digital music, videos, and integrated media. Today, artists can produce a digital recording, distribute it directly to consumers, and build a fan base, all online. Here, *disintermediation* is replacing a record company, record distributor, rack jobber, and retailer with a direct artist-customer relationship. If the customer knows which recording of which artist she wants, direct distribution may be very attractive to her.

It would seem, at first blush, that all artists should jump aboard the disintermediation bandwagon and distribute their music directly. They would not have to pay all of the middlemen their cuts, and would be able to establish a direct relationship with their customers. This direct relationship would enable all kinds of activities to create more value (and thus make more money eventually). The artists could create loyalty programs to reward and encourage their best customers. The loyalty rewards might include special seats for concerts or special merchandise. The artists could also reward current customers for referring new customers with similar added-value offers. However, the disintermediation decision is not this simple. There are other sides to this story that highlight the value of distribution channels.

One of the most significant considerations is building consumer awareness of the artist. Many websites and music services are spending tens of millions of dollars to get people to their sites and listen to artists' music. Generating this traffic is a significant challenge that may not make sense for the individual artist. In addition, customers may know they want a particular artist's song(s), or they may want to listen to a number of options before they make a purchase. Media offered to customers online may raise concerns about the quality of the digital recording they will download. Although many consumers are migrating to digital music, those that seek traditional fixed media may be excluded from an artist's desire to build a direct and digital relationship. These are just some of the myriad of issues that you must consider as you develop a distribution strategy. These distribution decisions can be at the same time the most difficult and the most important decisions you make when launching a new product, service, or business.

Revisiting Positioning in the Context of Distribution

All the functions described previously must be evaluated as part of the distribution options. If you have effectively positioned your product offering, then the distribution options to evaluate may be self-evident. However, as technology and the environment change the characteristics of existing options and generate new options, you must constantly review these options. Let's look at our digital music example in more depth to illustrate some of these issues.

The first element of positioning is understanding the target market segment the artist is trying to reach. Is he trying to reach a very small alternative group, or does he want to add value to a more mainstream market? The answer to the targeting question will have a very big impact on the distribution strategy. Alternate target markets may want to buy and consume music in different ways. If the alternative target market eschews mainstream digital media and consumption, iTunes or a direct sales website may not be appropriate for the alternative group. They may prefer to learn about music from attending live performances. They may value the artwork and liner notes of CDs and prefer to buy CDs directly from the artist. All of these behaviors can make the alternative target market valuable to the artist but only if they understand the preferences and behaviors of their target segment and adapt distribution (and all other aspects of the product and marketing) to that customer. These distribution choices can be evaluated by concept testing before the entrepreneurial marketer makes this decision.

The product-offering bundle that the end customer sees must reinforce your differentiation, the second element of positioning. A good distribution strategy enables the perception by the end customer as you have planned. Most artists categorize their work in specific genres and subgenres of music. Artists may also consider others' works as serving the same audience as their own. With the advent of streaming and Internet radio services, listeners have the ability to sample many artists' works. An effective distribution channel will categorize the artist's work in the desired manner, and recommendation engines will connect listeners with other music that reinforce the artist's desired positioning. Some channels may offer unbiased reviews of music by critics whom the artist respects. Others may sell both digital and fixed media versions of music, shipping the latter with preferred terms. They may offer multiple payment options. All of these distribution options may reinforce the positioning of the artist's work and desires and preferences of their target market.

The artist in our example may never get exactly the "optimal" product-offering bundle by the distribution system he has assembled. He makes trade-offs of less-than-optimal product-offering bundles versus the costs of the available distribution options. He is trading off potential revenue from getting it perfect versus lower costs from less-than-perfect distribution options. If the artist has done a good job with his concept testing (see Chapter 2, "Generating, Screening, and Developing Ideas") with target market participants and of considering the important concepts in this chapter, he should be able to make productive decisions on these distribution trade-offs.

Other Aspects of Distribution System Design—Direct Versus Indirect

The earlier disintermediation example of using the Internet to distribute music directly to consumers is only one example of direct distribution. Similar to manufacturers' reps and your own sales force, distribution options can run the gamut from direct to many layers of middlemen who handle your goods or services before they are bought and used by the end customer. The trade-offs you make in terms of direct or indirect distribution options impact your business in several ways, including fixed and variable costs, efficiency versus effectiveness of contacts, amount of control, mass coverage versus targeting ability, and level of customization provided to the end customer. Table 7-1 shows the directions of these trade-offs as a function of whether the distribution system is direct or indirect.

Table 7-1 Indirect Versus Direct Distribution Options

Indirect	Direct
Variable costs	Fixed costs
Efficiency per contact	Effective per contact
Control	Control
Coverage	Targeting
Customization	Customization

Although Table 7-1 reflects direct and indirect distribution as a choice, the reality is that distribution strategy and options lie on a continuum that reflects elements of each.

Owning Your Own Distribution—The Highest Control

Direct distribution allows you to capture the largest portion of profits for each sale; however, this strategy also incurs higher fixed costs and risk. Because distribution intermediaries may take title to your goods and then mark them up, or else take a fee for each item they handle, their costs are typically mostly of a *variable* nature. They do not usually charge you for the fixed costs of their operations. However, some intermediaries do have minimum quantities that they may handle—effectively imposing some fixed costs. On the other extreme, direct distribution typically involves *fixed costs* for warehousing, billing, and other administrative costs. Fixed costs add more *risk* to the venture because they will be incurred regardless of what level of sales actually occurs in the marketplace. Variable costs lower risk because they are only incurred when sales are made. Direct distribution typically entails more risk than indirect distribution, so you must ensure the additional profit potential justifies the risk.

Indirect distribution is typically more *efficient* in terms of physically getting goods from your company to the final consumer. By combining your product or service with other products and services, the middlemen are able to more efficiently perform the kinds of functions described previously. However, the middleman also takes some *control* over the product-offering bundle and may not provide the one that is best for your product because she is combining your product with others. When you are more in control, you will be able to portray your product in the best way you can—this is typically more *effective* in adding perceived value to the product-offering bundle. The added control also enables direct distribution options to develop a more customized product-offering bundle for each potential customer. The indirect distributor will not typically have the flexibility or ability to make changes for each customer because the indirect distributor has to keep in mind the needs of all of her products in her product-offering bundle strategy.

Victoria's Secret and the L Brands' "Own Store" Channel Strategy

An important element in the distinctive competence of the L Brands (formerly Limited Brands, Inc.) and Victoria's Secret is their ownership and complete control of all of their stores in the United States. The consumer store experience—including sales force attention, display, and pricing—are all key elements of their positioning. Because many of the L Brands' stores (including Victoria's Secret and Bath and Body Works) are in similar malls, they have a lot of power with mall owners to get good locations and probably good rental rates. For Victoria's Secret, it would be very hard and extremely expensive for competitors to duplicate their "own store" strategy. These stores and the consumer experience derived from them is a key source of sustainable competitive advantage for Victoria's Secret.

It is this "own store" strategy that dictates how L Brands and Victoria's Secret expanded globally. Les Wexner, the former CEO, wanted to use his corporate resources where they would contribute the best long-term return versus the resource costs for implementing the strategic initiatives. Going global with stores typically involves complex relationships with intermediaries in the various countries and a loss of control to brokers, agents, and other third parties. L Brands felt that it has other, better uses for its resources that have higher returns than global store expansion. They started new U.S. products that leverage their ability to very economically (compared with their competition) open new stores. For example, they introduced a new beauty line with Henri Bendel and C.O. Bigelow—an apothecary. C.O. Bigelow was created many years ago in Greenwich, Connecticut. L Brands has made it into a store concept with all of the original formulas for which C.O. Bigelow has become famous.

Victoria's Secret launched a new line of lingerie—Pink—for the college-age woman, which has been rolled out to all of the Victoria's Secret stores. The idea for the line came from a segmentation study of their customers and potential customers. They saw a need for a younger line for a more casual life style. There is a separate "Pink" room and environment in each Victoria's Secret store. The concept could eventually be spun off to its own stores, as was Bath and Body Works. The Pink line was first sold only in 10 stores, then modified based upon the customer reaction, then rolled out to 30 stores, modified again, then 100 stores, and then to all stores. This is a much better (that is, valid) and cost-effective way to test new products than the typical concept or in-market testing that other consumer products goods (CPG) companies that don't own stores do. Pink became a $500 million revenue product line in less than two years! It's hard to envision any export strategy doing anywhere near that well. The ability to do these controlled, cost-effective, extremely valid test markets for new store/product ideas is another sustainable competitive advantage that leverages VS distinctive competencies.

Victoria's Secret found that their website has been able to service demand around the world. They continue to service global customers through the Internet because the incremental costs (very small) are justified by the sales generated. They also retain complete control about how the products are portrayed and how the sales process works. They also experimented with catalogs with some success in some areas of the world, but there was not enough success to justify diverting resources from other initiatives domestically that were evaluated as more productive.

Indirect Distribution and Exclusivity Alternatives

The next distribution/channel option to consider and evaluate is lower on the control continuum than "owned" distribution but retains some of the benefits—distribution exclusivity. Many firms do not even consider distribution exclusivity options. They assume that they should use the same channels in the same way as everyone else in their industry. Marketers do not consider exclusivity options nearly as often as they could. The exclusivity options vary by how selective your distribution channel is and may vary over time. The two extremes are exclusive distribution and intensive distribution. In the middle is the selective distribution option. Exclusive distribution gives a retailer or other intermediary the exclusive right to sell your product in a defined "area" for a defined time period. Area used to mean geographical area—such as a country or metropolitan area—or focus of industry sectors, product lines, or other means of limiting scope of exclusivity. Areas in cyberspace can also be exclusive to one or a select few e-tailers. Selective distribution gives the right to distribute your product to some entities in a defined area but limits the number to a select group. Intensive distribution lets anyone who wants to distribute your product do so. There are a number of trade-offs that you must evaluate when you consider your choice of distribution channel exclusivity. First, as with almost all entrepreneurial decisions, creativity in terms of options is crucial. Exclusivity is just a subset of the distribution options that should be generated and evaluated as part of the venture initiation process. Table 7-2 shows elements of the trade-offs that are involved with different levels of distribution exclusivity.

Table 7-2 Distribution Exclusivity

Exclusive	Selective	Intensive
Possible easier sell in	Resellers compete	High coverage
Higher control	Less reseller loyalty	Convenience
Higher margins for all		Lower control
Less competition at point of sale		Less push in store
		More mass pull needed
More push in store		More coverage
Less coverage		Faster sales cycle possible
More association with channel members attributes		
Possible guaranteed minimum sales		

Exclusive Distribution

The exclusive distribution option has a number of advantages that most firms do not realize. The first advantage is that it is usually easier to sell into a distribution channel if you are able to offer exclusivity. Exclusivity adds value to your product-offering bundle to most intermediaries. Using the Internet as an example, if you can offer your product to only one website for resale, then that website operator does not have to worry about any price competition from other websites. This price competition is made easier on the Internet by the robots that automatically find the lowest price for purchasers among the competing sales sites on the Internet. Not only can you sell the product easier with exclusivity, but also in many cases you can extract valuable benefits for a struggling entrepreneur. Typically, exclusivity is negotiated with either some payment in advance for it, or some guaranteed minimum sales quantities that the distributor will have to sell in order to retain the exclusivity.

We must mention that some smartphone software apps are a unique, and extreme, example of exclusive distribution. As part of their business model, Apple created the App Store as a means to promote the standardization of iOS (iPhone, iPad, and iPod Touch) device software and capture a new and significant revenue opportunity. By making your app available on the Apple App Store, you gain access to hundreds of millions of iOS owners. As with the previous music example, the App Store facilitates search and categorization of your app. Recommendations and ratings provide users with the ability to explore and choose from more than one millions apps available. The success for Apple is astounding. In 2013, customers spent more than $10 billion in the App Store and downloaded almost 3 billion apps in December 2013, making it the most successful month in the App Store's history. However, relevant for us is the more than $15 billion that developers of apps have earned through the App Store since its inception.

Although this is a significant revenue opportunity, do keep in mind the cost of this exclusive distribution relationship. For access to the iOS market, Apple charges 30% of all app revenue, and only a very small number of apps generate significant revenue.

Google Play provides a similar exclusive distribution platform for Android app developers. Play has more than one million available apps and has had more than 50 billion app downloads.[3] Although Android has a much larger share of the smartphone market (estimated at 80% in 2014), the average Android user spends half as much on apps as an Apple iPhone user. However, analysts believe that Android app revenue will overtake Apple in 2018.[4]

The Apple App Store and Google Play provide a unique case in exclusive distribution. The following section revisits Anki, the company we introduced at the beginning of this chapter, to see how distribution exclusivity can help launch a product.

Anki DRIVE—Launched by Exclusivity

Anki agreed to an exclusive distribution agreement with Apple for six months. During this time, customers could only buy Anki DRIVE from the online Apple Store, through the Apple retail stores in the United States, or direct from Anki. Anki would not be able to expand to other channels, like Best Buy and Amazon.com, that the company felt would be required to gain market penetration. However, in return for exclusivity, Apple included Anki DRIVE in its coveted Holiday Gift Guide as well as provided prominent displays in the Apple stores.

This exclusive distribution deal gave Apple access to one of the potentially hottest high-tech toys of the holiday season. In addition, the Anki DRIVE allowed Apple to feature its implementation of Bluetooth LE (low energy) in its newest iOS devices. Bluetooth LE is a wireless technology that allows multiple devices to exchange information in small, personal networks with a much lower power consumption than Wi-Fi or earlier Bluetooth generation technology. Together with a design aesthetic that is consistent with the Apple customer, Anki DRIVE provided an engaging iOS device accessory that reinforced Apple's technology and design competitive advantage. And most importantly for Apple, it would not be available on the Android platform or through any other distribution channels (except for Anki's website) during the exclusivity time period.

In its inaugural selling season, Anki DRIVE became the top-selling accessory in the Apple 2013 Holiday Gift Guide. In May 2014, Anki expanded its distribution channel to sell Anki DRIVE via Amazon and at Best Buy, providing greater market reach and exploration of other channel options.

Evaluating Channel Exclusivity

By giving exclusivity, you enable the channel member to associate your product more closely with the channel member's other products. In many cases, this can be a win-win situation for both parties. If the positioning of your product is consistent with that of other products the channel member carries, then your product may reinforce the positioning of the other products and simultaneously benefit from the association. For example, many upscale products will have exclusive retailers in each geographical area who are "authorized" to sell their product exclusively. Even the adjective "exclusive" has been used to describe this kind of product. "Exclusive," very high-priced watches and certain haute couture designer fashions are examples of products that use exclusivity as one of their distribution leverage points.

If a channel member has exclusivity, she will typically have more motivation to "push" the product to the next level of distribution, or to the final consumer. "Push" involves promotion, distribution attention (for example, shelf space, display in store), advertising, and so on. Because she has exclusivity, the channel member can push the exclusive product and not worry about a competitive channel member capitalizing on the "push" by selling the product without paying for any of the "push expenses." In addition, if the exclusive product is attractive to consumers, advertising the exclusive product may get new people into the channel member's business and cause them to buy other products while they are there.

Because of the lack of interchannel competition, the margins on exclusive goods are usually higher, not only for the channel members, but also for the manufacturer. The manufacturer typically has some more control over what the channel member does with her product if she has an exclusive arrangement. In many cases, the exclusivity contracts will not only have guaranteed minimum purchase quantities, but also stipulations about how much and what kind of "push" will be performed by the channel member. However, the granting of exclusive distribution is not a one-way street.

If you give an exclusivity contract for a long period, you may end up at the mercy of the channel member to whom you have given exclusivity. During the contracted exclusivity period, as long as all of the exclusivity contract provisions are being observed, you may have very little leverage over the channel member. This happens a lot when a firm enters a new country using a full-service importer/distributor. These importer/distributors typically assume all responsibility for the product once the container leaves the firm's country. The firm may not be very knowledgeable about the sales potential and/or the potential perceived value of the offering to the end consumers in the new country. The importer takes advantage of this by negotiating a contract that has a competitive price that the importer pays for your product, but does not specify the price or other marketing mix elements that the importer will use in his country. There are also typically annual minimum purchases that are required to retain the exclusivity. The agreements may be very long in duration—10–20 years, or even lifetime. The importer/distributor is thus free to do whatever he wants with the product as long as he buys his minimums from the firm. Sometimes, the importer will second source an inferior version of your product to distribute alongside your product and unfairly leverage your brand equity. In other cases, the importer will develop a competing version of your product and limit his competition to the minimums he has to sell of your product.

One coauthor has been working with foreign companies entering the U.S. market for over 35 years, including a number of Israeli firms. He has seen a number of Israeli firms that wanted to enter the U.S. market and found someone who knew someone in the United States who spoke Hebrew. That person became the exclusive importer/distributor and told the Israeli firm that "standard practice" was to have very long exclusivity terms: 20–30 years in many cases. The Israeli firms lost millions of dollars in opportunity costs because of the treatment of their exclusive distributors for whom they had no operational recourse. Many American firms have had similar experiences when they attempted to enter other countries—especially those with different languages and culture. Just as it makes sense to generate and evaluate a number of alternatives for other elements of your marketing plan, it is at least as important for the distribution channel decisions.

Before getting into long-term exclusivity agreements, you should know your market, how the product offering should be perceived, and have some reasonable ideas about its perceived value and pricing options. The long-term exclusive distributor is crucial to your business—it's like a marriage. You should check out all alternatives and be sure of the ethics of your chosen distributor, if you choose the exclusive route.

Item Exclusivity

Some firms use exclusivity by item to help lower price competition between competing channel members or competing retailers. They will make small differences between models and give retailers or channel members' exclusive rights to one model for a geographical area. This exclusivity by item does not help as much with all of the advantages of exclusivity in Table 7-2. However, in a number of industries, it has become the way most firms go to market. For example, the medium- and high-end furniture manufacturers will have different models that are exclusive to different retailers in a U.S. metropolitan area. The biggest advantage the furniture retailers see from this tactic is that their potential customers cannot easily compare prices from one local dealer to another. Now that furniture is beginning to be sold on the Internet, it will become even more important for local retailers to attempt to insulate themselves by having exclusive items.

Intensive Distribution

Intensive distribution is the opposite extreme from exclusive distribution in the options described in Table 7-2. Anyone who wants to carry your offering is encouraged to do so. The objective is to be everywhere the end customer might be and possibly buy your product offering. Impulse purchases such as candy, snacks, and so on are typically well suited to intensive distribution. However, in order for you to be successful, the consumer needs to know your product is there and perceive its value. The product needs to be pulled off the shelves by the customer compared with all the other competitive products. The classic, non-entrepreneurial way for that pull to happen is for a company to spend millions of dollars on promotion and advertising. As entrepreneurial marketers, we know better ways. Our chapters on public relations, promotion, and advertising cover creative, cost-effective ways to pull products through intensive (and other) distribution channels. One of the most creative ways to use intensive distribution is with *fad* products.

Ken Hakuta was the master user of intensive distribution to support his launch of "Wacky Wallwalkers" in concert with the rest of his ingenious, creative, lucky marketing plan that he executed in the mid-1980s. Because of the amazing demand built up by his fortuitous national public relations "Blitzkrieg," every store in the United States wanted to sell Wacky Wallwalkers. Wacky Wallwalkers were exactly what their name hinted. They were little plastic octopuses that if thrown against most walls, would slowly walk down the wall, one leg over the other. Every retailer wanted to sell Wallwalkers after they were featured as the "newest fad" on the CBS Evening News.

Ken knew that time was of the essence and that he should take advantage of the extraordinary consumer demand by getting as many Wallwalkers into as many storefronts as possible as fast as possible. He was aware that cheap knockoffs would soon arrive to compete, even though he had an "exclusive license" from the Japanese manufacturer.

To accomplish mass distribution as quickly as possible, Ken authorized toy and novelty distributors to sell his product to the trade rather than have his own sales and distribution team. The distributors had the entire infrastructure in place to quickly get the product to all of the retailers who were demanding to be part of the Wallwalkers action. Ken gave an additional markup to these distributors to compensate them for their part in the distribution chain. He thus made less on *each* Wallwalker that he sold than he would have earned had he used his own sales and distribution system. However, he correctly estimated that his total number of units sold would be much higher with the indirect distribution system. The total profits he earned by selling over 200 million Wallwalkers in less than one year were much higher than he would have earned had he struggled to develop his own sales and distribution system. He also was able to capitalize on the consumer demand before the knockoffs were able to become a big factor.

The use of intermediary sales and distribution resources was appropriate for Ken for another reason. He correctly viewed Wallwalkers as a product with limited life and did not plan to follow Wallwalkers with any other products targeted at similar mass-market customers. If he were planning a long-term business where retailer relationships were going to be important, then more direct contact between Ken's people and the mass retailers would possibly have made sense. He was right to view Wallwalkers as a once-in-a-lifetime opportunity. He made "tens of millions"[5] of dollars on the Wallwalkers—not bad for a year's work and virtually no assets before he started!

Selective Distribution

Selective distribution is in the conceptual middle between exclusive and intensive distribution. Here, some, but not all, resellers are authorized to resell your product and/or service. By not allowing everyone to carry your product, you retain some control as to how it will be resold. The control mechanism is the implied threat to take away the product from those resellers who do not follow your rules for your product. You also may have a stronger say in how the end consumer may perceive you. The selective distribution option is best if it is integrated with the rest of the marketing mix to reinforce a sound positioning and segmentation plan. Brooks Sports found a way to compete with Nike that includes selective distribution as an important, integrated element of its marketing mix.

Brooks Sports—Integrating Selective Distribution with Effective Positioning and Segmentation

When Helen Rockey came to Brooks in 1994 after 11 years at Nike, Brooks was a mess. Brooks had been successful during the running boom of the late 1970s, but in the 1980s they tried to chase Nike. They expanded into other categories like basketball, aerobics, and baseball, and signed big name athletes like Dan Marino and James Worthy to sell their $70 shoes.[6] Brooks, like Superscope (discussed later), had committed the classic error of trying to move down the prestige of distribution channels to maximize revenue. According to *Forbes*,

> But in trying to become a mini-Nike, Brooks was stretched too thin. When business began to slow, it began using cheaper materials and selling its sneakers at rock-bottom prices to discount retailers like K-Mart, which sold them for as little as $20. Brooks lost credibility with joggers, and between 1983 and 1993 it lost some $60 million. "I don't think I really knew what I had gotten myself into," Rockey says.[7]

Rockey developed a completely different marketing strategy in order to differentiate Brooks from the rest of the competition. She went back to Brooks' running heritage and decided to reposition the product as the shoe for serious running enthusiasts. This revived positioning dictated all the elements of her new marketing mix, including distribution. This new strategy was consistent with what was left of Brooks' distinctive competencies—relationships with Far-East suppliers, design capability, and a new CEO who herself was a running enthusiast.

The best outlet for the newly positioned Brooks line was the specialty running store that catered to the running enthusiasts. Rockey had to make her product attractive, not only to the end purchaser, the running enthusiast, but also to the specialty running store retailers.

She did that with all the elements of her marketing mix—especially her product and pricing, and very selective distribution. She first limited the Far-East suppliers from 20 to the 3 best at producing high-quality shoes and redesigned the line to be attractive to serious runners. She next boosted the suggested retail prices significantly—to as high as $120. The margin to the running specialty stores was about 45%. This was a good margin for the stores—as long as the prices were not undercut by other retail competitors. This is where Brooks' selective distribution was critical. Rockey had to control all of the retail outlets to ensure that no one was undercutting each other. She did this by ensuring that only specialty running shops got the shoes and that the discounters were not able to carry the line. In the beginning of the repositioning, she had personally visited the major retail specialty running stores to convince them that she really was dedicated to having a brand that both Brooks and their partner selective retailers would make very good money on.

The other elements of Brooks' marketing mix also supported the new positioning. Their sales force helped their retailers to offer running clinics and trained the retail sales force about how to get the right shoe for the store's runner clientele. Brooks also had an extensive and professional presence at the major running trade shows. There are no more celebrity endorsements. Instead, the company has over 200 competing runners who are given free shoes. These runners are icons within the serious running community.[8] Because the target segmentation made mass media unnecessary, Brooks was able to take advantage of media that reached its target audience very efficiently. Brooks spends less than a million dollars per year in niche publications like *Runners World* and *Running Times*. This reinvented positioning and segmentation has been very productive for Brooks. According to *Forbes* in 1999, "Brooks' sales have been growing at a 30% clip for the past 4 years and should hit $100 million by next year. Operating income (net before depreciation, interest, and taxes) last year (1998) topped $4 million, from $3 million in 1997."[9] Some brands may not be suited for intensive distribution. Brooks was one of them, as it was developed over time. Brooks does not have the potential to outcompete or outmuscle Nike or Reebok. However, it does have the potential to make a lot of money for its entrepreneurial owners if they continue to understand its limitations and have a marketing mix (including selective distribution) consistent with its revised positioning.

Preservation Hall Jazz Bands—A Selective Distribution Example

Alan Jaffee, the entrepreneur who founded the Preservation Hall Jazz Bands in New Orleans, understood the importance of selective distribution in determining how his product-offering bundle was to be perceived. He founded the Preservation Hall Jazz Bands by personally finding old Dixie Land jazz stars and rehabilitating them and caring for them so that they could re-create Dixie Land jazz as it was in its heyday. His objective was to have the Preservation Hall Jazz Bands perceived as art, not just as entertainment. To ensure that potential consumers received the correct perception, Mr. Jaffee only let the bands perform in venues that were perceived as mainly artistic as opposed to entertainment. For example, the bands would perform at the Tanglewood or Wolftrap music festivals, but not at stadium rock or jazz concerts. If they performed on television, it was on the Bell Telephone hour, not on a weekly variety or entertainment show. If you saw the Preservation Hall Band perform in the late '80s or early '90s, Alan Jaffee was the rotund white man playing the tuba in the all-black band. Their home venue, Preservation Hall in the Bourbon Street district of New Orleans, also reinforces their artistic, authentic positioning. The "hall" is very simple, with benches for the audience to sit on, and no alcoholic beverages served. You are supposed to go to Preservation Hall to listen to Dixie Land jazz and appreciate it as an art form. Their home venue, their venues on the road, and their media appearances all support and are synergistic with that positioning. Perhaps it was because Alan Jaffee did marketing at Gimbels Department store before he founded Preservation Hall that prepared him to position his very successful "offering" so well.

Types of Intermediaries—Earn Your Partners in Distribution

As Figure 7-1 shows, there are many types of intermediaries that may be part of an effective distribution strategy. As you develop your distribution strategy, remember one critical fact: Intermediaries do not exist to reinforce your positioning, serve your customers, and build your business. Rather, they seek to accomplish all of these objectives for themselves. Throughout this book, we emphasize the importance of positioning in all aspects of marketing. As you evaluate and develop distribution options, you must position yourself with your chosen intermediaries just as you would with customers. Your product offering must enhance the perceived value of the intermediaries' customers and create value for their businesses.

To understand how best to position your product-offering bundle and capitalize on an intermediary relationship, you must understand each type of intermediary as well as which of the three basic distribution functions they perform.

Agents, brokers, and manufacturer representatives (reps) routinize transactions, facilitating transactions involving goods and services between two parties. These intermediaries usually earn a commission from sales made and do not take possession of inventory.

Wholesalers and retailers may perform any or all of the three basic functions. Unlike agents and brokers, wholesalers and retailers often take possession of inventory and may facilitate search as well as provide an array of goods and services to specific market segments. Wholesalers will often buy in larger volumes (at lower per unit prices), breaking up lots to sell to other customers or retailers at a markup.

Resellers and value-added resellers (VARs) provide a form of selective distribution in which they bundle an offering with additional products and services, enhancing the overall perceived value of the product-offering bundle. Often the reseller or VAR can deliver the "complete product" and a better customer experience in a manner that you cannot. Many technical products that need to be used together with other products in an integrated solution are best marketed through VAR, selective, indirect distribution channels. For some component product categories, the end customer does not expect to buy directly from the manufacturer, but wants to buy an integrated solution from a VAR. In those categories, the VAR can almost become the end customer to the entrepreneurial marketer.

Original Equipment Manufacturers (OEMs) provide a component, subsystem, or complete product that is then sold as part of a separately branded product. In the personal computer industry, Intel provides chips and Western Digital provides hard drives that may be sold as part of any number of branded computer systems.

Regardless of the type of channel, you must understand the end customer you are trying to reach, how your offering is differentiated from competitive offerings, and how the distribution partner can help you expand your market, more effectively reach your target customer, or increase the perceived value of your offering. It is also critical that you communicate how working with you will provide the same value creation activities to your distribution partner as it will to their (and your) ultimate customer.

Neat, Co.—Using Kiosks (Direct Sales) to Earn Distribution

The Neat Company (Neat) designed and manufactured scanners for the small office and home office markets. The company positioned their products very specifically to solve the problem that many small business owners and companies have—organizing the myriad of receipts, business cards, and documents that clutter offices. The company developed a set of personas for the customers of the target segment that would see value in the Neat scanners and software and sought channel partners that could help them reach this segment.

The logical choice of distribution partner was Staples and other office products retailers. These channels focused on the small and home-based businesses and had significant reach into the target market segment. In addition, these retailers carried many complementary products as well as a few competitive products. Neat felt it had a compelling solution that integrated optimized hardware and software that made scanning, organizing, and reporting a one-button operation. This solution had higher value than the broad range of scanners with weak or limited bundled software and the stand-alone software that could only provide parts of the scanning solution or forced users to pay for more capability than they needed.

However, the office products retailers were hesitant to give up valuable shelf space to an unknown brand, preferring to retain brand name products that may be less capable. Neat developed a unique distribution model that reflected a direct distribution with complete control over the product-customer interaction. Neat rolled out kiosks in airports that allowed customers to demo the Neat solutions using their own receipts and business papers. This approach had the added benefit of being located in close proximity to one of the key customer segments, frequent traveling business people. These customers are usually accumulating the types of paper that Neat manages and may find themselves with time in the airport to participate in hands-on demonstrations.

The kiosk program generated excellent visibility and awareness as well as provided a controlled ability to present the product bundle the way the company wanted. The kiosks also provided revenue without sharing profits with intermediaries. As stated previously for the direct distribution model, Neat did need to incur the risk and fixed costs associated with renting airport space, building the kiosks, and staffing them. However, the most important outcome of the successful kiosk distribution strategy was proof that Neat products were perceived as highly valuable to the market.

Armed with the data and results of the kiosk program, Neat returned to Staples and secured both the shelf space and broad distribution it sought. This allowed Neat to rapidly expand its presence in the market and increase revenue. Although the addition of the intermediary forced Neat to sacrifice margin, the ability to grow more rapidly and exit the kiosk business was more than worth it.

Nice Systems—A VAR Example

Nice Systems Ltd. is an entrepreneurial company started in Israel that has used the VAR channel all over the world to grow from less than $10 million in 1991 to nearly $1 billion in 2014. Their major product line has been integrated digital recording and quality control systems for telephonic voice applications. These are systems that digitally record phone or other voice sources and provide technology to financial services, telecommunications, and Internet service providers to monitor their interactions with customers. Even though the product is similar, or even identical for each of these markets, Nice has wisely chosen to have selective distribution with different VAR partners in each market. For trading floors, Nice has authorized firms like British Telecom, Siemens, IPC Information Systems, and so on. For call centers, they have associated with Alcatel, Aspect Telecommunications, Rockwell, Lucent Technologies, and so on. In each of these markets, their objective is for the VAR associates to integrate the Nice Systems products into their total communications offerings to their target markets. Nice could not have grown nearly as rapidly nor have as good a base of business had they not utilized a VAR strategy. The drawback to the strategy (if there is one) is that Nice must make sure that its product-offering bundle is not only attractive to the end customers in the call centers and air traffic control centers, but also attractive to their VARs as well.

Dynamic Distribution Management

Many entrepreneurs need to understand that distribution channels can sometimes be more valuable if they are changed over time. This is true especially for product lines that continually have innovation and change a lot and/or have new products or models that are introduced. The distribution channels need to change because the prestige you want to associate with your newest and most innovative product may be very different from the prestige you are able to associate with an existing product. If the existing product has been sold for a length of time and is no longer considered as the state of the art, it will not command as much prestige and status as the "newest and most advanced." Consumer electronics and fashion items are those for which changing distribution *by item* over time is often an excellent strategy. If you can associate the high-prestige items with high-prestige distribution channels, and the lower-prestige items with lower-prestige (and typically lower margin) distribution channels, you can often create win-win situations for both you and the distribution channels.

The reason this item change over time works has partly to do with examining the needs and values of the various types of channel members. The high-end channel members (for example, Sharper Image, Bloomingdales, Hammacher Schlemmer, in the United States) want to sell exclusive, high-perceived value items. They do not want to sell the same items that the lower-end, mass-market channel members (Walmart, K-Mart, and so on) sell. The high-end retailers do not want to have to compete on price with the same item in a lower-end, lower-margin store. The high-end stores perceive that their better service, the store ambiance, and so on justify higher markups than their mass-market competitors. They also do not sell the kind of mass volumes that the lower-end stores do. This also justifies their higher profit margins because their fixed costs are higher per unit of sales.

The lower-end channel members have just the opposite set of needs. They would like nothing better than to be able to sell the same items that the high-end stores do. They want to advertise that they have the same items as the high-end stores, but for less. Managing the delicate balancing act of the different channel hierarchies is a real challenge for many entrepreneurs. However, with careful planning and a bit of "chutzpah," an entrepreneur can successfully manage these conflicting channel priorities. The following sections cover two examples—one of an entrepreneurial company, Superscope, Inc., that mismanaged the balance of their distribution channels, and Franklin Electronic Publishers, which has managed the process very well for 15 years.

Superscope, Inc.—Couldn't Achieve Balance

In the late '80s, Superscope, Inc., bought the right to the Marantz label for high-fidelity components. When Superscope bought them, Marantz was a premier manufacturer of very high-end audio components—tuners, amplifiers, speakers, and so on. Marantz distribution was consistent with their high-end image. They had a very selective distribution channel—only the most prestigious and best audio/video "consultants"/dealers in each metropolitan area of the United States. The Marantz business had good profits but was not large in terms of sales volume. The Marantz positioning and pricing limited their target market to the high-income audio file market segment. With a limited, but very profitable, target market, Marantz was growing with the high-end audio market—around 10% per year.

Superscope was not satisfied with the growth potential of Marantz. They reasoned that the brand's perceived value was so high that it could sell much more if its distribution were broadened and its advertising budget increased. When Superscope talked with mass-market retailers and distributors, they got big intentions of purchasing and promoting the Marantz line. Retailers like Walmart and K-Mart or Circuit City would have liked nothing better than to get a high-end, high gross profit product line. Their modus operandi would have been to discount the list price to build volume and sell very large numbers of units. They might have even used the Marantz line as a loss leader to build store traffic. They reasoned that middle-market consumers would love to have an opportunity to buy high-end products at a good discount.

Superscope thus began an ambitious program to sharply increase the sales of Marantz by significantly broadening the line's distribution. They began offering the line to the mass-market retailers. They encouraged them with co-op advertising programs to advertise Marantz in their weekly circulars and newspaper inserts. Most of the circulars of retailers like Best Buy or K-Mart advertise temporary price reductions and other kinds of special pricing. Initially, the sales results of the increased distribution program were extremely strong. For the next two years, Superscope's Marantz sales volume more than doubled, and their corporate profits were up even higher because of economies of scale. Superscope was a hot stock in New York for about a year.

Then things began to unravel. The high-end, exclusive retailers got upset that they were being undercut on price and outpromoted by the mass retailers. The high-end clients were sophisticated and were willing to go to K-Mart to buy for much less what they used to buy at the high-end specialty retailers. So the high-end retailers began to lose business. What did they do? The high-end specialty retailers began refusing to carry Marantz and changed allegiance to other audio equipment makers who would respect the selective distribution to only high-end specialty channels that would not compete with each other on price. For a while, Superscope did not care about these distribution losses because the high-end business was more than being made up for by large orders from the mass retailers. However, once the majority of the high-end retailers stopped carrying Marantz, its cachet and prestige began to really suffer. The high-end retailers began to bad-mouth Marantz as "the cheap brand" that was being sold through K-Mart. The mass marketers began to also shy away from paying good wholesale prices for Marantz because it began to no longer fly out of their stores as it used to. This wholesale price pressure made a big impact on Superscope's profit margins. Superscope then decided to increase their profit margins by making Marantz offshore at much lower costs and somewhat lower quality. This manufacturing change held up Superscope's profits for a time, but it also added even more fodder for the high-end "Marantz Bashers" who created much word of mouth about the decline in Marantz quality. The mass-market retailers then began to cut back their orders because the consumer demand for Marantz was deteriorating. Superscope's volume began to drop precipitously. They tried to introduce a line of Marantz "Gold," made domestically, that would only be sold in the high-end stores. The high-end stores turned Superscope down flat because they felt betrayed by their Marantz experience. They would not trust Superscope not to do the same with Marantz Gold that they did with Marantz. Superscope is no longer in business, and the Marantz name lost most of its former value.

Superscope made a number of mistakes. They did not create long-term value for any of their distribution and retailing channels. They used the Marantz reputation partially built by the high-end retailers to hurt the same high-end retailers when they broadened distribution to price-oriented competitors. They lost the trust of the high-end retailers by not treating them with the exclusivity that they rightfully expected. They lowered the quality of the brand as they lowered the prices. They sacrificed their long-term positioning and perceived value for a short-term big revenue and profit spike. Their short-term thinking killed the company.

Franklin Electronic Publishers

Franklin Electronic Publishers' core business is handheld reference products like dictionaries, thesauruses, wine guides, and so on. Over the years, Franklin has had a spotty record with other product lines, but they have continually been able to slowly grow and make good returns on their core product line. Their dynamic distribution channel management by item is a big part of their long-term success with this core line. They use a tried-and-true formula to provide a win-win situation for all of their channel partners—from the high-end Sharper Image and Bloomingdales to the lower-end Walmart and K-Mart. They give each of them what they want without alienating anybody. Sharper Image and other high-end catalog retailers, as well as the high-end retailers and e-tailers, all want exclusivity to the high end for items that they sell. Sharper Image does not get too upset if Hammacker Schlemmer sells the same new Franklin translator at the same price. However, if K-Mart or the Heartland catalog are each selling the same item at 30% lower *at the same time as Sharper Image*, the upper-end retailers get very upset.

Franklin handles this conflict by *cycling its items* through the distribution channels *over time*. Their newest models get selective distribution to the high-end retailers for about six months. They then are released to the mid-level retailers, like Radio Shack, Macy's, and so on for another six-month period. After that period, the items are released to the mass-market retailers, the Walmarts and K-Marts. If Franklin has its plan working perfectly, they have new items every six months to feed into the channel to replace the items that have been released to the next prestigious levels. When they release the item that has been at Sharper Image for six months to the next level, they should have another brand-new item to take its place. Sharper Image and other high-end retailers are happy because they are always the first to have the newest and most advanced items that they can price at high margins because of their very selective distribution. The mid-level retailers are also relatively happy because they get to carry items at a discount that had just been in the Sharper Image at higher prices. The lower-level mass-market discounters are also happy because they get to carry items at a further discount that had just been in the department stores and other mid-level retailers at higher prices.

Franchising: Still Another Distribution Option

Many entrepreneurial marketers have used franchising to accelerate their revenue growth. However, as is the case with all distribution alternatives, franchising is better for some product/market situations than for others.

Different Types of Franchising

A franchise is usually permission or a license granted by the franchisor to the franchisee to sell a product or service in an agreed-upon territory and format. Franchising is typically a continuing relationship in which the franchisor provides assistance in organizing, training, merchandising, systems, and management in return for payments from the franchisee. Franchises are a big part of business in the United States. Approximately 1 in 10 businesses is a franchise and more than $1 trillion in revenue come from franchises.[10]

The different types of franchises depend on what rights are licensed to whom. Different forms of franchising are cropping up all the time. The following forms are examples of those that have been used by entrepreneurial marketers. These forms are not mutually exclusive. Many franchise forms can have elements of these different prototype forms:

- **Manufacturing franchise**—The franchisor provides the right to a franchisee to manufacture a product using the franchisor's name and trademark. The most prevalent examples of this form are soft drink bottlers. Other examples include companies who manufacture private label goods that have a retailer's label on them and firms that manufacture fashion apparel under license to a designer label. The Callanen Watch company (now a division of Timex, Inc.) had a license to manufacture watches under the Guess label.

- **Manufacturer-retailer franchise**—The manufacturer gives the franchisee the right to sell its product through a retail outlet. Examples of this form include gasoline stations, most automobile dealerships, and many businesses found in shopping malls.

- **Wholesaler-retailer franchise**—The wholesaler gives the retailer the right to carry products distributed by the wholesaler. Examples of this form include Agway Stores, Health Mart, and other franchised drug stores.

- **Business format franchise**—This is the most popular form and includes elements of the other forms. It is typically more all-inclusive. Here, the franchisor provides the franchisee with a name, an identity, and a complete, "proven" way of operating a business. Examples include Burger King and McDonald's fast-food outlets, Pizza Hut and Dairy Queen restaurants, Holiday Inn and Best Western Hotels, 7-Eleven convenience stores, and Hertz and Avis car rentals.

From the Franchisee's Point of View

For the franchisee, these franchise forms can be very helpful for some entrepreneurs who want to start a business but may not have the vision, creativity, resources, or skill to start a completely new venture. All of the forms provide for the franchisee to benefit from the market power of large-scale advertising and marketing expenditures. These large marketing budgets typically come from the collective resources of all of the franchisees. Many franchises also enable franchisees to band together and buy products and supplies at better prices than they could as individual entrepreneurs. Probably the biggest value of these franchises is the brand name value and equity that has been built up over, in some cases, many years by the franchisor. The different forms may also add unique advantages.

For *manufacturing franchises*, the franchisee may get a well-protected market that they have exclusively. Many manufacturing franchises may also permit the franchisee to obtain licenses from more than one company. For example, the Callanen Watch Company also had a license to manufacture Monet brand watches. Having multiple licenses can lower risk levels for franchisees, especially for items that may go in and out of favor. For Callanen, if the market for Monet watches was waning, perhaps the Guess brand could take up the slack.

The *business format franchise* adds a number of benefits to the franchisee that has little business experience. The best business format franchises have encapsulated all the relevant knowledge and experience of the franchisor into training and operating systems that take most, if not all, of the guesswork out of operating the franchise. McDonald's is famous for its "Hamburger University" that trains its franchisees in all elements of running a successful outlet. The franchisee basically gets to leverage on all the other experience of other franchisees and the franchisor in the past. The franchisee is helped in setting accounting procedures, facility management, personnel policies, business planning, and actually starting up. Most franchisors also help with outlet location and help arrange financing. Many business format franchises are in businesses like fast-food and convenience stores that are not very sensitive to business cycles and can make it easier to weather a poor economy. This franchise form is also available for a wide range of prices. Some business format franchises can also be operated from home—like aerobics instruction or direct marketing of cosmetics.

Following are the typical advantages of becoming a franchisee:

- Lower risk of failure
- Established product/service
- Experience of franchisor
- Group purchasing power
- Instant name recognition
- Operational standards ensure uniformity and efficiency
- Assistance in setting accounting procedures, facility management, personnel policies, and so on
- Start-up assistance
- Location assistance
- Help with financing arrangements
- Power of national and regional marketing

However, there is another side to being a franchisee. The franchisee is no longer her own boss. All of the preceding franchise benefits come at the cost of sacrificing much autonomy and often significant portion of potential profits. For most franchises, the franchisee has little, if any, control over the product/service they sell or the marketing decisions on advertising, public relations, or location. It may be impossible, for example, to drop or add products that may be more or less suitable to the particular needs of your market area. Local public relations may be under the franchisee's control, but with constraints from the franchisor. The franchisees may have a cooperative governing organization that decides on national advertising and promotion policies together with the franchisor. Each franchisee is limited to one vote in these organizations. There are also usually strict rules and regulations on all aspects of operating the business.

Aside from autonomy, there are other typical disadvantages of becoming a franchisee. You pay for the privilege. There usually is an initial franchise fee, ongoing royalty payments as a percentage of revenue, as well as a percentage of revenue to a cooperative marketing fund. The marketing fund is administered by the cooperative franchisee-franchisor organization. These fees are all "off the top." The franchisor gets paid before the franchisee may make any profits. The franchise agreements may also impose restrictions on selling the franchise if things go badly, and may also restrict how the business may be passed on to your heirs. Because the business depends on the franchisor's success, there is also a risk that the franchisor may fail. Visible franchisor failures have been Arthur Treacher's Fish & Chips and Boston Market.

Following are the disadvantages of buying a franchise:

- Payment of an initial franchise fee
- Ongoing royalty payments "off the top"
- "Off the top" payments for cooperative marketing fund
- Cannot add or drop products unilaterally
- Little say on national marketing policies and tactics
- Must conform to operating procedures—even if you have a better way
- You depend on the franchisor for much of your success
- Some large franchisors have failed
- May be restrictions on selling the franchise
- May be difficult to pass the business to your heirs

Besides considering all of the preceding benefits and disadvantages, before selecting a franchise, the potential franchisee should carefully read the Franchise Disclosure Documents (FDD) for each franchise being evaluated. FDD is required by the Federal Trade Commission's Franchise Rule, and replaced the original *Uniform Franchise Offering Circular* (UFOC) in 2007. The FDD governs disclosure requirements by the franchisor to the franchisee, and it contains the information that is needed to make a well-informed decision about the franchise as well as some not-as-useful information.

The FDD is much like a prospectus that is required as part of an initial public offering for a company's securities. Its major purpose is to keep the company making the offering from getting sued by people who buy the securities (or in this case, the franchise). The lawyers thus make the issuing company disclose any possible risks that the franchisee might be taking when they buy the franchise. Because of this bias in the way the document is written, it should be read in a special way. If you took all of the possible risks the lawyers put in these documents literally, you would not buy any franchise or any new public security. The lawyers get paid to invent risks to worry about. Most of the risk stuff is "boilerplate" that can be found in most of these documents. There is, however, much very important information in the FDD that is crucial for evaluating a franchise. The following sidebar provides the items required in the FDD and listed in the table of contents. The prospective franchisee should *scrutinize* the information before entering into a franchise agreement.

Important Items from the Table Of Contents in the Federal Trade Commission Franchise Disclosure Documents

(Adapted from the Franchise Rule 16 C.F.R. Part 436 Compliance Guide Table of Contents)[11]

- The Franchisor and any Parents, Predecessors, and Affiliates
- Business experience (of the franchisor and its affiliates)
- Litigation
- Bankruptcy
- Initial fees

- Other fees
- Estimated initial investment
- Restrictions on Sources of Products and Services
- Franchisee's Obligations
- Financing
- Franchisor's Assistance, Advertising, Computer Systems, and Training
- Territory
- Trademarks
- Patents, Copyrights, and Proprietary Information
- Obligation to Participate in the Actual Operation of the Franchise Business
- Restrictions on What the Franchise May Sell
- Renewal, Termination, Transfer, and Dispute Resolution
- Public Figures
- Financial Performance Representations
- Outlets and Franchisee Information
- Financial Statements
- Contracts
- Receipts

Because there are many fly-by-night franchisors around, it really pays to do your homework before buying any franchise. The FDD can be helpful. Under *no circumstances* should you buy a franchise *without scrutinizing the FDD.* Some franchisor salespeople can be overzealous. From the franchisee's point of view, *caveat emptor* (let the buyer beware!) is the point of view that is necessary.

From the Franchisor's Point of View

Just as the consumer viewpoint is often quite different from other channel members, the franchisor's viewpoint is very different than the franchisee's in most cases.

Advantages for the Franchisor

Franchising is a distribution option that should be considered by more entrepreneurial marketers. Many of the aspects of franchising can be attractive.[12] Franchising enables rapid expansion without large investments by the firm. The alternative ways of expanding involve both selling equity and losing some control or borrowing money, which adds leverage and may encumber some assets. When the entrepreneurial marketer successfully franchises, she effectively leases a sliver of the business and in return receives the franchisee's capital, energy, and entrepreneurship. The more rapid expansion that franchising enables may allow the franchise to take advantage of some scale economies. Large networks mean collective buying power. Franchisees can compete with other chains because they can buy in larger quantities and vendors recognize and reward the franchise's growth. Franchisees often also set up their own advertising and promotion cooperatives to obtain scale economies.

The scale economies also increase the venture's access to real estate. Single location businesses have difficulty obtaining access and credibility with mall developers, leasing agents, and limited access locations such as stadiums and contract food-feeding operations. These landlords are looking for name brands and consumer recognition, as well as repeat leasing in multiple locations. Franchising eliminates these entry barriers.

The "employees" that become franchisees are typically highly motivated to succeed because their own money is on the line. For most entrepreneurial companies, recruitment, training, and retention of great managers is key to successful expansion. The best managers are typically hard to retain unless they are offered equity. Franchising gives managers their equity with their own investment. The franchisee's investment is always at risk. This causes commitments of time and energy that typically cannot be bought with a salary. If particular skills are needed for the operation of the venture, franchisees can also be sources of highly skilled employees.

As discussed previously, the franchisor typically gets paid "off the top" as a fraction of revenue and also gets an initial franchise fee. This is typically a more predictable cash flow source than profits from an owned business. Thus, the franchisor can make profits, even if her franchises may not be profitable. It is this inherent conflict between the franchisor's incentives versus the franchisee's that causes some of the questionable and unethical franchises to arise. Conflicts between franchisees and the franchisor also come from this potential conflict of interest. Franchising works best when the entrepreneur has a proven business model that can be replicated in different areas or venues and in which both the franchisee and franchisor are better off financially than they would be if they were not together. In this manner, the franchisee/franchisor relationship is similar to that of the company/channel partner.

Franchises are typically easier to sell than the equivalent business that is not franchised. Think first about a traditional business with 50 managers with hundreds of employees in 10 cities with 100 leases. Contrast this with a franchise business that has 10 managers responsible for 50 franchisees with 100 locations. The franchise business is more attractive for an outsider to buy and may become an easier exit strategy than a traditional business.

Disadvantages for the Franchisor

There are also drawbacks to franchising. In order to attract many franchisees and generate good long-term word of mouth, the franchisees should do well financially. These franchisee profits are sometimes sacrificed when the franchise form is chosen. Obviously, if the entrepreneurial venture is really best suited for franchising, the franchise fees should more than make up for these foregone profits as returns on resources invested in the venture. Because the franchisees are independent businesses, the franchisor has only the control given explicitly by the franchise agreement. The franchisor is thus banking the image and positioning of his franchise on the franchisees. The franchisor cannot just fire those "employees" who do not keep up the firm's image and positioning. This is the same conceptual problem that users of independent sales representatives also have. It takes constant vigilance and many programs to convince the franchisee partners to handle the image and positioning as if it were their own—which it really is. Successful franchises have reduced the fundamentals of operating their businesses to a cookbook, or operations manual. Their training programs succeed in transmitting the founder's intended positioning through the franchisee to the ultimate consumer.

The franchisor also must put in suitable systems and controls to ensure that the franchisees pay the correct amount of ongoing franchise fees based on revenue of the outlet. When in doubt, the franchisee would rather report lower revenues. In many franchises where lots of cash changes hands, this control problem can be very big.

The franchisee and franchisor will typically have different incentives for pricing. For the franchisor who gets paid as a fraction of revenue, maximizing revenue becomes the objective. For the franchisee, profits are the objective. The franchisee may want to raise prices in order to increase profits at the expense of lower revenues. These pricing conflicts add a constant level of tension to many franchises.

As a franchisor, it is not as easy to change the channels of distribution because you no longer own them. Your franchisees will get very upset if they think you are going into another channel of distribution that may compete with the franchisees. For example, GNC franchises natural food and herbal remedy stores around the world. GNC has not been able to successfully use the Internet as a distribution channel because their franchisees rightfully objected to the company competing with its franchisees. This is just one example of a *distribution channel conflict* that needs to be managed and planned for very carefully. We discuss management of these conflicts later in this chapter.

Another potential disadvantage of franchising is that you may be creating a new set of competitors that learn the business through your franchise and then replicate the operation under another name. In this case, it is very important for the franchisor to maintain brand positioning, image, and other proprietary assets that would make it difficult to replicate the franchise under a different name.

Rita's Water Ice—A Successful Franchising Venture

Rita's Water Ice is an entrepreneurial venture that has succeeded very well using the franchise form. They have been able to leverage the benefits of the franchise form and minimize the impacts of most of the disadvantages. Robert Tumolo, a former Philadelphia firefighter, started Rita's in the summer of 1984. Bob and his mother, Elizabeth, experimented with various new recipes for Italian Water Ice—an ethnic summer refresher that was popular in Philadelphia. Their first store was opened in Bensalem, Pennsylvania, a working-class suburb of Philadelphia, in the summer of 1984. By 1987, Bob and his brother, John, opened three more locations to service demand. In 1989, the company made the decision to franchise, and by 1996 Rita's had more than 100 locations in nine states.[13]

For a small entrepreneurial venture begun with little capital, franchising made sense from a resource requirement point of view. Rita's could not afford to rapidly expand to more stores without going out and raising equity capital. Each franchisee invested between $135,000 and $242,000 initially to start a new Rita's outlet. That investment included an initial franchise fee, finding and leasing a site, constructing the store layout, equipping the store, and working capital. In 2005, Rita's had over 330 outlets in the Northeast and Florida. The capital needed to open all of those outlets at minimum would have been $100,000 per outlet or 330 × 100,000 = $33 million dollars. In 2005, the Tumolo interests held all of Rita's assets privately and had not had to take in public funding to expand. In addition, the firm took in over 330 franchise fees from each newly opened franchise. They also get an ongoing 6.5% of the gross sales of each franchisee. For this kind of operation, franchising was a very good distribution channel choice.

Rita's also developed a very smart way to collect their ongoing franchise and collective advertising fees, without having to audit or monitor their franchisee's sales. They just add a charge of 9% (6.5% royalty fee + 2.5% advertising fee) of the calculated gross sales for each gallon of Rita's mix that is shipped to each franchisee. The only way a franchisee can get around paying the royalty would be to buy their mix from another supplier. All Rita's personnel need to do for control is to spot check to make sure that each outlet has only Rita's authorized mix in use. Many franchisors must put in elaborate control systems to make sure that they are getting the right amount of ongoing revenue-based franchise fees.

Another constraint for expansion of company-owned stores was the ability to find, retain, and motivate real competent help to run the stores and serve customers. The stores were not open all year—just in the spring through early fall. (Most people don't crave water ice in the winter in the Northeast United States.) As hard as it was to get restaurant and fast-food employees, it was even harder if you weren't going to be open all year. An unwritten requirement for getting a Rita's franchise is that family members want to work in the outlets. One of the neat benefits of owning a Rita's franchise is that the franchisee and her family only need to work during the late spring through early fall. The franchisee has the late fall and winter to relax. Rita's was not only selling franchisees a business. They were also selling a lifestyle.

Rita's, like most franchises, had two (at least) target markets it needed to satisfy to be successful. The first was the ultimate consumers, who bought the water ice experience at its outlets. The second target segment is the franchisee, who must invest, in many cases, their life savings to buy a Rita's franchise. It is not inexpensive to sell franchises. The first few franchises were sold by word of mouth to customers at company-owned stores who really liked the Rita's product. However, in order to expand to areas outside of metropolitan Philadelphia, Rita's had to get their franchise product-offering bundle exposed to potential franchisees. In any new area, the first Rita's to open was a company-owned store. This company-owned store attempted to replicate the original Philadelphia experience, using word of mouth to expose customers both to the end product at the Rita's outlet, but also to the possibility of becoming a franchisee. Just like most business-to-business products need a sales force to help close the big sales, Rita's required a franchise sales force to follow up and close all of the leads that came into the new areas.

Like most franchises and other distribution channels, it is important for the franchisor to continually manage the channel relationships so that each franchisee continues to perceive the value proposition that they are getting from the franchise relationship. Rita's, like most successful franchisors, attempts to have franchisees perceive themselves as members of Rita's extended family. If you as a franchisee perceive yourself as a "family member" of a very successful family, then many conflicts between franchisor and franchisee don't seem to crop up. Franchisees who perceive themselves in this way are going to be the best source of positive word of mouth for attracting new franchisees. Good entrepreneurial marketers know that *word of mouth* is the most *powerful, cost-effective marketing lever* a venture can have.

Rita's franchise has been able to counter one possible disadvantage of franchising in the best way. Rita's is not very worried about their franchisees opening up competitive outlets for a very simple reason. According to Bob Tumolo, Rita's CEO, the average Rita's has almost twice the revenue of competitors in the same area.[14] This is because the product's reputation, the expanded product line (including gelati and crème ice), and the cooperative marketing campaign have created perceived value for consumers that is much higher than Rita's competition. Rita's has been able to create a win-win situation in which *both the franchisor and the franchisee are better off with each other than they would be if they were not together.* This synergy objective should be the essence of not only effective franchise management, but also effective management of all distribution channel relationships.

By 2005, Rita's franchising had created a significant business for the family and franchisees, alike. In that year, Rita's was sold to McKnight Capital Partners, a private equity firm led by two brothers that owned and operated high-performing restaurants for another well-known franchise, Wendy's.[15]

From franchising, the following section next turns to a different aspect of channel management—how to manage and anticipate channel conflict.

Managing and Anticipating "Channel Conflict"

Entrepreneurial firms can get in major trouble if their channel members perceive the firm as beginning to compete with them when they had not been competing before. Channel members are used to relating to their competitors and usually consider it "part of the game" to compete with their channel counterparts. For example, the specialty running stores that sell Brooks running shoes are used to competing with each other on the basis of service, location, and assortment, but typically not on price. If Brooks were to try to sell directly to runners and bypass the retail channel (using a catalog or the Internet), their retailers would get really upset and many would probably stop supporting Brooks. The retailers would feel that the implicit rules by which they had been operating had changed without their consent. Like any human being, that gets them very angry.

Managing channel conflicts leverages all of the marketing concepts discussed in this book. You need to define roles for every channel member that are not conflicting and are easily understood. These roles should be consistent with the venture's segmentation and the product-offering bundle that is appropriate for each segment. The benefits that are added by different channel partners will not be valued the same by all of the target segments. The channel partners will end up making the most money if they are matched with the segments that value the channel partner's benefits the highest. The channel partners also want to perceive that they are being treated fairly—which means being adequately compensated for the value that they add.

There is a big difference between channel conflict management at the beginning of a venture than when the firm wants to change the rules in the middle of the game. When a venture is beginning, the channel members should understand their role and any potential conflicts before they become a partner. If you have done your job well of marketing the role of the channel member, and the channel member signs up, then there usually will not be any conflict problems. As long as the channel member perceives that his or her role has not changed and that you have not done anything to change his role or competitive situation, he will feel that he is being treated fairly. Human beings are comfortable when their expectations are fulfilled and not changed. However, if the firm wants to change the roles of the channel members after all the expectations have been fulfilled, there can be very big problems.

For example, when vineyards began to supply firms like Virtual Vineyards and Wine.com, which sold wine directly to consumers over the Internet, the existing distributors and brick-and-mortar retailers became incensed. They pressured state legislatures all over the United States to outlaw alcohol sales over the Internet. So far, Florida, Georgia, and Kentucky have made it a felony to ship alcohol directly to consumers, and at least 17 other states prohibit such sales.[16] The recent Supreme Court decision that outlawed some of these prohibitions in states that let their intrastate wineries ship to consumers may level the playing field in some states. Rumors also go around that some distributors will refuse to support those vineyards that sell over the Internet. These distributors felt that the Internet e-tailers jeopardized their positions as exclusive representatives of vineyards in each state. If the e-tailers were already part of the picture when the distributors were signed, it would not have been a problem for the vineyards. Depending on the strength of the distributors and their importance to the venture's success, the entrepreneur may have to creatively pacify the existing distribution partners in order to change or update the channels. The Internet causes many entrepreneurs to creatively deal with channel conflicts as they try to leverage the Internet's benefits.

The best alternative is if the entrepreneur can restructure the roles of all the distribution partners so that every member of the channel becomes more productive and adds more value. This is the best "win-win" scenario. Herman Miller, Inc., seems to have found this win-win scenario in the way it has restructured its distribution channels to take advantage of the Internet to target a new segment.[17] Herman Miller's core business is selling its sleek, ergonomic premium cubicle office furniture systems to major corporations under big contracts at volume discounts. According to *Sales and Marketing Magazine*:

> The emphasis is on **big**. The company's network of more than 250 contract dealers typically nab five-year purchasing contracts to configure, deliver, and install millions of workstation components to thousands of a single customer's employees. They also go to extraordinary lengths to serve those customers. Dealers reupholster furniture, reconfigure workstations as needs change, move employees' workstations to new offices, and provide ergonomic consultations.[18]

These big dealers are not able to sell ones and twos of chairs or workstations very economically. The burgeoning small office-home office (SOHO) market was not being served well by the big partners Herman Miller had for its core business. To serve the SOHO market, beginning in 1994, Herman Miller put a few items in Office Depot and other retailers targeted at that market segment. In June 1998, Herman Miller introduced its full-fledged online store targeted at selling to the SOHO segment. Before Herman Miller management communicated with its core dealers and released its programs to help its core dealers using the Internet, the dealers were furious. When the website was first started, the dealers' perceptions were very different than Herman Miller's. Because Herman Miller had not done the appropriate marketing with their dealers, the dealers assumed that Herman Miller was out to directly compete with them. Herman Miller, to their credit, quickly realized they had a problem and began an intense program of communicating to the dealers that the online SOHO customers were a very different market segment from the major corporations in their core dealer market. They also communicated to the dealers that the same underlying configuration engine of their website was also available to help corporate customers more easily and efficiently deal with their Herman Miller partner dealer. The site was designed so that corporate customers, through their own customized intranets, would be able to develop their own configurations and price them in a much more efficient and productive manner. The dealers would still handle this corporate intranet business, but it would lower their costs significantly.

"But even if they don't go after new business, the system will significantly lower operating costs because information only needs to be entered once," says Gary Ten Harmsel, senior vice president of distribution. "A dealer's average operating expense level runs in the 16% to 18% range, and this system can help [him] lower it to 12%. If you can take six points out of your operating expenses, pass some of that on to the customer, but also keep some for your future investment purposes, it's a win for everyone."[19]

Sometimes it is not possible to segment your market clearly so that different channels can be used for the different segments. If you are changing channels, to go on the Internet and sell direct for example, it may be the best policy to make your existing channel your partner in the new channel. Ethan Allen is typical of many ventures that have been selling through selective retail distribution and decided that the Internet was too big of a potential channel to ignore. Ethan Allen owns 25% of its brick–and-mortar retail outlets. The other 75% are independently owned and operated under license. To use the Internet effectively and to not alienate their licensees, Ethan Allen had really no choice but to make their licensed retailers partners in their Internet operation. If they had opened up an independent Internet operation, their retailers (to whom Ethan Allen is their sole supplier) would have been upset with the new competition. The Ethan Allen CEO, M. Farooq Kathwari, made the only reasonable decision under the circumstances. "In exchange for a cut of the Internet revenue, the store owner would deliver much of the merchandise, accept returns, and handle the minor repairs often needed when furniture comes out of the crate."[20] Stores were also to be encouraged to make contact with people in their area who visit the website and express an interest in having decorating help.

Mr. Kathwari also realized that his dealers needed to correctly perceive the new role of the Internet in their partnership with Ethan Allen. Before the website was launched, he met personally with each of the dealers (in groups) to explain to them how "We'll do this in a partnership... We don't want to bypass you."[21]

For established ventures with existing exclusive distribution, it is difficult to bypass them without doing something like Ethan Allen did. On the other hand, if Ethan Allen did not have well-defined territories for its dealers, the preceding partnership would have been difficult to implement. However, if Ethan Allen had multiple dealers in an area, then the dealers would be used to competing with each other, and adding an Internet competitor would not have been seen as such a direct threat to each dealer. Auto companies, for example, are not having as much trouble dealing with web retailers for this reason.

Concept Testing to Channel Members

If you use all the concepts and paradigms in this chapter and decide on your optimal distribution strategy and tactics, you still may not be successful. If the distribution channel members you have chosen won't do the part you expect, then the plan and venture may fall apart. It is at least as important to get channel members' reactions to your new entrepreneurial product(s) or services, as it is to get the reactions of the ultimate consumers. Just like consumer concept testing (see Chapter 2, "Generating, Screening, and Developing Ideas) is best when the consumer is exposed to the product in the most realistic manner possible, concept testing to the channel members is completely analogous. The channel member should be exposed to your concept as realistically as possible. A nice website or brochure mock-up and descriptions of all the services you will supply to the channel member should typically be part of the concept. You also should let the channel member know explicitly what functions you expect him to perform as well. All tentative prices and terms should also be shown. If you have done concept testing with customers of this channel member, it can be helpful to summarize those results as part of the concept. Consumer concept testing results can be powerful arguments for convincing a retailer to carry your product.

The channel member should answer a similar type of question so that the end consumer is asked: "How likely will you be to buy and carry this product or service?" "What do you like best about this concept? What about the concept could be improved?" If the channel members are all "extremely likely" to buy and carry your product, then you can feel confident that the distribution channel plan will work as you hoped. On the other hand, if only a small fraction of the channel members are excited by your offering, you have problems that need fixing before introduction. Just as testing a product with real consumers can give you excellent feedback that may be very different than your logic and planning, the concept testing to the channel members can be even more valuable. There may be aspects of your product-offering bundle that you never even considered that are very important to the channel members.

Summary

The concepts, options, and examples in this chapter should encourage you as an entrepreneurial marketer to give the attention, creativity, and resources to the distribution channel decisions that they deserve. The creative juggling of different items for different time periods juxtaposed with decisions on direct, exclusive, selective, or intensive distribution can make big differences in how your offering is perceived by your target segment(s). These differences in perception can have significant impact on your ultimate profitability. Just as with the end customer, concept testing the offering with channel members is typically a cost-effective way to "reality check" all of your major distribution plan assumptions.

Endnotes

1. Leyland Pitt, Pierre Berthon, and Jean-Paul Berthon, "Changing Channels: The Impact of the Internet on Distribution Strategy," *Business Horizons* 42, no. 2 (March–April 1999): 19–28.

2. Ibid., 20.

3. C. Welch, *Google: Android app downloads have crossed 50 billion, over 1M apps in Play*. (2013, July 24). Retrieved from The Verge: http://ben-evans.com/benedictevans/2014/6/25/market-shares?_ga=1 .227055449.515846885.1408972657.

4. B. Evans, *Market Shares and ecosystem value*. (2014, June 25). Retrieved from Benedict Evans: http://ben-evans.com/ benedictevans/2014/6/25/market-shares?_ga=1.227055449.51584688 5.1408972657.

5. Jillian M. Marcus, "Eight Legs and an Amazing Feat," Harvard Business School, Note 394–444, 1994.

6. Leigh Gallagher, "Runner's World," *Forbes*, February 22, 1999, pp. 96, 98.

7. Ibid., 98.

8. Ibid.

9. Ibid.

10. U.S. Bureau of Census (2010, September 14). Retrieved from U.S. Bureau of Census: https://www.census.gov/newsroom/releases/ archives/economic_census/cb10-141.html.

11. Federal Trade Commission. (2015, April 25). Franchise Rule 16 C.F.R. Part 436 Compliance Guide. Retrieved from Federal Trade Commission: https://www.ftc.gov/system/files/documents/plain-language/bus70-franchise-rule-compliance-guide.pdf.

12. Some of these advantages and disadvantages come from discussions with Craig Tractenberg, an experienced franchise attorney with Buchanan, Ingersoll in Philadelphia, 1999.

13. Ritasice.com Website, 2015.

14. Personal communication with Leonard Lodish, 1999.

15. Ritasice.com Website, 2015.

16. Garner, Rochelle, "Mad as Hell," *Sales and Marketing Management* (June 1999): 55.

17. Ibid., 58.

18. Ibid.

19. Ibid., 58, 59.

20. James R. Hagery, "Ethan Allen's Revolutionary Path to Web," *Wall Street Journal*, July 29, 1999, p. B1.

21. Ibid.

8

Sales Management to Add Value

Plantronics

Plantronics is a global leader in audio communications for businesses and consumers. The company's primary sales channel is a large distributorship that sells to value-added resellers (VARs). Plantronics didn't have many direct relationships with the VAR channel. Erna Arnesen was hired as VP, Global Channel & Alliance Marketing to grow their revenues. She quickly surmised that the market dynamics had changed. Plantronics' products used to be sold primarily through audio specialists who understood the feature/function benefits. Now Plantronics devices were squarely in the technology arena being sold by generalists. Feature/function superiority was not enough. To understand how to create the right value proposition for the channel, Plantronics initiated market research. They interviewed partners and the Plantronics field personnel, conducted a brand survey across international markets, and took input from their distributor councils.

The research showed a big opportunity for Plantronics to grow their VAR channel through their distributors if they made their offerings easier to sell and lowered the financial risk for the VARs. The VARs had to buy the devices from distributors, resulting in a capital outlay. Many of the VAR unified communication offerings to their customers were packaged as services paid for in a subscription model that was an operating expense (OPEX). Forcing their customers to pay for the devices in a separate way from the service wasn't acceptable to the VAR's customers. So Plantronics launched a new "Plantronics as a Service." This service provided Plantronics devices and customer support via their distributors to SMB-focused (small medium business-focused) VARs in a monthly payment structure funded by Plantronics. This eliminated the upfront capital outlay and aligned the payment structure to their services subscription model.

Not only is Plantronics attracting new partners at a significant rate, but a new channel has emerged. Global integrators who didn't want to resell just headsets are now interested in incorporating headsets into their unified communications services because the cost structure is OPEX, not capital, which fits their customer's business model.

The Role of the Sales Management

The previous chapter focused on distribution channels, and many of these channels are also responsible for sales of products and services. Sales management is a key section to include in a marketing book. Although sales and marketing are quite different, they are inextricably entwined. Writing about marketing without including sales management would be the same as building a house without an initial design. The challenge, of course, for these Siamese-twin disciplines is that both of them believe they are the dominant one. Without marketing, sales wouldn't have leads and collateral. Without sales channels, closing deals and transactions wouldn't be possible. So there is a natural friction. Plus you have more sales channel options available than ever before. Have you ever seen two people dance when both are trying to lead? Now imagine ten people trying to do it. Therefore, defining the appropriate sales channels to use in the marketing mix, the role of each, and the execution plan is critical. The organization of this chapter is as depicted in Figure 8-1.

Sales management has become more complex. Sales management used to mean only managing a sales force of people. Now it means holistically managing the complete set of sales channels defined by the marketing mix.

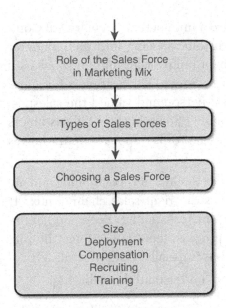

Figure 8-1 Sales management issues

All elements of the marketing mix should be based on the marketing-driven strategy of the venture. The sales channel decisions must be consistent and derived from the positioning (segmentation and differentiation) decisions that are the core of the strategy as well as the economics of the channels. In particular, the positioning usually implies a role for different types of sales channels in the marketing mix as part of the product's position and as a mechanism for targeting the desired market segments.

For example, the Tandem's East firm uses the owner, Mel Kornbluh, as its prime salesperson. His perceived expertise and experience with tandem bicycles and his willingness to satisfy customers is the bulk of his offering to potential customers. He also performs part of his firm's targeting functions by asking qualification questions during his first interactions with potential customers. On the other hand, some e-commerce companies have no role for personal sales in their marketing mix. Amazon.com customers have no interaction with any human salespeople when they make their purchase evaluations. However, the information and very personalized software Amazon.com has developed imitates what might happen if a customer went into a good discount variety department store and asked an experienced salesperson for information and recommendations. When Dell Computer first introduced direct-to-customer selling into the computer industry, the company used a mix of online sales and personal sales depending on customer preferences. Some Dell customers felt more comfortable interacting with a real person and valued the salesperson's perceived problem-solving ability. Some bigger Dell customers felt that they deserved special prices and/or had special circumstances that needed a personal touch.

The question you need to answer is: Given my positioning and my product/offering economics, what is the right sales channel mix? If your thinking has been clear and your research has been good in the segmentation and differentiation process, then determining the role of the different sales channel options is usually straightforward.

The first steps are to review and understand the following:

- How do your buyers behave—are customers willing to buy the product/service that you are offering?
- What is the gross margin of your offering, and how much can you spend on sales while providing the right net margin to the company?
- What is the expected length of the sales cycle?
- How complex is the sales process?

It is important to select a sales approach that is consistent with the answers to the preceding questions. For example, you can't afford to pay a salesperson $200,000 a year for selling products that generate $20 of gross margin, such as in the previous Amazon.com example. Similarly, a customer is going to expect more than the self-help of a website or tele-salesperson when selecting a multimillion-dollar enterprise software solution. The key is not just analyzing how customers currently buy, but testing to determine how they might be willing to buy. Amazon.com bested the traditional bookstore because they adopted a channel that customers hadn't used before, but were willing to use for the right economics. Options are evolving, and the effective marketer will analyze and test options to find better approaches. The continuum between marketing actions and sales action is getting tighter and tighter. In our social, local, and mobile world, many customers are halfway through their buying process before ever engaging with a company directly.

Type of Sales Forces

In addition to being consistent with the product and market dynamics, a company wants to deploy the most cost-effective sales model. If a product can be effectively sold over the phone, there is no reason to have external reps make in-person sales calls. Chapter 7, "Distribution/Channel Decisions to Solidify Sustainable Competitive Advantage," discussed distribution channels and types of intermediaries. Many of these channels play an important role in sales as well. Let's review the basic sales approaches to getting your product to an end user:

- Direct (to end user)
- Indirect
  - Resellers, distributors, and retailers
  - Value-added resellers (VAR)
  - Agents, brokers, representatives (often referred to as contract agents, manufacturer's reps, or just "reps")

Direct to End User

Direct to end user sales models are owned or directed by the company to sell the company's products to the entities that will use the product. Dell is an example of a company with a direct to end user sales model. Their products can only be purchased through Dell via many different media, including online, telephone, in-person, and even in partner store locations. Other companies may focus on a single means of communication for sales, including a corporate website for self-serve purchasing (Amazon.com), smartphone applications (Uber.com), telephone sales (L.L. Bean catalog), and even via direct sales representatives (IBM).

In direct to end user sales models, the company can completely control the end-user experience throughout the sales process, and the company receives customer feedback directly. The direct model can be more responsive to reflect changes, such as pricing, strategy, and messaging. The company's products are the first sales priority. However, the direct to end user model usually has high start-up costs and significant personnel management and infrastructure requirements. In many cases, it is harder to expand quickly with limited resources.

Resellers, Distributors, and Retailers

These companies resell your product in its current state to the ultimate end users. They typically sell products/services from multiple companies to a set of target markets. They buy the product/service from the entrepreneur and resell it to customers, keeping the margin between cost and price. These intermediaries include traditional retailers like Best Buy, which buys products from manufacturers and resells them, or third-party websites that may resell offerings without taking possession of inventory, like Expedia.

One relatively new variation of reseller is the store-within-a-store concept. In this channel relationship, a manufacturer provides products, personnel, and sales and marketing support in a section of a store dedicated to selling the manufacturer's products. In fact, Best Buy currently has sections of its stores dedicated to the offerings of a single manufacturer, including one each for Dell, Samsung, and Apple.

Using a reseller or distributor model may get your offering into the market faster and gain broader market reach by leveraging the marketing and sales efforts, as well as providing access to the customer base, of an established channel partner. This model may also lower your start-up and transaction costs because the reseller has responsibility for the process and paperwork in closing an end-user sale.

The marketer must consider the disadvantages of this sales channel. You may lose complete control over the customer experience during the sales process. However, you still retain responsibility for training the sales force, and you must build marketing and support programs for this channel. This support may take several forms, including product training, tools/collateral needed to sell your product, technical support, and order placement/management support.

Simply stated, much of what you need to support your own sales operation also may be needed for this channel. The difference is that you need to provide modular materials that can be incorporated into a reseller's own materials—for example, providing PDF-formatted product diagrams that the channel can incorporate into its own product catalog. Likewise, you might want to have a special section of your website where information, collateral, self-directed training modules, and so on can be easily accessible for resellers/distributors to reduce your cost of supporting this channel. A FAQ (Frequently Asked Question) section with appropriate answers can be very helpful for your channel.

The same support discussed here is required for value-added resellers/distributors as well, which are discussed next.

Value-Added Resellers

Value-added resellers (VARs) provide a form of selective distribution in which they bundle your offering with additional products and services, enhancing the overall perceived value to the customer of the offering. An example is MetricStream, a Governance, Risk, and Compliance (GRC) software company. MetricStream resells the Oracle database product as part of its solution. Customers buy MetricStream's Sarbanes-Oxley Compliance solution to ensure that they comply with the SEC regulation. The MetricStream software solution requires the Oracle database. Therefore, the end customer buys the Oracle product, but in a way that allows him to solve compliance problems. The advantages and disadvantages of this channel are the same as reseller/distributors.

Agents, Brokers, and Representatives

Agents, brokers, and representatives (all often referred to as *reps*) are independent companies or individuals who sell your product offering on your company's behalf, usually do so on a commission basis, and bear all of their own sales expenses. They are generally local or regional with a defined territory they cover. They generally do not carry competing lines, and their contracts are not usually guaranteed for a long term. The rep's role is to either replace, or in some cases, supplement, the direct sales force. However, they are not a substitute for a distributor because they do not hold inventory or take title, invoice or ship, or take credit.

These reps provide several advantages. The assets these reps have are their relationships with their customers. In many cases, they have been providing their customers a number of products for many years. The good reps have achieved positions of perceived trust and reliability with their customers and understand their customers' needs very well. The rep may be able to achieve synergy by bundling your product with other products they are already selling. Also because of the economies of combining products, it is typically more economical for reps to call on smaller buyers or call more often on a single buyer than it is for the typical direct salesperson. Because the reps' asset is their customer relationships, reps typically are more permanent and have less turnover than direct sales forces. Companies of reps also pay more than you may pay direct salespeople and may retain their sales forces longer. Reps are also likely to be nimble, sales focused, and very conscious of their sales costs. Reps also add a lot of flexibility—their low overhead (almost all variable costs) makes it easy to forecast sales costs and provide downside cost protection if revenue is lower than anticipated. It is also much easier to terminate reps than an internal sales force.

However, reps also have disadvantages. Because they have many masters ("principals") whose products they must juggle, getting focus on your product may be difficult. This is especially true if you have one or a small number of products and other client companies of the reps have many complementary products. Reps may give greater focus to companies with many products versus one or a few. The reps may also be too diversified to devote appropriate attention to the subset of their accounts that find value in your products. Some products may not have existing rep networks that are appropriate for your product. In other cases, a competitor may already have secured contracts with the really good reps. The biggest trade-off that needs to be evaluated, however, is the loss of control that is part of being with a rep. The control issue applies to all the indirect channels. This is why it is so important for marketing to understand the needs of your indirect channels and establish a specific value proposition for them.

The Control Issue: Choosing Your Sales Force

When your firm directly employs the salesperson, theoretically you can direct the salesperson to do whatever you want. However, in actuality, there's a continuum of realized control that depends on the kind of compensation and supervision system the entrepreneur chooses. Figure 8-2 shows this continuum.

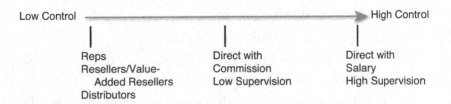

Figure 8-2 Control continuum

The figure underscores the relation between the compensation method and the ability to control the salesperson. If your salespeople are on a straight commission with a low or non-existent base salary, they will also not be easy to control. If you tell a salesperson compensated by commission to do something he does not feel will add to his commissions, he will not want to do it. The rep is even harder to control because she has many masters and possibly conflicting activities she can do for each principal. On the other hand, if you pay the salesperson some kind of base salary, you can expect him to do some noncommission activities in return for his salary.

Control is important depending on the product positioning and the appropriate role of the sales force. If your sales force plan requires activities that have unspecified payoff, then rep organizations (or straight commission) are probably not appropriate. If you have a product that requires single-minded dedication, then a rep might not be appropriate, but straight commission might be a viable option.

What Situations Favor Direct Versus Rep?

A very interesting study by Erin Anderson[1] analyzed how 13 firms in the electronic components industry decided on the rep versus direct decision in 159 different sales district/product combinations. These companies had a broad range of products from commodities to new, innovative, "glamour" products. The companies used reps when in doubt between reps and direct, and they used reps for the "normal," nondescript sales situations. However, there were lots of situations in which companies went direct, including the following:

1. Situations where it's difficult to evaluate the salesperson's results "by the numbers," for example:

   a Measure of sales results are inaccurate.

   b It's difficult to assign credit for the sale because of multiple influences on the customer.

   c Performance means much more than current sales—for example, there are long-term implications to short-term sales.

2. Situations where product and applications knowledge are difficult to learn, important, and/or complex. These include:

   a Highly complex, unusual, or difficult to understand or explain products.

   b Highly complex, unusual, or difficult to understand or explain applications.

3. Situations with highly confidential information in which salespeople come to learn sensitive information about their company and customers.

4. Situations where support activities are critical—for example, marketing research, trade show participation, after-sales service, and engineering support before the sale.

A situation that favors reps over direct salespeople is global expansion. When an entrepreneur is planning to expand into different countries, there are many risks that can be mitigated by leveraging local, in-country reps to start. One of the biggest risks is hiring. Hiring an employee in a foreign company exposes you to foreign labor laws, taxation rules, and the legal and consulting expense to deal with these issues—not to mention the cost and legal risk of firing an employee in many countries if you made a mistake in the hiring process.

An in-country rep is a proven sales professional, with a Rolodex of prospects and an understanding of how local business gets done. They represent a low-cost, low-risk approach to opening sales in a foreign country. However, the challenges associated with getting the rep's right focus and attention on your product and its positioning when she is balancing other companies' products still remain.

Choosing Reps

If you decide to choose reps, the decision on which reps to choose is very important and should not be taken lightly. What you are buying with the rep is market reputation, relationships, and positions with complementary products. There are two criteria to trade off when choosing a rep. The first criterion is the rep's market position. Is she selling top brands in the market, or does she represent the less-attractive products? The second criterion is whether the rep will have enough resources and use them to push your product or service versus the other products she sells. The best reps might not make enough time to push your new product, especially if the new product is small compared with the rep's current line. On the other hand, if your new product is really innovative and valuable, reps may use it to gain more access to their target accounts by introducing them to a new, valuable product.

How can you efficiently get the information to make these trade-offs? The way is similar to other recommendations in this book. *Talk to market participants.* Specifically, as part of the concept testing for a new product or service, ask also about which reps the target market prefers to buy from. Most market participants are quite willing to recommend people they prefer to buy from. Finding out how well the rep will push your product, if you choose her, is not so easy. Finding out how excited a rep firm will be with your product is comparable to finding out if the end customer will buy your product. Concept testing can be helpful. You should interview rep principals from alternative rep firms and show them your product, tentative sales aids, and any possible advertisements for the product. You want to present your product to the rep in its most positive light. Then monitor the rep's reaction and compare across all the reps you interview. Your ideal rep is one who is excited about how your product will help the rep's business and a rep who is highly valued as a resource by the market-place for your product. Your judgment, after having talked both with alternative reps and with a sample of market participants, should provide a productive rep choice.

An important caveat—the rep choice is crucial to the financial viability of many businesses and should not be taken lightly. Above all, choosing a rep should *not* be done opportunistically. *Do not choose the first rep who approaches you.* It is almost always productive to invest some time and money to find the best rep. Even when time and money are scarce, it makes sense to get information *from market participants* before making a decision like choosing a rep that has a very long-term and pronounced effect on your venture.

Effective Rep Management

If you have decided to use reps, they will not be successful without you managing and motivating them very carefully. Reps are another group that needs marketing attention. Just like the end customer, you need to understand what makes the rep tick—what her objectives and goals are and how your product offering can add perceived value for the rep. Anderson, Lodish, and Weitz studied how 71 independent reps actually allocated their time to their principals' products.[2] They found that, in general (and no surprise), reps allocated time to maximize their commission income from their principals. However, reps also deviated from solely resource allocations that maximized their commission income in order to favor principals who they perceived had similar *goals, good communication,* and *mutual trust.* Reps also favored principals who had *active involvement* in the reps' activities. The authors' findings imply some specific tactics that help obtain more of a rep's attention, as follows:

1. Make your products easier for the rep to sell. Make its price/perceived value better for the end user. Provide sales training for reps. Develop and implement promotions toward the end user that the rep can use to make her job more efficient. In short, provide effective marketing!

2. Increasing commission rates will increase the sales effort toward your product. However, keep in mind that it will have diminishing returns.

3. Reps favor products that are synergistic with other products in their portfolio.

4. Principals should develop trusting relationships with their reps.

5. Principals should improve communication through recognition programs, product training, and consultation with the reps, as well as by informing reps of plans, explicitly detailing objectives, and providing positive feedback.

6. Principals who have a hands-off approach to reps lose time for their products.

7. Even providing critical or negative feedback to reps is better than not providing feedback at all, as it will cause reps to spend more time on your product.[3]

Rep Management and the Perceived Value Proposition

Many of the preceding tactics cost either money (for example, end-user promotions, sales training) or margin points (for example, improving the price/value relationship, increasing commission rates). If you have an excellent business plan that has a positioning strategy that succeeds in creating incremental perceived value to the end user compared with competition, then you should have "room" to share some of that value with your outsourced intermediaries in the channel.

Franklin Electronic Publications, Inc., is a manufacturer of electronic, handheld reference tools—spelling correctors, dictionaries, and so on. For the past 18 years, they have successfully used reps to sell their products in the consumer electronics channel. Especially when they began as an entrepreneurial company with few resources, but with a new unique product (the Spelling Ace spelling corrector), reps were a crucial part of the marketing plan. Because the Spelling Ace could be sold to the consumer at prices that gave very good manufacturing margins, Franklin was able to "share" some of those high margins with their reps and retailers. The reps got excellent commissions for selling the products, and the retailers got better margins than from comparable products that competed for scarce shelf and display space.

This Franklin example underscores the importance of including all elements of the marketing mix as part of the initial business plan. The positioning decisions have a big impact on the viability of the venture partly because they have an impact on what is possible for other elements of the marketing mix. The management of reps is only one element in which the positioning decisions have a crucial impact.

Direct Sales: Personal Versus Telephone Versus the Web and Other Nonpersonal Sales

A direct personal sales force may be effective for navigating the sales process. However, the telephone, the Internet, and other media may be more efficient, cost effective, and allow greater scale for accomplishing needed tasks in the direct marketing and sales process. You should first determine the tasks and activities that are required for each step in the sales process. Understand a buyer's process for acquiring your type of product offering. Then you should evaluate the costs and the benefit of alternative ways to accomplish those sales tasks. Tables 8-1 and 8-2 show the evaluation of two alternative sales processes for a venture. Table 8-1 evaluates a personal sales process, and Table 8-2 evaluates how the same process might be accomplished by telemarketing instead of personal sales. These are disguised real examples.

Table 8-1 Field Sales-Oriented Sales Process

Sales Activity	Prospects Remaining	Delivery Vehicle	Elapsed Time (wks)	Activity Cost	Total Cost
1. New lead	100	Mail/Telephone	0	$25	$2,500
2. Literature fulfillment	100	Mail	1	$10	$3,500
3. Quality prospect	100	Telephone	2	$15	$5,000
4. Initial meeting	30	Field visit	4	$200	$11,000
5. Follow-up call	20	Telephone	5	$15	$11,200
6. Demonstration	10	Field visit	7	$250	$13,700
7. Proposal	5	Overnight service	8	$100	$14,200

Sales Activity	Prospects Remaining	Delivery Vehicle	Elapsed Time (wks)	Activity Cost	Total Cost
8. Additional follow-up	3	Telephone	12	$50	$14,350
9. Approval/ Purchase	3	Telephone	16	$10	$14,380
10. Post-sale follow-up	3	Telephone	20	$30	$14,470

Table 8-2 Telemarketing-Oriented Sales Process

Sales Activity	Prospects Remaining	Delivery Vehicle	Elapsed Time (wks)	Activity Cost	Total Cost
1. New lead	100	Mail/Telephone	0	$25	$2,500
2. Initial literature	100	Mail	1	$10	$3,500
3. Quality call	100	Telephone	2	$15	$5,000
4. Second literature	30	Mail	3	$10	$5,300
5. Consult/Sales call	30	Telephone	4	$25	$5,800
6. Payback worksheet	20	Telephone	6	$5	$5,850
7. Configuration call	10	Telephone	6	$10	$5,950
8. Proposal	5	Overnight service	8	$100	$6,450
9.–12. Additional follow-up	3	Telephone	12	$100	$6,750
13. Approval/ Purchase	3	Telephone	16	$10	$6,780
14. Post-sale follow-up	3	Telephone	20	$30	$6,870

In Table 8-1, the entrepreneur, who we can think of as Sarah in this example, has estimated the "sales funnel" for her typical personal sales process. Starting with 100 prospects, she estimates how many will remain after each stage in the process. For example, of each 100 prospects who have been qualified, 30 will remain as prospects after the telephone qualification call. She also estimates the elapsed time for each activity and the costs of each activity. It is usually pretty easy to get good estimates for the timing and costs of the various activities and sales calls. The most difficult estimate is the success rate for each activity—that is, what fraction of the people in the funnel will proceed to the next stage. For example, there is an assumption that five out of ten, or 50% of prospects, will ask for a proposal after a demonstration. Before one begins business, it is pretty difficult to get good estimates for that kind of response percentage. However, once the business is going, it is conceptually easy to measure these percentages by keeping track of the number of people in the funnel at different stages, their treatment by the sales process, and the fraction who go on to the next stage after each task is performed. The challenge is to keep track of the data in the middle of launching a new product or service.

Notice that in Table 8-2, there are different activities in the tele-marketing-oriented sales process. The funnel also has different costs and different fractions progressing from stage to stage. However, if the assumptions are reasonably correct, in this case, the telemarketing-oriented sales process will be much more efficient for accomplishing the sales process. The personal sales approach may convert more prospects per 100, but it costs over 50% more to get each completed sale. Only if the number of prospects is very limited does it make sense to use a personal sales approach for this example.

What these examples should illustrate is how important it is to determine all the stages of the sales process and then to estimate the costs and benefits of performing them by different vehicles. In many cases, it will be difficult to construct funnels like Tables 8-1 and 8-2 with no sales experience. What then makes sense is, as you begin your operations, to *experiment* with the sales process alternatives that make à priori sense. As the sales process is performed, keep track of the number of prospects in the funnel for each stage along with elapsed costs and timing. After a suitable length of time, you should be able to infer which approaches to the sales process are most efficient and use those on an ongoing basis.

It is important to evaluate many options for accomplishing the sales process. Not every prospect should necessarily be put through the same sales process. Some market segments may respond differently to different sales processes. Depending on the costs and potential value, in many cases, it makes sense to experiment with different sales processes for different market segments. Again, depending on the circumstances, some potential prospects might want to choose the sales process that they prefer.

IndyMac: Using Both Direct and Indirect Sales Channels

The IndyMac Bank developed technology to automate the underwriting and risk-based pricing process for home mortgages. The technology was distributed and sold in two ways to capitalize on two types of consumers that the IndyMac management had defined: "low tech + hi touch" and "hi tech + low touch." The first segment was much more comfortable with a personal intermediary to help them apply for and go through the home mortgage purchase process. So a mortgage broker (personal salesperson) sat with the client and typed information about the proposed loan and the loan applicant. Within five minutes, the IndyMac e-MITS system came back with an underwriting decision and a price for the mortgage that had been uniquely determined for the potential purchaser based on his credit history, and so on. The system also printed out, right at the computer, all of the closing documents that would be needed for the loan to be closed.

The same e-MITS technology was used in indymac.com, the direct-to-consumer website that IndyMac introduced for the other "high tech + low touch" segment. The website performed almost the exact same functions as the technology available on the Internet for mortgage brokers, but it is presented directly to consumers who felt confident enough to apply for and close on a mortgage without relying on a mortgage broker intermediary. These customers got to pay less for their mortgages because they were not paying the sales commissions for the mortgage brokers.

Many other creative entrepreneurial marketers have also realized that one sales/distribution system might not fit all of their customers. Just as product and service offerings should be tailored to the needs of market segments, so should the sales and distribution process that is a part of what the end consumer finally perceives. Barnes and Noble does the same thing as IndyMac. They sell the same books at stores with personal assistance and over the Internet at Barnes and Noble. com. Their competitor, Borders, did not take advantage of this segmentation opportunity and lost much potential business to Amazon. com and BarnesandNoble.com.

Sales Force Size, Deployment, and Organization

Once you have decided to use a personal sales force, your decision making is just beginning.

Sales Force Size and Deployment

When you decide to use a personal sales force, a number of questions quickly surface. How big should the force be, and how should it be organized and deployed? The conceptual answer to these questions is easy. A sales force is like any other investment the entrepreneur makes. If adding resources to the sales force is the most profitable place to use the scarce capital, and if the use is more profitable than putting the money in the bank, then the funds should be added to the sales force. Funds should be added until they are no longer the most profitable place to put capital. The sales force is the right size when the "last person added" brought in more of a return on their investment than any other investment opportunity.

In many cases, the appropriate sales force size can be dictated by the market segment(s) that are being targeted and the costs and incremental benefits associated with the role of the sales force. In many cases, a salesperson is a necessary part of what the channel expects from the entrepreneur. For example, if you expect to sell through retailers such as department stores or mass merchandisers, these firms have expectations about terms of sales and service from their suppliers. It is typically not possible to change the customary way in which other suppliers have set the retailer's expectations. Interviewing buyers from the retailers as well as salespeople (or reps) who service the retailers can get you enough information to roughly estimate the sales time associated with the various activities that are required by the potential customers. You can then also estimate the incremental revenue associated with those activities. It is then straightforward to calculate the marginal revenue and marginal costs of this sales force activity.

For other sales situations, it makes more sense to evaluate the activities by estimating directly the impact of sales calls on the revenue of clients and/or prospects. For example, "What would happen to the revenue of a typical customer of type 'A' if we called four times per quarter instead of twice?" This kind of question should be asked for alternative levels of sales force size and deployment levels that you are evaluating. Once the revenue associated with the alternative levels of sales efforts has been estimated, then the incremental revenues and incremental costs can be applied to roughly determine the appropriate sales force effort to use toward each type of client and prospect.

There are three ways to estimate the sales response to alternative call frequencies. Judgment of the salesperson along with her manager (who may be the entrepreneur) has been shown to be better than deploying salespeople without considering sales response to different levels of call effort. By evaluating judgments of the sales impact of different call effort levels to different segments of accounts, it is straightforward to allocate time to those segments where it adds the most incremental profit contribution and then continue to add time to that segment and/or other segments until the incremental return does not justify the sales force costs. Before the business begins operations, experience is probably the only way to determine the best sales force size along with some guidelines on deployment over account segments. Without experience, competitor activity can provide a reasonable starting point.

Once the venture has begun and the sales process has begun, the entrepreneur can evaluate any naturally occurring experiments that may have happened. These naturally occurring experiments happen when different accounts in the same segment get different amounts of sales effort. If you have planned your information system to keep sales as well as salespeople call reports, you can evaluate to what extent different levels of sales force effort have seemed to cause sales changes. The problem with this procedure is that the sales force may be choosing who to spend more or less effort on within a segment based on other factors such as prior relationships or specific knowledge about that account's situation. The analysis may attribute sales changes to the wrong causes. The most accurate, unbiased estimates come from the third way of getting sales response to alternative levels of sales effort—structured experiments.

Instead of letting naturally occurring changes happen to sales force effort levels on accounts, it can be valuable to *randomly assign* different levels of effort to different accounts within a segment. If there really is a random assignment of different levels of sales effort to accounts, then other possible causes are mitigated by the randomization. The same concerns and issues for designing experiments that we describe for advertising decisions are also appropriate for sales force experiments. See Chapter 5, "Promotion and Viral Marketing to Maximize Sustainable Profitability," for additional information.

Deployment with Limited Sales Force Size

Many entrepreneurs do not have the luxury of evaluating many different levels of sales force sizes and appropriate deployment levels as described previously. They are limited in resources and cannot afford to have many salespeople. In these cases, it is crucial to "skim the cream." Using the judgmental method described earlier, you must only spend your sales force effort where it contributes the highest amount of incremental revenue and profit. However, keeping track of the sales effort, and associated incremental sales generated from it, can be an excellent way to show a source of financing what to expect if more resources were made available for increasing sales force effort.

Travel costs and entertainment expenses also need to be considered when the size and sales force resource decisions are made. If the location of some accounts will necessitate extra trips, then these costs should be prorated over the accounts to be called on during the trips. The sales force organization decision will also impact travel costs if it means that different people will be calling on different accounts in the same geographical area.

Sales Force Organization and Travel Costs

Sales force organization typically encompasses how the force is structured vis-à-vis markets and geography. The trade-off of most alternative organizations is conceptually simple. Is the specialization of sales efforts more beneficial to the firm than the increased costs associated with the specialization? The increased costs of segment specialization are typically travel costs and the opportunity costs of time spent traveling. For small entrepreneurial companies with their own sales forces, the organization that is appropriate is usually obvious. If there is only one target market, then a geographical sales organization is the only reasonable option. A geographical sales organization has territories that are geographically determined, with each salesperson covering accounts in one territory. If there is more than one target segment, another possible organization is to have a sales force for each segment. Each segment sales force would have its own geographical organization. It would then be possible to have more than one salesperson covering the same geographical area, with each salesperson calling on accounts in different segments. The more specialized the sales force, the larger geographical area each salesperson's territory will cover.

Compensation

Compensation is one of the topics most senior sales managers are always fretting over.

Matching Incentives

If you remember one idea from this sales force chapter, it should be this one: People (and especially salespeople) do what they think will make them *the most money* for the time they spend at their jobs. Your compensation system should make sure that you and your salespeople have *matching incentives.* If you both are trying to do the same thing, then it's difficult to get into situations in which your salespeople do the wrong thing. The appropriate compensation also depends on the role of the salesperson. For example, if the salesperson has some control over the price she charges, then the compensation should have the salespeople negotiate as good a price as you, the entrepreneur or business manager, would negotiate. Auto dealers are classic examples of this type of compensation. The salespeople at most car dealerships who negotiate a price with each consumer have a commission that is based not on the sold car's sales price, but on the gross margin (sales price-variable costs) for the car. If the commission were on just the sales price, the salesperson would likely be selling cars to maximize revenue by selling more cars at the lowest price she could quote.

This same argument is pertinent to situations in which your sales force is selling more than one product. If each product has quite different contribution margins, you want the salesperson to be incented, not on revenue, but on contribution margin (revenue-variable costs). In these multiproduct situations, you do not have to actually share your gross margins with the sales force. All the sales force needs to know (and have incentives based on) is the relative profitability of one product versus another. You can have sales compensation based on "points" for each product. The points just need to be proportionally correct; that is, if product A has four points per sales dollar, and product B has two points, then product A should have twice as much gross margin per sales dollar as product B. The salespeople don't have to know the exact margin figures in order to allocate their effort to where they will get the most margin per hour of their time. Many firms have not compensated their salespeople in this way and have foregone some profit by not treating revenue differently from different products. In extreme cases, one author has seen firms give sales awards to the top revenue-producing salesperson. After some analysis, it was determined that that person was actually *losing money* for his company. He was selling products that were not profitable after his sales costs were considered.

The salespeople will visit customers who are perceived to be most likely to value the products they can sell. If the salespeople are trying to find accounts that will most likely buy the products with high contribution margin, then the salesperson and the firm both have matching incentives, and the salespeople will naturally gravitate to the accounts that will be most profitable for the firm.

Outback Steakhouse—Perfectly Matched Incentives

Outback Steakhouse has been very successful in an extremely competitive restaurant industry. One reason for their success is how they compensate their store managers. Each store manager invests $25,000 in "his or her store." For that investment, they get 10% of the profits that store generates. These store managers report to regional managers who have made similar investments in return for a piece of their region's profits. The incentives here are matched perfectly. These managers will try to use the resources in their control to maximize their income—that is exactly proportional to the income of the Outback Steakhouse Corporation. By maximizing their income, the managers are simultaneously maximizing the income of their "parent" corporation. This compensation scheme is a creative blend of some aspects of franchising with corporate control. If the managers leave, there are prearranged values for buying back the managers' equity interest in the restaurant.

Incentives Versus Control Versus Time Horizons

The preceding Outback example points out one concern about matching incentives. Profit can be short term or longer term. You may have different time horizons in mind than members of your sales force. Even if you both are trying to maximize profits, a salesperson may want to maximize short-term profits, whereas you, the entrepreneurial marketer, may be more concerned with longer-term profits and building the value of the company. Some sales force activities may be helpful to long-term profits but take away from short-term profits. These include market research and call reporting. Our experience is that it is easier to have some portion of the fixed component of the salesperson's compensation specified as payment for these kinds of activities. You thus *tell* the sales force that they are being *paid to do market research* and/or *fill out call reports.* Most salespeople will not see the value to their future income of these kinds of activities and need to perceive that they are being directly paid to perform them.

It is important to set these expectations at the beginning of the relationship. If the salesperson is told when he is hired that part of his base salary is for call reports and other "paper work," he will feel that this becomes part of his job for which he is being adequately compensated. The base salary can also be used as a way to control the salesperson to do activities that may not be maximizing his short-term income. You may want the salesperson to call on some accounts that will not be ready to buy, but you need their feedback now on the next-generation product or service design.

Just as the discussion of reps had control as an issue, the same issues occur in compensation. The more straight commission you have, the lower your control. Our experience has shown that for many businesses, it makes sense to have some element of base salary as a justification for requesting the salespeople to do activities that may not be maximizing their short-term commission income. Many of the suggestions throughout this book for continually experimenting with different elements of the marketing mix will be thwarted if the sales force will not cooperate. By its nature, experimentation will show that some activities are more productive than others. You don't want your sales force to feel that they are being penalized if they happen to be in one experimental treatment that doesn't perform as well as another treatment. You need to set these expectations at the outset of the relationship. You should tell new salespeople that they are joining an entrepreneurial, adapting, learning, and continually experimenting organization. By their nature, some experiments will work better than others, and the salespeople should expect that. If you couch their base salary as compensation for these learning and experimental activities, you will avoid possible problems later on.

Compensation for New Versus Existing Customers, a Possible Festering Problem

Many entrepreneurs will start their businesses with a straight commission sales force. This option has the lowest variable costs. If more than one product is involved, the commission rate should be proportional to the gross profit margin of each product. However, another phenomenon is happening with straight commission sales forces that most entrepreneurs don't realize until it has begun to affect their growth and profitability. By then, it is typically too late to solve easily.

If the commission is high enough, and the product potential large enough, a straight commission sales incentive plan can result in amazing sales force effort and motivation—up to a point. The first salesperson to sell your product (let's use Sarah again as our example) will typically "bust her butt" to open up many accounts in her territory. She will view this as an opportunity to be entrepreneurial and develop these accounts as her "own little business." However, in her mind, she has an idea of what she needs to make in order to "make a good living." Once the salesperson has gotten the territory to the point where her commissions generate this "good living," the salesperson will then tend to *coast* with her established accounts and protect them from any management gerrymandering.

It is usually much easier to maintain accounts than to get new ones. The straight commission salesperson will get to a point where she will be content to just maintain her current accounts and not spend much effort generating new accounts. The previous scenario has been validated as typical by over 3,000 sales managers who have attended the Wharton School's executive program in sales force management.

One solution to the problem is to have *different rates* of commission for generating *new accounts* than for maintaining the business. The commission rate would thus be higher for the first year's business with an account and lower on succeeding years. Alternatively, some firms will have a different commission rate on sales until last year's level is reached and a different level on sales higher than last year's.

The Shadow Broadcast Services Example

The Shadow Broadcast Services (Shadow) story, in which one coauthor (Lodish) was a minority investor and advisor, provides examples of the sales force compensation issues faced by the company and are illustrative of the preceding concepts. Shadow gathered traffic information using planes, helicopters, police scanners, part-time drivers, and cell phone messages from citizen volunteers. The company then would create, broadcast, and barter the traffic reports (and eventually, local news, sports, and weather) for advertising time. Shadow then would sell the advertising time to advertisers. Shadow advertising was typically a 10-second spot read at the end of the traffic report along with a lead-in, when all of the other advertising time on the radio stations was sold to advertisers in units of 30 and 60 seconds. Shadow had research that showed that listeners paid more attention to traffic broadcasts than to any other element of a radio show, making the 10-second spots more valuable.

Given this model, Shadow and their customer stations both were selling advertising. Shadow focused on selling 10-second spots and the radio stations focused on 30- and 60-second spots. The radio stations did not want to add another competitor when they took on a traffic service. Almost all stations stipulated that the advertisers the traffic service obtained for their network should not overlap with either the radio station's current advertisers or any advertisers to whom the radio station had made a recent pitch. The stations were told that the money for traffic ads would come from different budgets than for traditional spot radio advertising—things like promotion funds or co-op vendor funds.

The Shadow sales force's role was pretty difficult. They were charged with convincing nontraditional radio advertisers to use a new kind of ad (10-second) in a new submedium (within live traffic reports) in a new network. This role is quintessential missionary selling—taking the gospel out to convince new people to convert. To attract and motivate the best people for this role, Shadow paid pretty big draws against commission and pretty high commissions (around 10%) on revenue. The really effective salespeople were making several hundred thousand dollars per year. However, many salespeople could not accomplish the job adequately and were asked to leave.

After a few years in the first two cities, New York and Chicago, Shadow managers began to see the "coasting" phenomena set in on some of the best, most experienced salespeople. Once these salespeople had gotten enough accounts so that the commission on those accounts gave them the standard of living to which they aspired, they cut down severely on their new account prospecting and spent whatever time was necessary to maintain the revenue (and commission) from their current accounts. They also spent less time selling but maintained their income and even improved their standard of living because they had more leisure time. Maintaining revenue from current accounts typically requires less sales effort than getting an equivalent amount of new business. This was definitely true for Shadow.

To improve the situation, Shadow changed its compensation to a higher commission rate for the revenues from an account for its first year (over 12%), but a lower commission rate on succeeding years' revenue (less than 8%). Theoretically, the commission rates for new versus existing business should be roughly proportional to the effort required for each task. In this way, the salesperson should be indifferent to spending time with current accounts or trying to penetrate new accounts. A compensation system like Shadow's new one helps to control the "coasting" problem. If the salesperson coasts and just services existing accounts, she will get a lower income level. As you might have forecast, convincing the experienced salespeople to adopt the changed commission plan was difficult. The salespeople rightly were concerned that their initial expectations to which they had agreed had been changed. A number of the experienced, best salespeople had performance problems adjusting to the new arrangement. They had to work hard again!

When Shadow expanded to other cities, management initiated the tiered commission plan from the beginning—paying a higher commission for the first year of revenue and lower on succeeding years. It was no problem to get salespeople to buy in to the scheme when it was introduced *at the beginning* of their relationship with Shadow. In fact, the better salespeople were able to accelerate their compensation growth. If they ended up "coasting," they at least did it at a much higher revenue level and had to work harder to keep a compensation level. Hindsight and experience in the newer markets convinced Shadow management that it was much more productive to *introduce the differential commissions at the beginning.*

Salespeople are human beings just like any other person (or buyer of something). They are much more satisfied if their experience matches or exceeds their prior expectations than if they are told to change their expectations in the middle of an experience. This is one example of using marketing thinking to manage more than your relationships with customers. Your sales force also needs to be approached with careful marketing thinking. Just as it is crucial to manage the buyer's expectations when you or your sales force sell your product or service, it is also just as important to manage your employee's expectations when you "sell" them on working for your company.

Recruiting, Training, and Retention Strategies

Once you have made all of the preceding decisions about your sales force, recruiting the right people is a difficult job. Chapter 11, "Entrepreneurial Marketing for Building Teams," looks at this process as another marketing problem to solve. For most entrepreneurial ventures, you will not be able to have the luxury of training raw recruits from scratch. You just won't have the time or available resources to train them. Raw recruits won't have the market contacts to "hit the ground running." Thus, most initial sales force hires will come from other companies that have operations in markets related to yours. Remember, the salespeople you hire will be the representatives of the company to the marketplace. The entrepreneur needs to be diligent and thoughtful in the hiring process.

B.J. Bushur, owner and president of Unlimited Results who has hired hundreds of sales reps throughout her career, has found several key factors (in addition to experience) to look for in successful sales reps:

- **Drive**—Highly motivated to excel.
- **Love of learning**—Self-improvement focused. Continually add value to their clients by sharing their knowledge and keeping up to date with market trends.
- **Solution-oriented**—Problem solvers who can link their customers' problems to their solutions (for example, products and services).
- **Positive people that others like to be around**—People buy from people they like, and they buy more from people they like to be around and who add value in some way to their lives: by giving them more knowledge to do their job more effectively, by helping them enjoy life more, or by making them "look good" (in many different ways).

One of the toughest trade-offs in hiring salespeople is sales experience versus drive. If given the choice, hiring the person who may be a bit lighter or equal on experience but has the higher drive is better over the long term. In every interview, ask: "What drives you?" And, of course, money drives all salespeople. But you also want to hear about motivation besides money. Chapter 11 discusses more entre-preneurial approaches to this hiring/marketing challenge.

Another important consideration in the hiring of sales reps relates to the newness of the products being sold (or of the company sell-ing them). According to Leslie and Holloway, a company must learn how customers will acquire and use a product—they call this the sales learning curve. When the product is ready to launch, sales reps' focus must be on learning as much as possible from customers on how they will use the product. This informs product development and may help to refine the offering and how it is brought to market. Once the prod-uct breaks even and/or reaches a critical mass of customers, the sales reps' focus changes to developing repeatable sales models. Finally, when the company is ready to scale sales rapidly, it must use "coin-operated reps," who can execute a process and simply need a terri-tory, sales plan, and marketing materials. Each of these phases has different objectives and therefore requires different sales rep skills to successfully achieve its goals. Hiring a sales rep skilled at executing a sales process when the company needs to learn how customers use and buy a product will result in failure.[4] Thus, you must not only hire the right sales reps, but also the right sales reps for the right stage of the sales learning curve.

Training the sales force will be idiosyncratic to the role of the salesperson in your marketing mix and the role of the salesperson in the product-offering bundle that you offer. As a small, entrepreneur-ial company, you will typically do better with someone who already knows how to sell. Your job is to make sure that this person knows your product inside and out as well as how the market will benefit from the product. It will usually be beneficial for you to do anything you can to help the new salesperson learn about the buying process at her customers and prospects, the competition, and any other mean-ingful parts of the positioning of your offering bundle.

When *not* to retain salespeople is a decision that is not made nearly as well as it should be by entrepreneurs (and other managers as well). There is a trade-off to be made that most managers and entre-preneurs rarely consider. If you have a limited sales budget and/or limited prospects on which to call, then you have a limited size of sales force to deal with. One way to possibly improve sales productivity is to fire lower-performing salespeople and replace them with new recruits who might prove to be higher performing. The trade-offs are costs of hiring and training, the "burn-in" time of the new recruit, plus the chance that the new recruit may not be very good. In the only analysis we've seen of this phenomenon (on U.S. Navy recruiting salespeople), the answer was clear. The venture was keeping mediocre people when they would have been much better off "raising the bar."

Summary

Sales management is a marketing issue. Determining the right mix of sales channels is based on buyer behavior and the product economics.

Determining the type of salesperson needed and the role and size of the sales force are decisions derived from your work on segmentation and differentiation. The sales force concepts and paradigms shared are useful for entrepreneurial marketers to understand and embrace so that marketing can work with the management team to ensure good decisions are being made. These include the ways to evaluate different sales approaches, handling the rep versus direct issue, and deciding which functions to do in person versus which sales functions to handle impersonally.

Once the appropriate type of sales force has been deployed, ensuring continuous improvement in productivity is important. Analyzing alternative options for sales force size, deployment, and organization are areas where marketing can assist. Because sales priorities are driven by their compensation structure—that is, sales plans—marketing needs to understand options and approaches to compensation and motivation systems. Shadow Broadcast Services was used as an example of not only a good compensation system, but also entrepreneurial thinking about its product positioning and perceived value to its different market segments. Shadow also exemplifies how much easier it can be for the entrepreneur if she gets her compensation system correct in the beginning and manages employee expectations appropriately.

This was not meant to be a complete summary of management techniques for sales forces, but a compendium focused on key sales management ideas that have been demonstrated to help add lots of value for entrepreneurial marketers.

Endnotes

1. Erin Anderson, "The Salesperson as Outside Agent or Employee: A Transaction Cost Analysis," *Marketing Science* 4 (Summer 1985): 234–254.

2. Erin Anderson, Leonard M. Lodish, Barton A. Weitz, "Resource Allocation Behavior in Conventional Channels," *Journal of Marketing Research* XXIV (February 1987): 85–97.

3. Ibid., 95.

4. Leslie, M., and C.A. Holloway, "The Sales Learning Curve." *Harvard Business Review* (July-August 2006).

9

Marketing-Enabled Sales

MetricStream, Inc., and the Marketing-Enabled Sales Strategy

MetricStream is a market leader in enterprise-wide Governance, Risk, and Compliance (GRC) and Quality Management Solutions. MetricStream solutions are used by leading global corporations in diverse industries such as Financial Services, Healthcare, Life Sciences, Energy and Utilities, Food, Retail, Consumer Packaged Goods (CPG), Government, Hi-tech, and Manufacturing to manage their risk management programs, quality management processes, regulatory and industry-mandated compliance, and other corporate governance initiatives. In early 2013, MetricStream was growing. Their value proposition, target market segments, and positioning were defined. MetricStream's products were being successfully used by hundreds of enterprises all over the world. Now it was time to scale sales even more.

MetricStream's focus was on growing sales but with a limited budget. Therefore, the marketing investments were directed toward making it easier for customers to find MetricStream. Although inorganic or paid lead-generation campaigns were also run, special focus was made on programs that would enable customers looking for GRC solutions to find MetricStream easily, review information to evaluate if the apps met their needs, and then reach out to MetricStream. Organic search traffic, website conversion, social media interaction, customer videos, and so on were optimized to ensure that if someone was looking for information on GRC solutions, they were sure to find MetricStream and could easily contact sales teams. These leads came in the form of direct inquiries on the phone or e-mail for demo requests, requests for proposals (RFPs), and so on. These leads were labeled *hot leads*.

In Q1 2014–15, 20% of the total leads were hot leads. But when the analysis of leads converting into qualified opportunities for sales was done, it turned out that over 70% of the qualified opportunities came from these hot leads. Moreover, sales found these leads to be of much higher quality in terms of their readiness to buy compared with opportunities from other leads. Earlier, the focus had been on increasing the total number of leads. Inorganic or paid lead-generation programs were seen as scalable as more leads could be acquired by spending more at a certain cost per lead. But hot leads, which were smaller in numbers, were contributing disproportionately to the number of qualified opportunities. Moreover, in analyzing lead source of new customer wins, 65% of the wins were from the hot leads in Q1, 2014–15. The company decided to set goals and direct investments in activities that generated such hot leads and lower the goals for total leads. Two quarters later, Q3 2014–15, although the total number of leads reduced by 10%, the number of hot leads increased by 25%. The result was an overwhelming 65% increase in new customer wins of which over 90% came from hot leads.

Clearly, the marketing investments going into placing the right content and marketing assets where prospective customers would find it and making it easy for them to reach out to MetricStream gave a significantly better result from a cost of sales perspective.

Marketing Tools to Support the Sales Process

Once you have made the sales channel mix decisions, marketing needs to focus on how to best enable sales. This is a step that is frequently forgotten. Once you have a sales force and/or sales channels and a presentation, you send the sales reps out to the market to sell and then are disappointed when sales cycles are longer than anticipated, win rates are not as high as expected, and prices are lower than planned for. What went wrong?

Salespeople are not marketing people. Salespeople need marketing tools to support the process of selling (see Table 9-1).

Table 9-1 The Sales Process and Marketing Needs

Sales Process Steps	Marketing Needs
Help prospects find you	Content placement
Gain prospect interest and trust	Customized presentation
	Product demonstrations
	Relevant case studies
	White papers
	ROI tools
Qualify prospects and identify prospective buyers	Lead generation
	Analytics
	Target customer profile
	Product collateral: datasheets, brochures
Drive toward the close	
Submit proposal	RFP checklist
	Proposal template
Check references	Reference customers
	Customer testimonials/quotes
Handle objections	Company viability presentation
	Detailed product spec sheets
	Implementation methodology
	Competitive comparisons
Close the deal	Contract
	Support materials

Every step in the sales process can be much more productive if appropriate marketing tools are used. Buyers of every type have significantly changed their behavior over the past decade due to the abundance of information and choices in our digital, social, mobile world, and, therefore, marketing has to change too. It used to be that marketing focused on finding prospective customers, and so they prioritized outbound lead generation for the sales channel mix. Today, according to Sirius Decisions, 70% of the customer's buying experience is completed before the first contact with a salesperson is made.

Fundamentally, the shift for marketing is from thinking about driving the sales process, to better understanding and supporting the buying process. This will make the sales process more effective and efficient. Marketing has to make it easier for prospective buyers to find their company's offerings. Now it is all about getting found by prospects, versus finding prospects. That changes the focus of marketing in the early stages.

Help Prospects Find You

Relevant, engaging content is king. Today, strong marketers focus on placing content where their prospective customers will find it as the customers move through their self-directed research steps. Blog postings, white papers, contributed articles, social media engagement, and so forth all represent ways to get your content in front of prospects. But it is not just any content. The content needs to enlighten, educate, excite, and engage prospects. It has to tell a story. Facts, functions, features, and the basic commercial pitch are being rejected. Marketers have to make the shift to telling stories or, better yet, getting others to tell the stories on their behalf.

Pathbrite is a Portfolio Platform start-up that allows people to showcase a lifetime of learning and accomplishments, as well as empowers enterprises and universities to assess and institutionalize the achievements of their employees and students. Pathbrite has achieved success by creating situations whereby prospects can find them. They operate in the world of academia and, therefore, have focused on thought leadership-driven white papers and e-books. Their research stems from conference feedback, customers, and LinkedIn. Heather Hiles, the founder and CEO, posts voraciously on LinkedIn. Pathbrite analyzes the feedback on the different posting topics from followers and responders to determine the hot topics. Topics get 25,000 to 50,000 followers, sometimes over 100,000. These hot topics then turn into website content, white papers, and/ or e-books. Heather Hiles has become a top influencer on LinkedIn as a result of this activity, and Pathbrite will get four to five real leads from each hot topic. The team analyzes the LinkedIn metrics to build their marketing content approach. The vast majority of their customers are inbound leads. In fact, a strategic partnership with Cengage, a multibillion-dollar player in this space, was a direct result of this activity. Cengage told Heather Hiles, "Pathbrite is everywhere."

You might not have heard of Pathbrite. You are probably not in their targeted audience. The fact is, they are putting their content where their target buyers can find them. Marketing must do the research to understand where their prospective buyers spend time online as well as offline so they can ensure the right content placement.

Gain Prospect Interest and Trust

One of marketing's key roles is lead generation. Its primary goal is to find customers who have an immediate need that your product can fill or to establish and maintain relationships with qualified prospects so they will consider your products and services first when a need arises in the future. It is crucial that lead generation is based upon your positioning, the targeted segmentation, and differentiation that should have been determined first. Knowing whom you are trying to attract not only allows sales to remain focused on the right prospects, but also enables marketing to focus their activities more precisely. However, the way to do this effectively in this buyer-driven process environment is changing. The tactics used in lead generation are the same, but their content and focus needs to change. The goal is to entice and engage the prospective customer to come to you by gaining their interest and trust.

Marketing needs to maintain an "outside in" mind-set versus an "inside out" mind-set. "Outside in" means to critically evaluate all prospect communications from the prospect's vantage point. It is not important to the prospect that your product is made of high-quality components. However, it is important to them that your reliability is better than the industry norms, which results in less downtime. The latter example is "outside in"—it explains the benefit to the prospect explicitly of having high-quality components.

Marketing tools that support gaining a prospect's interest are those that answer the following questions from the prospect's point of view:

- What is the latest thinking in the area of my problem?
- How will the product offering benefit me and my company?
- Why is it better than other options out there?
- How does it work?
- What is the user experience? How does it look and feel?
- What do other people/companies say about their experiences with the offering?
- Why should I buy now?

Many prospects first look to be educated about the problem area they are trying to solve with a purchase. They will turn to industry resources and credible experts for help. Creating blogs, articles for industry publication, regular social media posts, and niche portals are some examples of tactics to build your company's profile and discover who is researching both. The key is to create this content in an engaging manner without overtly pitching your company or product. Heather Hile's blogs as the CEO of Pathbrite are a great example.

Customized presentations, ROI tools, and company websites are excellent tools for explaining benefits and differentiating your product over others. Nothing beats a demonstration in showing prospects how your product works. There are several ways to handle a product demo. Video demos are a recorded demonstration of your product that can be put on the company's website and viewed by prospective customers on demand, at their convenience. Slideware demos can be created using PowerPoint software and a recorded voice-over. Whether it is video recording or recorded slideware with a voice-over, a story needs to be told. Prospects will only watch content that is engaging, and telling a compelling story that is relevant to your customer engages them more effectively. According to Carmine Gallo, best-selling author and communications coach, effective stories accomplish three things:

- They make an emotional connection with their audience.
- They are novel, providing something unexpected.
- They are memorable.[1]

In addition to posting on your company website, you may broaden the reach of videos and demonstrations by posting on public services like SlideShare and YouTube. These services also provide tools to allow viewers to refer your demos to others via e-mail and social media sharing.

Sharing customer references is another powerful tool to gain prospect interest and trust. Press releases that contain customer quotes, case studies of a customer's experience, and inclusion of quotes in other marketing materials, including the website, are extremely powerful. However, remember you can't control all references. Social media reviews and posting carry tremendous weight especially in the business-to-consumer arena and more and more in the business-to-business space. You need to monitor these sites, encourage happy customers to participate, and respond to negative feedback.

Answering the "Why buy now?" question takes an understanding of the individual prospect's needs, wants, and situation. However, tools that can assist sales include ROI calculators, pricing/service promotions, and special treatment programs. Special treatment programs put customers in a position to get benefits such as access to provide requirements directly to development, participation in an advisory council, joint participation in publicity events, and so on.

Moka5 is a Bring Your Own Device (BYOD) service provider who delivers a secure, device-aware, digital workspace across any network with significantly less overhead. Moka5 faced two key marketing challenges. Their leads contained too few buyers, and the sales cycle was much too long. They were using traditional marketing tactics focusing on finding prospects instead of helping prospects who want to buy find them. Kris Bondi, the new VP of marketing, did some research into the existing marketing approach and found several key opportunities to improve marketing. Although industry events generated a lot of leads, Moka5 wasn't attending the right ones. They shifted from large thought leadership events to small regional events where attendees are gathering information for an upcoming purchase. This alone removed three to four months from the sales cycle.

The second challenge that Moka5 faced was that their target buyers were attracted to educational media formats. So they redesigned the website, shifting it to operate more like a media site with lots of pictures, infographics, and video. Product information is reformatted to read like articles, and content from employee-written blogs is pulled through the site. Marketing can now watch a prospect come into the site through social media to a specific blog post, then go to a related product topic, and then to a related solution and either fill out the form to request a contact or engage inside sales via web chat. These leads are highly engaged and get categorized as likely buyers. These changes to help prospects find Moka5 are working. The average time a person is on the Moka5 website is now 4.5 minutes. A web lead that has registered on their website has a 70%+ likelihood of converting to a likely pipeline candidate. Within a year of creating this new approach, the average length of Moka5's sales cycle has been cut in half.

There are many ways to generate and cultivate leads, as discussed in the following sections.

Company Website

To optimize your company's website for lead generation, it needs to be simple to navigate, enticing, and interesting. They can't read or see information about your wonderful products and services if they don't spend time on the site. You need to convince your visitors that your products/services can deliver value where they need it in an engaging manner. Ensure that your site is "meaty"—that it contains information on the industry segment you operate in as well as focuses on what is truly important to your prospects, such as the problems that you can solve for them, costs that you can reduce, or new revenue opportunities that you can enable. Remember, when prospects are browsing, they glean information that will help them make the best decision. Your website needs to make it easy for them to do that.

Navigation and layout are very important to lead generation as well. If a visitor can't quickly determine what your company knows about the domain and what it can do for her through valuable content, you won't generate a lead. Design the navigation so prospects can easily find the information they are looking for and easily contact the company to ask for additional information.

Tools such as Monetate or Optimize.ly allow you to continually test the small changes to layouts that can dramatically affect conversions or click-throughs. Colors, placement, sizes of type, and so forth can and should be honed through testing in a dynamic manner.

Finally, your website content should be dynamic, changing content frequently and adapting to site visitor preferences. Nothing sends a customer away quicker than a website that appears dated, stale, and static.

Traditional Advertising

Advertising is nothing more than the paid-for, public promotion of your product or service. As discussed in Section Two, "Demand-Generation—Lead Your Customers to Your Offering," successful demand generation activities need a well-defined audience, objective, call-to-action, and measurable outcome. Traditional advertising to prospects occurs across a wide spectrum of media: TV, radio, outdoor, embedded product sponsorship, and more. The key to lead generation when using traditional advertising to drive sales is getting your prospects to act. The call to action is critical and must contain the following:

- The action you want the prospect to take: call the company, sign up, register, or engage in some way
- The reason they should take it: free valuable content, free trial, free gift, discount pricing, exclusive opportunity, and other promotions perceived as valuable by the customer
- A reason why they should do it now: limited time offer, price increase coming, or something else to indicate urgency of action

Pay per Click (PPC) Advertising

Pay per click (PPC) advertising is a fast-growing advertising tool. Whereas most advertising is priced based on the number of impressions/eyeballs/exposure your ad will get, PPC only costs your company money when someone actually clicks your ad. The ad clearly must define the value you can provide your prospects in a creative manner that encourages them to click your ad. Keep the advertisement message clear and concise and specify to the prospects the action you want them to take. For example, "Click here to reduce your cost of Sarbanes-Oxley compliance up to 25%." The example has a clear call to action and a clear message.

When prospects click your ad, you must have a landing page that continues them on the route to becoming a prospect. It is this step that will determine if they become a lead or not. Continue the same value message. Your goal is to get them to give you their contact information if they want to save money on Sarbanes-Oxley compliance. The landing page should focus only on that. It should provide content that gives credibility to the value offered. This can be done with customer quotes or a short ROI example. It should briefly explain how you deliver the value promised—that is, cut costs. Then it should have a place to enter the minimum amount of information from the prospects and give them options for follow-up: Do they want a salesperson to call? Do they want some product collateral? Do they want to attend a seminar?

Regalix Collaborating to Increase Advertising and Selling Effectiveness

Regalix is a digital and online marketing company that helps its clients improve the results of online engagement with customers. Regalix takes advantage of the fact that today's consumer is engaged and proactive in communicating online about the companies and brands with which it interacts. This has led to advertisers needing to be more sophisticated in how they deploy PPC advertising. Rather than advertisers improving by trial and error, they are actively engaging with their online advertising providers to improve results.

Regalix collaborates with online advertising providers and their advertising customers. In one such relationship, the online advertising providers work to drive up advertising efficiency for advertisers, telling them what will work, what keywords are trending, how to reallocate the budget, and which keywords are not performing and should be removed—all of this based on what the customers are doing in real-time online activity. When the advertisers reach out to the provider via phone, chats, social media, and e-mail, Regalix consults with the customers, understanding their needs, and advising them accordingly. All of these conversations and follow-ups are tracked using a social CRM (customer relationship management) platform.

In this manner, there is never sales pressure on advertisers to buy more than they need. Performance metrics are used to measure how well advertisers' needs were captured and the quality of the solution that was offered. The objective is to delight the customer, not to sell more advertising. Regalix has been running this program for one client in more than 14 countries on four continents. This new approach of a bidirectional communication and consultative guidance is resulting in happier customers and a demonstrated 20% to 30% increase in advertising spend each year. Consultative selling, which has traditionally been the province of direct sales, has moved into the online and digital world of PPC advertising.

Social Media

With social media, a company can both participate and advertise. Social media properties, such as Facebook and Instagram, offer targeted advertising. Ads can be displayed based on user profiles. Social media is one of the least expensive costs per impression. But the marketing opportunity is far beyond advertising. Having a company Facebook page, an interest group on LinkedIn, or a following on Twitter gives you a way to engage prospects that is unparalleled. For example, a business Facebook page provides analytical data that helps you understand how users are interacting with the business page. This data can be used to adjust the page content to make it more appealing. Examples of the measurements available are

- **Demographics**—Provides location, language, gender, and so on
- **Likes**—Provides the amount of "likes" and "unlikes" a page has received
- **Page views**—Provides information about the number of Facebook users who actually visited the page directly and where they came from

- **Page posts**—Determine:
  - *Reach*—The number of users who viewed the post
  - *Engaged users*—The number of users who actually clicked the post
  - *Virality*—The percentage of users who commented, liked, or shared the post

The analytics allow for a continual communication and dialogue as well as testing concepts or messaging with your audience.

According to a study by InsideView, over 90% of CEOs said they *never* respond to cold e-mails or calls. When a potential customer is looking to buy, they are far more likely to engage with a salesperson who responds to their questions on social media than a cold call pitching a product.

Webinars

A *webinar* is a web-driven workshop or seminar where prospects can participate simply by logging in to an event via their computer versus having to travel to participate in person. Webinars offer an easy means for participants to engage with the speaker as well as one another. Using discussion group technology, all participants are able to explore issues and share knowledge effectively. Webinars can be hosted "live" or can be taped and viewed at a prospect's convenience.

As a result, webinars can be excellent lead-generation vehicles. Offering webinars targeted at providing valued educational content to your prospects will encourage them to register for the webinar and thus identify themselves and their interest. For example, Metric-Stream, the GRC software company mentioned earlier, offers weekly webinars on topics such as

- Creating effective risk management frameworks
- How IT controls fit into the enterprise risk management framework
- Enterprise risk management, making our investment count

Each of these topics not only provides value to the participants, but people interested in these subjects may also be interested in software that automates risk management to increase effectiveness while reducing costs, which is what MetricStream sells.

Trade Shows

Trade shows are gatherings of companies with similar products or companies with different products serving the same markets. Companies showcase their latest offerings, meet customers, learn new trends, and identify new prospects. To generate leads at a trade show, you must create a specific marketing plan. It is not enough to just show up. An effective plan includes the following:

- **Targeting the right trade show**—There are over 10,000 trade shows annually. Do your homework to identify those shows that will attract your ideal prospect as the Moka5 example demonstrated. The difference between the right event and the wrong one can significantly impact your sales effectiveness.

- **Setting clear objectives**—We are discussing lead generation; therefore, specific objectives to support lead generation should be set. These could include building a mailing list of quality names for your offering and/or qualifying prospective buyers. Your objective will guide your execution.

- **Staffing your booth properly**—You need at least two people to staff a booth. A good rule of thumb is to add another staff person for each additional 100 square feet of exhibit space. The staff should be trained on your offering and should be well groomed and friendly.

- **Focusing your message**—You have little time to make an impression. Establish one or two key messages and ensure the booth graphics, collateral, show prepromotion, and the staff stay on message.

- **Following up on leads**—Ensure you build a plan for following up with leads generated at the show prior to the show. Leads are perishable. Timely and appropriate follow-up is critical. Also keep all promises made at the booth. A trade show is one of the few times prospects actually engage with the company prior to a formal selection process. The impression you make will affect whether they consider your company in the future.

Keep in mind that many of the most valuable trade show interactions may *not* happen on the exhibit floor of trade shows. Serving on panels or leading plenary sessions may provide access to prospects as can many of the receptions and off-floor gatherings. Regardless of the format, the same requirements for clear objectives, messages, and follow-up remain critical for engaging prospects and generating interest.

Blog Posts

Blogs can provide real business value as a communications tool that helps define your image and brings you closer to your customers. Blogs are simple and easy-to-use vehicles to communicate. Each blog should have a focus to set expectations with the readers and encourage them to return to the blog. Blogs can range from industry focused, to technology focused, to just covering a set of specific topics. The informal nature of a blog can be inviting and personalized, which differentiates them from other media types.

E-Mail Campaigns

An e-mail campaign for lead generation is a program of sending a planned series of e-mails to your prospective targets with the objective of generating interest. Campaigns should comprise more than a one-shot e-mail. But don't be a spammer—use good lists, ones from a reputable company with contacts that fit your target profile and give recipients the ability to subscribe/unsubscribe. Make the e-mail personal to the recipient, addressing him by name and including content that is pertinent to the individual. Make the e-mails short and concise and always have a call to action that provides a clear connection to move the prospect along the route to becoming a lead. Like any marketing tactic, test it. Run tests against 10% of your target using different subject lines, different calls to action, and content design. Be sure to change only one variable at a time to ensure you know what works/doesn't work. Then launch the most effective e-mail—the one with the best results.

The key to make any lead-generation approach successful is targeting. Many marketing departments spend 80% of their time on the creative aspects of a lead-generation campaign, for example collateral creation, venue, messaging, and so on. But little time is spent on the audience. An average piece of collateral directed at the right audience performs far better than an outstanding collateral piece directed at the wrong audience. Spend time to define your target and research how to reach your target. It is important to be found where your customers are looking for information so you can place your collateral in the right place at the right time.

Contrary to what salespeople might demand, you don't want to create tons of leads. First of all, if you generate too many, they can't be properly processed and cultivated. Many will wither and die, which is just a waste of money, time, and effort. What you want to do is generate the right high-quality leads in numbers that can be properly handled by the company.

What is proper handling? Leads need to be captured, ideally in a system. They need to be assigned an owner responsible for qualifying and nurturing the lead. Lead data needs to be added to a marketing database so you can market to them in the future. And, finally, monitor each prospect interaction for impact and outcomes.

Qualify Prospects and Identify Prospective Buyers

The sooner prospects are qualified from the sales process, the better. Fewer resources are consumed, less money is wasted, and, most important, the more realistic the sales pipeline is. A quality pipeline enables sales management and company executives to plan and predict business results and take corrective actions when needed.

Marketing's role in qualification is twofold. First, marketing needs to provide as clear and precise a definition as possible of the target prospect. This definition should include as much detail as possible. To do this, marketing needs to analyze the product's benefits to determine what companies need it, which ones can afford it/justify it, who in the company specifically makes the buying decision for it, and so on. For example, a company selling supplier quality software with an average price point of $1 million needs to select a target market. Obviously, companies with multiple suppliers are a target, and given the outsourcing trend in manufacturing, manufacturing companies could be a target. But that is not specific enough. There are many manufacturers who would not be good prospects. By selecting a target that is too broad, marketing dollars will be wasted by delivering messages to companies that wouldn't ever need your product. Selecting U.S. discrete manufacturers with sales in excess of $500 million and more than 30 suppliers in the automotive industry is an example of a target prospect. See Table 9-2 for more examples of target market descriptors.

Table 9-2 Examples of Target Market Descriptors

Business to Business	Business to Consumer
Industry segment	Demographics
Revenue size	Income/net worth
Employee size	Geographic location
Geographic location	Gender/age
Growth rates	Hobbies/interests
Experience	Experience
Individual titles	Profession

For each target group, marketing should create appropriate collateral to assist both the sales channel and the prospect in qualification. Examples of collateral include brochures, data sheets, web-based demos, sample pricing sheets, and so on.

A quick note on collateral: Don't print it until you need it. Collateral design and content should evolve as your understanding of the market improves. Print only what you need so that you don't end up with stacks of unused, wasted collateral. Also with today's technology, a good quality color printer, and premium paper stock choices, printing in-house and on demand is a cost-effective alternative. In the business-to-business market, the PDF format is actually preferred as it can be easily shared electronically.

8x8 Reinvigorating Dormant Prospects

8x8, Inc., is the trusted provider of secure and reliable cloud-based, unified communications and virtual contact center solutions to businesses operating all over the world. The company was looking to nurture a database of dormant (more than one year old) leads to yield better prospects. 8x8 put together a six-month nurturing program with a mix of e-mails that addressed different parts of the prospect journey. They did not know where the dormant leads were in their "journey" and tried to create a blend of approaches. 8x8 also needed to get the lead scoring in place in order to prioritize lead routing and follow-up.

To determine what might work, 8x8 went back and looked at their previous marketing campaigns from a "first-touch" and "last-touch" wins perspective. The company examined which campaigns were good at creating a "first-touch" but didn't drive to an immediate sale, and which campaigns were complementary and tended to be the "last-touch" before a sale. This simple analysis looked at the "path to conversion" and the average number of touches before a sale. 8x8 used these metrics to determine a lead scoring methodology.

When a dormant lead responded to a "nurture" campaign, but the response was to download a thought leadership white paper using a Gmail address, it would get a score of "5" because the data suggested this was a tire-kicker and not quite ready to engage with a salesperson. Marketing would continue to do its thing to get the lead closer to sales ready. The threshold for prioritizing the lead for immediate follow-up would have been "15" or higher. However, if that same lead came to the 8x8 website within a specified period, the prospect would get "30" points, and it would get prioritized for follow-up. The website visit suggested they were clearly aware of 8x8 and were interested in what we were doing. White papers were always a key indicator. If the lead downloaded a white paper on 8x8's HIPAA compliance with a company e-mail address (not Gmail), then the score would reflect that the lead was more interested in 8x8's capabilities and more sales ready.

Within six months of implementing the lead scoring methodology and marketing automation, 10% of all new sales were generated out of the dormant database at no additional marketing expense to the company. 8x8 learned the steps and characteristics of quality prospects and used that knowledge to increase conversion.

Drive Toward the Close

Once a prospect has been qualified, the appropriate sales channel needs to develop the prospect's interest in the company's product. Here again, marketing needs to provide effective tools. The goal of the tools is to simply explain why a prospect should buy your product instead of buying someone else's or instead of doing nothing. It is imperative that these tools are built from the prospect's perspective. It is not effective to explain why your product is so great, although many marketing tools do just that. It is very effective to explain why a prospect should care about your product and how it benefits the prospect's company.

Unlike a recording of an actual demonstration, you may create PowerPoint slides that show different aspects of using the product, and a sales or technical person may explain the process while showing the slides. For example, if selling software, the slides could include pictures of the screens that users would interact with and reports that would be generated. Sales or sales support people can do live demos, but they are risky unless personnel are well trained. A failed demo, or one that the prospect perceives is irrelevant, can hurt far more than no demo at all. One of the author's software companies would challenge the sales force to qualify prospects (and even close a deal) without ever demonstrating software. This forced the sales force to engage with the prospect and focus on their needs and wants rather than the company's products.

Submit the Proposal

In business-to-business selling, the proposal or response to a request for proposal (RFP) or request for quotation (RFQ) can truly differentiate competitors in the sales process. Submitting a proposal is usually left completely up to the sales organization. It shouldn't be. For some prospects, the proposal is the most widely distributed piece of material from the company. Care needs to be taken in developing the proposal template to ensure that the company's brand and messaging come through. However, as with other aspects of marketing and sales, the focus and perspective of the proposal must be the prospect's business, not yours.

It is easy for companies to fall into the habit of using boilerplate proposals that simply search and replace the prospect's name in a generic proposal template. Winning proposals lead the prospect to believe that you crafted the proposal for their specific needs and requirements. You may still use boilerplate text, but using it in the context of client-specific overview, problem statements, objectives, and requirements will demonstrate that you have listened and reflected the prospect's specific needs.

In addition, it is rare that prospects consider just one proposal. Your proposal should include a checklist of key evaluation points that a prospect should consider, as well as how your company addresses those points. Obviously, you want to include criteria that highlight the strengths of your product offering. The ultimate goal is to have the prospect use your criteria when evaluating other options. To accomplish this, you need to establish a collaborative relationship with the prospect prior to a request for proposal.

Table 9-3 shows an example of a checklist used by MetricStream.

Table 9-3 Sarbanes-Oxley Checklist

Companies should look for solutions that enable them to sustain their compliance efforts, improve their internal control environment, and leverage technology to achieve a competitive advantage. This document provides a checklist of features required from a SOX-404 solution and can be used to compare solutions from various vendors.

	Requirement	**Vendor Support (Y/N)**
1.0	*Solution Overview*	
1.1	Support for COSO and Enterprise Risk Management frameworks	
1.2	Support for end-to-end management of Process Design, Assessments, Improvements, and Monitoring	
1.3	Easy to configure and reconfigure organizational processes	
1.4	Embedded best practices in out-of-the-box software	
1.5	Reduction of costs and support for ongoing compliance activities	

1.6	Can be leveraged to strengthen the internal control environment by documenting controls around other operational business processes
1.7	Can be leveraged to comply with other industry-specific mandates and government regulations
1.8	Can be leveraged to provide enterprise-wide risk assessment and management
1.9	Provides a business process management platform that can be used to improve all business processes
1.10	Matches the phases and steps being used to organize the SOX-404 program
2.0	*Usability*
2.1	Web-based application
2.2	Configurable portal-based user interface
2.3	Real-time status tracking of remediation plans via dynamic e-mail workflows
2.4	E-mail-based access to application
2.5	Role-based menu access controls to simplify usage
2.6	Easy to configure and customize forms, reports, and dashboards by business users
2.7	Personalized home page for each user who lists pending tasks in a To Do list
2.8	Ability to add company logo on pages
2.9	Drop-down list of values for appropriate fields
2.10	Help function
3.0	*Analytics and Business Intelligence*
3.1	Embedded analytics and business intelligence capability
3.2	Built-in reporting engine
3.3	Preconfigured standard SOX reports
3.4	Tool to configure standard, ad hoc, or scheduled reports
3.5	Ability to include any field into a report
3.6	Generate reports in printable, easy-to-read formats

3.7	Export reports into standard formats like Microsoft Excel, Adobe PDF, and so on
3.8	E-mail reports as attachments
3.9	Executive role-based dashboards with drill-down to details

4.0	*Compliance Platform*
4.1	Workflow and collaboration
4.2	Document management
4.3	E-mail-based access to application screens
4.4	Built-in integration capabilities
4.5	Integrated notification and alerts
4.6	Built-in analytics and reporting (no additional licenses required)
4.7	Auditability
4.8	Support for electronic signatures
4.9	Robust authorization and authentication controls
4.10	Highly scalable and available
4.11	Portal-based user interface
4.12	Support for offline access
4.13	Multilingual support
4.14	Multiple time zones support

The checklist is just one component. The following is a proposal outline:

- Thank you and introduction
- Restatement of prospect's needs and checklist of evaluation criteria
- Summary of how your company addresses the preceding items
- Pricing summary
- Details of proposal
- References
- Recap of proposal summary

Quality proposals not only help win competitive bids, but also may provide a solid foundation for project implementation.

Check References

In the business-to-business market, most customers will want to speak with reference customers. Although your existing customers may be quite happy, it does not mean that they will be willing to field frequent calls from prospects. When you receive requests for references, make sure you spread the requests around your customer base so no one customer gets overused. Otherwise, they will stop participating. An alternative to a "live reference call" is to ask customers for a written or videotaped testimonial that can be shared. This saves them time and effort, and it can be very effective.

Prepare your reference customers prior to them taking a reference call. Let them know what kinds of questions they are likely to get. Give them background on the person calling. The better prepared they are directly correlates to how comfortable they will be during the call.

Handle Objections

When a salesperson demonstrates a feature, talks about a benefit, or asks for the order, their customer may well respond in the negative, giving excuses or otherwise heading away from the sale. The salesperson then needs to handle these objections. Although there are numerous techniques that salespeople can use to handle these objections, in some instances appropriate marketing tools can help their effort.

Marketing needs to engage with sales to understand the current or expected sales objections and to determine what tools could be beneficial. For example, if the company is a relatively new or a small company, a prospect might be concerned with the company's viability. A viability presentation would be an appropriate tool for sales. Table 9-4 shows a list of common objections and possible tools that marketing could develop to assist sales in overcoming the objection. The key, however, is not to focus on this list, but to build your own based on input from the sales organization.

Table 9-4 Sales Tools for Handling Customer Objections

Objection	Possible Sales Tool
Viability	Viability presentation targeted at financial executives: • Show strength of company: number of customers, financial investors. • Show growth history and plans (sign non-disclosure). • Show customer satisfaction data. Customer case study: • Depict successful implementation process. • Explain measurable results. Bio sheet of key implementation personnel showing experience prior to joining the company: • Build confidence in the team that will support the prospect.
Competitor is cheaper	Total cost of ownership profile sheet: • Demonstrate that the total cost of product, implementation, training, and so on is comparable or cheaper than competitor. Product benefit sheet tailored to competitor: • Present argument that benefits achieved due to your superior product are greater.
Purchase risk too high	Trial program: • Give prospect a chance to see how the product will work and the benefits derived prior to fully committing.

One word of caution in handling objections: Avoid responding with only product information. One of the most effective responses to an objection about a specific feature or attribute, including price is simply to ask, "Compared with what?" For example, if a customer says your product is too expensive, the natural tendency for a salesperson is to reinforce the value proposition and excellent results the prospect will get. However, asking, "Compared with what?" will allow the prospect to share their comparative framework and help the salesperson understand how the prospect perceives the product, positioning, competition, and overall value. This information can help marketing understand how best to focus marketing activities to yield more favorable perceptions.

Close the Deal

A common oversight is the final contracts that a prospect sees. Just as with your collateral and proposal materials, your final contract and subsequent support documents reflect your company's brand. Proofread, proofread, and proofread. Many times, contracts are assembled from prior proposals, and multiple people are contributing content for the final product. Therefore, it is common for typos to be missed or other customer references to be accidentally left in. In addition to proofreading, take the time to make the final contract professional and consistent with your brand. Include your logo and company graphic if you have one. Print the proposal in color and have it bound. Another benefit of having professionally created customer-facing documents is that customers give them more respect. They are less likely to modify and change documents or contracts that are formal and well structured.

Training Is Necessary

Creating your marketing tools is the first step—training the sales reps to use these tools is the second. Training sales reps on how to deliver the presentations, use the ROI tools, or walk a prospect through a demo is a step often ignored. The value proposition must come through in each presentation, conversation, or piece of collateral set before her. Do not skimp on the training, though it won't be easy. Salespeople want to be in front of customers; they tend to minimize the value of training. Here are a few techniques that have worked:

- For newly hired sales reps, make training outcomes part of their initial objectives and compensation. Set a date for the rep to give a product demo or sales presentation to members of senior management. Ensure that new sales reps learn from experience by being taken on sales calls that other top-performing reps are making.

- Don't call it training. There is typically a regular sales meeting; ask for 10–15 minutes of the meeting to "update" sales on marketing. Use this "update" time to review new marketing tools and how to use them.

- Leverage a "loss review." Rolling out a tool after a review will typically meet with a more receptive audience. After losing a deal, good sales organizations review why the deal was lost to learn from the experience. In fact, if possible, have a follow-up call or meeting with the prospect to get additional perspective from them why they went in a different direction.

- Work with sales management to hold a quarterly or at least semiannual sales meeting to focus sales on the objectives ahead, share best practices, educate sales on new marketing tools, and ensure that they are accurately reflecting the company's positioning in their selling.

The Relationship Between Marketing and Sales

The relationship between marketing and sales is usually a healthy tension. In an entrepreneurial company, the sales organization is typically being asked to grow revenue at upwards of 100%–200% a year. As the pressure mounts, sales wants more from marketing—more demos, more collateral, more leads—while marketing wants to see sales do a better job of leveraging the good tools, and so on, that have already been provided. Respectful tension is normal and productive. If the relationship becomes adversarial, void of respect, or dysfunctional, then changes need to be made.

How should marketing and sales be structured? Although almost any structure can be made to work, based on experience, positive results are more likely when the following considerations are taken. The advantage of having marketing and sales report to the same senior manager is that there is someone in addition to the CEO who has the appropriate oversight and perspective to truly optimize the cost of sale. The disadvantage of joint reporting is that sales has a short-term, quarterly focus. Marketing requires a long-term perspective. A senior staff member responsible for both can end up spending a disproportionate amount of time on sales. In early stages of an entrepreneurial venture, it is best to keep marketing and sales separate. Once the company is more mature and has senior experienced people in both organizations, there is strong synergy that can result from combining the organizations.

Loudcloud, a website managed service provider (renamed Opsware and acquired by HP), hired an executive to help the company sell its services to large enterprise customers. This EVP of Sales and CMO was responsible for both sales and marketing. At the time, Loudcloud had approximately 320 people and roughly 40 people in marketing and sales. Sales was going through a transformation, the target customer was changing, the product offering was being repositioned to better match the new target audience, and the economy was beginning to stall. In this case, the EVP and CMO had nine direct-line reports. It was too much. With the short-term quarterly focus, sales overshadowed marketing. Marketing suffered.

NorthPoint provides a case study of benefits that can be derived from combining marketing and sales. In 2000, NorthPoint had 1,000 employees and approximately 100 people in marketing and sales reporting separately to the CEO. While NorthPoint's business was growing, its cost of sale was too high. A CMO was brought in to continue to grow the top line but to significantly reduce the total cost of sales. By combining the two organizations, eliminating duplicate work, holding marketing more accountable for the sales pipeline, and streamlining the sales process to take advantage of marketing's capabilities, in six months, the cost of sale decreased 30%, and subscriber count doubled. The CMO had five direct-line reports.

Summary

Marketing plays a crucial but often overlooked role in properly enabling sales success. From identifying prospective customers through lead generation, to providing tools to the sales force to handle prospect objections and close deals, marketing needs to be in lockstep with sales. Marketing needs to understand the sales process and inhibitors to moving prospects through the process to close as well as sales does. Ensuring that the right tools are created to assist sales at each step is a critical responsibility of marketing. This chapter provided checklists, examples, and questions to be answered for the marketing professional to help jump-start marketing's effectiveness in enabling sales. Through the NorthPoint and Loudcloud examples, the issue of the relationship and reporting structure of marketing and sales was also addressed. As long as marketing and sales share a common vision and strategy, significant sales leverage can be gained and sustained by driving close working relationships between the two functions.

Endnote

1. Gallo, C. (2014, June 11). *The unbreakable laws of storytelling*. Retrieved from Khosla Ventures: http://www.khoslaventures.com/the-unbreakable-laws-of-storytelling.

Section Three

Execution—Cultivate the People and Resources to Make Your Marketing Work

So far, we have discussed how to develop and refine product and service offerings as well as generate and fulfill demand with effective marketing and sales strategies and tactics. However, success of your offering in the marketplace is defined not by the launch, but rather by the scale of growth, a rapid increase in numbers of units sold, and the resulting revenue and profits. Achieving scale in marketing requires resources. In her discussion of capitalizing on entrepreneurial opportunity, Applegate describes three types of resources that are appropriate for our marketing objectives as well: ecosystem, people, and capital.[1]

Building an ecosystem requires cultivating employees, suppliers, customers, channel partners, evangelists, and other stakeholders and ensuring that they all are committed to creating a successful competitive advantage and capturing the value from it. Closer to home, your team leads the efforts, and you must recruit and develop the most important asset in business, your people. We provide keen insights on building effective teams within your organization. Of course, relationships and human capital require financial capital to fuel the activities to succeed in the marketplace, and marketing can help to secure financial resources. This section and the book conclude with a final chapter focused on the building of a brand, which is the culmination of successful marketing.

All of these concepts and activities are unified by the core premise of this book—effective positioning leads to great results. The marketer is most effective when resources are deployed with a common vision and shared set of values. When your ecosystem, team, and financial capital are all directed to capitalize on an opportunity; when you have a clear sense of the segment you are targeting; and when you are able to leverage these resources to build a sustainable competitive advantage, then you are able to create a strong and compelling value proposition and build value of your brand.

Endnote

1. L.M. Applegate, *Attracting Talent and Building Ecosystems* (Cambridge: Harvard Business Publishing, 2014).

10

Create an Ecosystem to Maximize Product/Service Lifetime Profitability

Pebble: The Start-Up Taking on Multibillion-Dollar Global Companies

In May 2012, Pebble Technology Corporation not only set the record for the most funds raised in a Kickstarter crowdfunding campaign—$10,266,845—but it also kicked off the development of a dedicated smartwatch ecosystem. The Pebble Watch was positioned as a customizable smartwatch for those who wanted to join the early rush to the emerging wearable technology market. Pebble Watch reflected several design choices that resonated with the early adopters on Kickstarter. As a companion to the iPhone and most Android smartphones, the Pebble Watch was a timepiece and accessory for the smartphone, not a replacement. Pebble used the eInk screen technology that provided high readability in any lighting combined with low power usage. Bluetooth LE (low emission) allowed sophisticated communication with your smartphone while drawing very little battery power and providing a wealth of capabilities beyond telling time. These technology choices (and use of both proprietary and standardized technologies) combined to deliver an offering with many capabilities and a much longer battery life than competitive smartwatches, and the Pebble Kickstarter campaign helped to build an actively engaged user community.

Pebble's early success was in direct contrast to other smartwatch entrants by large competitors, like Samsung. The Samsung Gear tried to replicate smartphone functionality to realize the familiar science fiction vision of the 1940's Dick Tracy two-way wrist radio. The result was a product that may have overpromised and underdelivered. The Gear had good capability, but an extremely limited battery life and really could not be used without a Samsung phone. As a result, it gained limited market adoption. After all, we are not used to charging our watches at all, much less charging them every day and pairing them with our phones!

Pebble's product launch did not stop with early adoption, an avid user community, and strong supplier network. The company was equally effective at engaging and cultivating distribution channel partners, developers, and even the educational community. Pebble was able to leverage its success on Kickstarter into broad distribution that yielded more than 1 million units sold. Because the company secured almost 69,000 backers and delivered the product that they promised on Kickstarter, they were able to establish distribution through AT&T, Amazon, Best Buy, and Target stores, as well as equally noteworthy wireless companies and retailers in Canada and Europe.[1, 2]

To secure their sustainable competitive advantage, Pebble needed to build a commitment to their smartwatch that went beyond unit sales and broad distribution. Pebble actively cultivated a developer network by providing a software development kit (SDK), which provided the tools, instructions, and samples to support a community of enthusiastic developers who would not only create watchfaces and apps for the Pebble Watch, but could also generate their own income by selling the fruits of their labor. Pebble has created a community of more than 18,000 developers and further fuels the ecosystem by cultivating young developers.

The year after their Kickstarter campaign, Pebble donated more than 4,000 watches and developer resources to several computer science programs at leading universities. One of the authors was fortunate enough to build a relationship between Pebble and Penn Engineering. Pebble provided hundreds of students with access to the technology and resources required to enhance their computer science and embedded systems curricula. Penn Engineering hosted Pebble Watch boot camps, which were supported by Pebble, and that gave participants instruction in app development and provided participants with free Pebble Watches. In addition, by supporting and sponsoring PennApps, the premier student hackathon that Penn Engineering hosts twice each year, Pebble expanded its young developer core to an even wider audience and created evangelists for the company and its products. In addition, Pebble received outstanding press that told the story of Penn Engineering's (and other leading academic reference customers') use and support of Pebble's products.[3]

The success on Kickstarter together with the strength of an expanding ecosystem has helped Pebble launch a successful first product offering and secure a strong position in the nascent smartwatch industry. In the early 2000s, Apple created an ecosystem that brought together the music industry, software developers, and distribution to establish the iPod's dominance in music devices. The company then did it again with the iPhone by bringing together wireless providers, great hardware, software, and accessories together with developers and distribution, to dominate the smartphone industry. Today, Pebble has unified a growing collection of stakeholders behind the vision of a well-designed product and well-executed marketing plan. They have achieved early success in unit sales and market engagement, and are well positioned to battle Apple, Samsung, and the other large smartwatch competitors. Of course, only time will tell if they create a long-term sustainable competitive advantage.

Engaging Your Customers in Product Launch

The most crucial time in the marketing of a new product or service is the initial rollout. Because "first impressions last," it is essential for an entrepreneurial venture to successfully launch its product. In fact, in our social media-fueled world, the difference between an initial rollout being a success or a dud can mean literally billions of dollars in market capitalization. Today, prospective customers are able to get information from a variety of sources and platforms. A successful product launch requires an integrated approach: one that includes traditional, social, and online marketing tools to engage customers. Much can be learned even before the launch of a new idea, using the *beta test* process to gather feedback and jump-start the customer acquisition process.

A great example comes from Virgin America, a Silicon Valley–based airline, which wanted to create a new website to increase the number of tickets purchased directly from the Internet. The company conducted research to get feedback on its website and also reviewed social media where its customers were quite vocal. The feedback was clear: Fliers found the website to be cluttered and cumbersome. Many would use travel agencies instead of booking online. Online buying habit studies showed online shoppers buy more from simple, intuitive sites.

Instead of revamping the website in one step and then unveiling it to beta users and finally the full market, Luane Calvert, Virgin America's CMO, enlisted the help of Work&co to re-create the website in a simple and clean way using the Agile methodology. This allowed them to apply the same principles of adaptive testing we preach throughout this book. Agile development enabled them to work and test in parallel. They broke customers into different segments and released it to employees first. They modified the website. Then they released the site to Google employees and their entrepreneur advisory board second. These were savvy people and represented top-tier fliers. They modified the website again. Then they finally released it to media bloggers and frequent flier writers to help build coverage. They continually incorporated the feedback and, finally, rolled out the new site to the general public.

Research and sequential testing using the Agile method made all the difference in ensuring a smooth rollout, great website performance, and strong user acceptance. Virgin America has experienced a significant increase in web traffic while experiencing much lower call center activity due to meeting customer expectations. Marketing must continually optimize the sales channels to achieve desired results.

Engaging your customer is just one part of building a successful product launch program. Product launches should contribute to a sustainable ecosystem that brings together several stakeholders, all of who add value to and are able to capture value from an offering's success in the market. Table 10-1 outlines elements that are important for a supportive ecosystem.

Table 10-1 Product Launch Checklist

Confirm and monitor product development timelines.

Secure initial reference customers.

> Identify target reference customers.
>
> Create a strategy to reach these customers.
>
> Establish a compelling offer for these initial customers. Test and refine the offer.
>
>> What benefits do they receive beyond the product benefits?
>>
>> What do you expect from them in return?
>
> Determine an internal resource plan to ensure successful implementations.
>
>> Sales
>>
>> Account support
>>
>> Technical support
>>
>> Escalation process
>>
>> Product/experience feedback process
>>
>> Social media monitoring
>
> Execute.

Utilize a phased launch approach that enables multiple cycles of launch, test, improve, launch.

Secure external support for your product.

> Analysts
>
> Industry experts
>
> Consultants
>
> Influential bloggers for your target segment

Establish your product's online presence.

> Create specific landing pages to optimize SEO
>
> Social media leverage
>
> Blog
>
> Analytics

Define partnering opportunities.

> To add credibility that the product will be successful
>
> To extend your reach into the target market segments
>
> To improve the opportunity for publicity
>
> To better optimize cost

Include your channel/distributors in the product launch.

> Create supporting marketing materials and collateral.

The Beta Process

Most products go through many revisions between the concept and final versions, similar to the Virgin America example. The changes are often stimulated by real user feedback to the engineering and product management teams. The process that helps this to happen is the beta process. The terminology is in common use in engineering hardware and software areas, where the first versions of a product are called *alpha* versions, the first versions that can go to customers for testing are called *beta,* the almost final versions are called *release candidates*, and the final versions are called the *released product.*

At each stage, successively more users and/or customers have the product in hand and are making comments to the product management team. This process is normally run by, and of benefit to, the engineering department. Properly managed, however, it can be a great help to the marketing of the product.

In today's Internet world, beta users provide the buzz and amplify the presence once the service is launched openly to the world. Whereas in the past beta testing was usually limited to a few customers, or a few dozen, there are now cases where the number of beta users is in the tens of thousands. Microsoft Windows 7 had over 8 million beta testers, and Google usually offers both a current shipping (or "frozen") version and a beta version that allows users to test the newest features.

When customers agree to join a beta program, they usually agree to spend some minimum amount of time using the product, to respond to questionnaires about the features and benefits of the product, and to be available for calls from the press or other customers. In return, their questions and problems should be dealt with at high priority, and they can gain visibility to their peer groups as thought leaders, as well as the psychic income of seeing their name in print in interviews and articles about the product.

Choosing the right customers is important because they will not only influence the press, but also provide the most cogent feedback at a key time when the offering may still be changed. Customers whose needs are not aligned with a majority of intended users could skew product features in an undesirable direction. In the software world, beta customers are often chosen from existing users of previous products. Such customers are already predisposed to a company and can get the extra benefits of additional support and relationships to help if they have problems with any product.

On the Internet, many offerings are completely new, and there is no customer tradition. In this case, make a list of the key target customers—whether they are Fortune 500 companies, Inc. 500 newcomers, consumers of certain demographics, and so on. Then network to a decision maker who is willing to listen to the benefits of a new product and convince him that his company will benefit from being a first mover—not only through discounts, but also through having a several month advantage over any competitors. For consumer sites, there may be specific discounts and the ability to say, "I've been there first."

TaskRabbit is a sharing economy company that connects buyers with safe and reliable help for errands and general tasks in your neighborhood. TaskRabbit was preparing to launch a new product to address a couple of major customer concerns. The primary one was scheduling between a buyer and provider. There was too much friction caused by back and forth between buyers of the service and providers of the service. For example, the buyer suggesting 2:00 p.m., the provider suggesting 3:30 p.m., the buyer replying that after 3:00 p.m. isn't possible, and so on. TaskRabbit wanted to test the new product in a fresh market—one that wasn't exposed to TaskRabbit before, but reflected the demographics and behavior of their primary target markets, large U.S. cities. They chose London. The new product forced TaskRabbits, the service providers, to publish their available hours, removing the back and forth. Upon testing, they learned that real-time communications capability was needed. People didn't want to share personal information like phone numbers with strangers. To solve this challenge, they added an in-app chat capability allowing buyers and TaskRabbits to communicate securely in real time. They also learned that buyers would get frustrated not knowing when a Task-Rabbit would respond to a request. So they implemented a 30-minute response time SLA and trained the TaskRabbits to respond within the timeframe.

This in-market beta test enabled TaskRabbit to refine their offering without compromising existing users. This set them up for a successful launch in the United States. It also paved the way for an international expansion.

iExchange.com, a site that permits people to share stock market advice and rates them on the accuracy of their predictions, needed to beta test for two reasons. The first involved the usual issues of making sure the programming was properly done and that the servers could handle the loads. Second, in order for the site to be attractive to general users, there needed to be enough predictions, about enough stocks, to give interesting content to new users. As an Idealab company, iExchange.com first called on all the people in the Idealab building (about 150) and asked them to post recommendations. The incentive offered was free pizza and T-shirts. After two weeks of building several thousand recommendations, these people were asked to virally expand the beta test to their friends and family members, by sending them e-mails promising prizes for their entries.

During this beta period, users were periodically asked for comments about the user interfaces, their interactions, and their overall comments about the site, including look and feel, mission, and effectiveness. Their movements through the site were tracked with software that could show each successive click, and determine when they were leaving the site. All this information was fed to the product managers and developers each day, and changes were made to improve the length of time and number of page views per visit, as well as the overall performance of the site.

As you reach the later stages of the beta process, it is important to have critics, as well as friends, test the site or the new product. People with a real need and use for the product will provide a less-filtered set of responses than those who are merely friends doing a favor. It is often the harshest critic who provides the spark for a feature change that turns her into a fan—and makes the site that much better for all other users.

InsiderPages.com, a website tagged "the Yellow Pages written by your friends," allows people to rate local merchants, either positively or negatively, and have those ratings accessible by their friends and others. For this type of site to be useful, it has to have a meaningful number of reviews and categories. This attracts new users, who then post their own reviews and further build the network. A beta test period was necessary to make sure it was easy for users to get their reviews in. For example, the system is designed to scour your Outlook contacts looking for words such as *doctor, engineer, plumber,* and so on. Making that process simple and intuitive took several retries on the code during the beta process.

Users were asked for feedback throughout the process and were observed while using the system (for those users at the InsiderPages. com facility). After several weeks, the internal users were able to invite friends from outside the Insider Pages and Idealab communities. The spread of new users was carefully monitored, and comments fed to the product and development teams. This led to the creation of a marketing program that offered a $5 Starbucks card for the first three reviews posted. Once a critical mass of reviews (about 5,000) and users (about 2,000) was achieved in Los Angeles, the product was opened up from beta. The beta period allowed many adjustments to be made without the fear of a very large user community being unhappy with any particular change.

Autodesk, an extremely successful software maker for Computer Aided Design and Manufacturing, understands how important their beta accounts are. They have a department whose responsibility is only to follow up every comment, suggestion, or problem that arises during the beta test process. This group is charged with communicating to the reference account about exactly what happened with every suggestion made during the reference, beta test process. Each reference customer is never left hanging about whether his suggestions or feedback were integrated into the released version of the product. Even if the suggestion is not implemented, the reference account is told why it wasn't. For many organizations, this step of saying what *was not implemented* in the new product is not completed. It is human nature not to want to give your important reference account bad news. However, such news is still valuable to the account. This kind of communication adds a tremendous amount of credibility to the Autodesk organization and gives their reference accounts a big signal that Autodesk is trustworthy. This management of the reference, beta test process is one reason why Autodesk has maintained the clear leadership in its marketplace for more than 20 years.

For business-to-business (B2B) products or services, finding initial customers may be more difficult. You have to convince them to try something that might not succeed, and hence could leave them stranded if they are not careful. And the growth might be much slower. This is why it is so important to choose influential innovators and early adopters to be the initial customers. It also is critical to market to them in the best way.

The need for reference accounts is tied to a product, not to the company. The process for securing reference customers takes place with each new product introduction. Buyers don't attribute references across product lines; they want to know that others have successfully used the specific product they are considering. MetricStream, a Governance, Risk, and Compliance software provider, had been selling software to large companies to manage their operational compliance needs, such as those dictated by the FDA, ISO9000, and Six Sigma. Despite the fact that they had customers such as Pfizer, Procter & Gamble, and UBS successfully using their software, when they launched their Operational Risk Management module, they needed references for that specific module in order to successfully sell it. They established a charter customer program that provided pricing discounts, enhanced support, and consulting. This program enabled MetricStream to obtain their first few customers for the Operational Risk Management module.

This practice is not limited to small companies. Companies as large as IBM establish incentives to acquire their first set of customers for a new product. These incentives are targeted at the sales force and at prospective customers. Salespeople are typically offered bonuses or accelerators to their commission plans for selling new products. Likewise, customers are offered discounts or attractive benefits for being early adopters.

Reference Accounts

In selling any product, nothing helps as much as strong references and referrals. This is especially true for products that are highly priced, mission critical, or perceived as risky. Enterprise software is a good example. Customers take a great leap of faith to believe the value proposition that you communicate via advertising or promotional materials. For them to believe what they hear from other experienced users is merely an act of trust that those users have no incentive to lie about your product's virtues and faults. Reference accounts provide for an organized word-of-mouth campaign so that when the press and key targeted accounts need to hear from noncompany sources, there are users to call.

The benefits to the company from a good reference account are great—credibility with peers of that account, spokespeople to talk with the press, and examples to use in advertising and public relations (PR). In essence, you are trying to create "Cow Bell" accounts, the accounts you want the world to know are your customers. You want to create as much noise as possible about the fact that they chose your product. Therefore, care should be taken to identify the ideal reference customers. The choice of who to get as initial reference accounts can have a huge impact on how fast (or whether) the product is adopted by the market. For Trust-Aid (see example later in the chapter), if the initial reference account had been a bank that other banks looked to for guidance on new technological innovations, the sales progress of Trust-Aid would have been much faster.

In most markets, there are individuals and entities that are known as early adopters and leaders in technology application. If these leaders are first to adopt your product, then the going will be much easier than if your first reference accounts are not respected as leaders. The medical market is probably the best defined in this dimension. For most new prescription drugs or new medical devices, who the first users are is crucial to whether they may become successful. Doctors have a "pecking order" of prestige and respectability. They will be much more likely to try a new innovation if it is first adopted by the physicians they perceive as highly influential in their field.

One caveat to these early adopters as reference accounts is the concept of the chasm, as described in Geoffrey Moore's excellent book, *Crossing the Chasm*. While early adopters may be influential, the mainstream market are pragmatic and may not perceive them as referenceable. The mainstream market has a lower threshold for the risk that might accompany adopting new products, preferring to wait until products are well-established in the market. However, the early adopters are still important customers for the entrepreneurial marketer.[4]

Reaching Target Reference Customers

After you have identified reference customers, you need to create strategies to reach them. In addition to leveraging your existing network, don't hesitate to use your board of directors, your investors, your advisors, or even your vendors, such as accountants, to establish introductions into your targeted companies.

Although many new companies rely on these networks for introductions that lead to their first set of customers, it is amazing how many companies don't. It is not professional, nor will it be productive, to ask investors or board members for a list of people and companies they know. The company must do the work to narrow a target list of potential reference companies. With this narrowed list, it is then appropriate to ask your network if they can assist you with introductions. This request should not be made via an e-mail distribution list. People's relationships are typically guarded. When you ask someone to make an introduction, you are asking that person to take a risk. That person is risking that you will have something valuable to offer her contact and will be able to deliver. Relationships are always stronger when value is perceived by all parties.

Vendors such as law firms and accountants can be excellent sources of introductions. They typically organize their firm's professionals around industries and geographies. Even if the person who serves your company can't help, he might be able to find someone in the firm who can. Because you are his customer, he is usually willing to help where appropriate. And an introduction that yields good results strengthens your perceived value as a professional service provider.

Establishing a Compelling Offer

Once identified, the venture must secure these initial reference customers. The targeted reference accounts themselves need a compelling reason to take the initial risk associated with being a first customer of a product. They need to understand what benefits they receive and what you expect from them in return. Remember, the benefits received must outweigh the natural inertia to wait for someone else to try your product first, or worse, for them to use a competing product. These benefits must go beyond the standard offering and often take the form of reduced pricing (at least for a long initial period), increased training, and far greater and more responsive support than later customers may find (although hopefully the product's bugs will have been ironed out and less support will be needed).

It is also critical to communicate and ideally to contractually commit a targeted reference account to what you expect from them in support of your product launch. It's not helpful to have a successful implementation, only to learn your customer has a corporate policy prohibiting joint press releases with product vendors. The following is a list of examples of marketing support you can request from your customers:

- Joint press release announcing use of the product
- Use of their name as a product user in marketing materials and on the website
- Participation in a case study highlighting benefits of the product
- Participation in a seminar or webinars
- Willingness to take calls from the media and prospective customers

Sometimes, the value to a venture of an initial customer is important enough to make a deal with a customer that would otherwise pain the CFO. In the 1970s, an MBA student at Wharton who had developed a time-shared computer program to automate the trust accounting process for banks started what became SEI Corp. He wanted to commercialize the software and an associated support service for bank trust departments to use. His competition during that time was in-house accounting machines and manual calculations, for the most part. Without his product (called Trust-Aid), when IBM declared a dividend, someone manually had to go into each different trust account to enter that event so it was accounted for correctly. Conceptually, adopting Trust-Aid should have been a very easy decision for any bank based on very high value in use. However, as the student quickly found out, no bank was going to put its "family jewels," its trust accounts, onto a system that no one else had shown to be reliable and to actually work. He asked his teacher, one of this book's coauthors, for advice. The advice was simple: "You need to get a very credible reference account, and even if you have to give the software and service away for free, it'll be very worth it." That is exactly what the student did to get his first customer. He gave it away for free for over a year to his first "customer." He was not very happy about not having any initial revenue for a year, but it was probably the only way the company (now with a market cap in the billions) would have gotten started.

It wasn't until that first customer had run the system for nine months without using the old manual system as a backup, that the student got his first paying customer (at still reduced "charter rates"). The first customer was really only a credible reference after he had put his trust department "family jewels" in the care of the Trust-Aid software and service and had stopped using the old manual system. Even when the reference account had both systems running (with Trust-Aid running very successfully), he was not a credible or convincing reference site until he had demonstrated his own faith in the software and service.

Building an Internal Resource Plan to Ensure a Successful Launch

The SEI example highlights the importance of ensuring your first customer(s) are completely satisfied with your product and their experience with the company. This doesn't happen by accident. Spend the time up front to establish your internal resource plan to ensure a successful implementation.

The plan starts with sales and understanding the needs of customers in different phases of the sales learning curve, which was discussed in Chapter 8, "Sales Management to Add Value." Most companies that are willing to be first users tend to be early adopters. Because these innovators know that they are taking a risk, they prefer to work directly with the company to mitigate additional risks associated with going through intermediaries. Regardless of the distribution channel decisions you've made, the best approach is to ask the potential reference account how they want to be treated. You may have to either hire a direct sales force if the number of initial customers requires it, or as the entrepreneur, you and other senior managers may assume the sales role directly.

In *Crossing the Chasm*, Geoffrey Moore also recommends a small, top-level sales force as a way to deal, in particular, with those innovators he terms "visionaries,"[5] to manage their expectations during the sales and initial usage process.

> Because controlling expectations is so crucial, the only practical way to do business with visionaries is through a small, top-level direct sales force. At the front end of the sales cycle, you need such a group to understand the visionaries' goals and give them confidence that your company can step up to those. In the middle of the sales cycle, you need to be extremely flexible about commitments as you begin to adapt to the visionaries' agenda. At the end, you need to be careful in negotiations, keeping the spark of the vision alive without committing to tasks that are unachievable within the time frame allotted. All of this implies a mature and sophisticated representative working on your behalf.[6]

Once the sale is finally closed, the venture must be ready with plans to provide account support and technical support. Many times, the person responsible for the initial sales takes responsibility for ongoing account support. He must make sure that whatever happens, the initial client's expectations are exceeded. As discussed in Chapter 8, salespeople tend to respond directly to the financial incentives inherent in their compensation structure—that is, they focus on the tasks that will generate the most income. During this phase, it is important that the salesperson is compensated not only for the sale, but also for customer satisfaction. This can be measured and paid when the customer agrees to be a reference. Many companies forget this step and don't understand when the salesperson is off selling the next accounts and not adequately focusing on ensuring that the current customer is being well managed.

The referrals of these initial users are what the business will live on. If this initial salesperson is not a senior manager, this person should have direct authority from the CEO to do whatever is necessary to exceed this customer's expectations. Likewise, engineering and development must be prepared to respond very quickly to technical issues or problems that arise.

A successful Israeli high-tech company had established a very nice North American business selling products and services to call centers through VARs (value-added resellers) and large equipment vendors. They had a different new product targeted toward security departments of large firms. The firm originally planned to use the same type of sales and distribution (VARs) to introduce the new security product and large equipment vendors. However, after interviewing the potential innovators, the company had to change their initial marketing plan. The innovative potential initial customers were not receptive to dealing with intermediaries. They wanted to deal directly with the company. The company used its senior managers as direct salespeople and began a successful rollout of its new, innovative, security product. If they had not asked their initial target customers how they wanted to be treated, they would have had significant problems in penetrating the market.

One mistake that entrepreneurs sometimes make is to neglect to put in place processes for escalation of issues and for customer feedback on the product or experience with the company. Although it is important to make the product work as represented, it is equally important to solicit feedback on the overall value received and what could be done to make the product even more valuable. Today, many users are comfortable with social media. It is important to ensure there is a plan to monitor and address social media–based feedback as well.

Securing External Support for Your Product

In addition to having strong reference customers, external support and awareness from unbiased entities is quite valuable. Use social media to help build this awareness by being visible in places where they spend time—Facebook, Twitter, LinkedIn, Pinterest, and so on. Set up a presence. Add links from your website or blog. Remember social media is a two-way communication opportunity. A company needs to add value in their communication. Value can be educational, promotional offer–based, or entertaining. In a relatively short period of time, you can build an active audience.

Now you need to engage them. Update your social media outlets regularly. Ask questions or get prospective customers to interact through contests, simple surveys, content posting, and so forth. The key is understanding that each time your target audience engages with you, it is an opportunity to expand your visibility and awareness.

In addition to social media, many industries have analysts whose opinions are valued by potential customers when making a purchasing decision. Establishing a good review from one or more of these analysts can provide excellent credibility to your product.

Analysts can deliver real value for a company launching a product. Analysts have two main constituencies: vendors selling a product and companies that need help and assistance in selecting products. Most analysts publish research and provide a list of vendors that they have evaluated and are recommending. Getting on those lists and being included in the research can expand your visibility tremendously. Analysts are also aware of companies in the buying processes and can introduce your company into a sales process. They can also provide your company with information on purchase trends, marketing direction, and competition.

To take advantage of these opportunities, you need to educate them about your company strategy and products. You need to provide the information in the framework of the industry you serve. Analysts strive to be the expert in their area of focus. They will be less interested in hearing about why your product is so great and more interested in understanding what gap currently exists in the marketplace and your company's approach to filling it. Even when you aren't a paying customer of an analyst, you can get their attention. Analysts will typically meet with nonpaying companies in their focus area once a year. Why? Because as experts, they need to be aware of what's happening in the market and who the players are.

Industry experts represent another avenue to consider. Although it might be difficult to get an explicit product endorsement, there are other ways to leverage them for credibility. Invite them to speak at a key event during your launch. You can also consider recruiting them as board members or advisory board members. NorthPoint is a classic example. NorthPoint communications was a telecommunications DSL provider that was purchased by AT&T in 2001. In the early days, following the founding of NorthPoint, they needed to establish credibility in the telecommunications industry. Their competitors were the well-established Baby Bells and other new upstart companies. To add credibility and break out of the pack, NorthPoint successfully recruited Reed Hundt, the former FCC chairman, to join their board. His participation on the board of directors indirectly gave validity and notability to NorthPoint over competitors.

Partnering for Launch

Intel and Microsoft have been masters of cultivating ecosystems to support and increase the sales of their products. Each time one of these companies announces a new product, it releases a list of companies that are "supporting" the new processor or platform. These partners help validate the eventual success and hence make it easier for a large company customer to take a chance. Once they know that others will be using it also, they feel less afraid of being left stranded or of being unable to convince the supplier to fix the product if it isn't working.

Smaller companies can also improve their chances of success on a product launch by including the testimonials and support of a number of key strategic and tactical partners in their announcements.

When Viewpoint.com prepared to launch its new Viewpoint 3D format, which allows low bandwidth streaming of 3D content on the Internet, it wanted the credibility that strong partners bring to a new effort. Two months prior to launch, a concerted effort was undertaken to sign up partners who could participate in the launch event. Microsoft, Intel, and AOL all had an interest in seeing 3D proliferate on the Internet. For Intel, it meant a need for more processing power; for Microsoft, a leg up for its Internet Explorer browser; and for AOL, better e-commerce. In addition, a number of companies that wanted to use the technology on their websites, including Nike, Sony, and CBS, all agreed.

Each of the partners got strong press exposure, the ability to add to their own leadership and forward-thinking images, and early use of the technology. Viewpoint.com, because it was linked with such powerful partners, got coverage in the *New York Times*, CNBC, and other prime media venues that probably wouldn't have covered the story, or featured it, without the names associated with the launch.

The business development and technical organizations, rather than the straight marketing and sales forces, had to make the introductions and connections to the partners because those organizations had to be convinced that the technology would succeed before they could approach their own marketing and public relations operations. The lead time for such endorsements is long—typically two to three months—and it pays to create the relationships between your company and possible partners even sooner.

Channels of Distribution

When creating your launch plan, don't forget your channel/distributors. If you've decided to leverage these entities, ensure that they are part of your launch plan. For example, they will need training and lead time for creating their own marketing materials and go-to-market plan. They need to be brought into the planning process as early as possible so that they can be an effective sales engine when the product is ready.

These channels also represent publicity opportunities—to coordinate press releases, public relations plans, and event participation. In some cases, your channel may be better established than your company is. Therefore, they may be more likely to get extended press coverage. By coordinating, you can ensure that these opportunities are leveraged and that the messaging is on target with your positioning and strategy. These activities can create not only better reach into the marketplace, but will also strengthen your relationships with your channels.

Summary

You must build ecosystems that engage stakeholders in the support of your offering, including customers (especially reference customers), technology and business partners, press, and distributors. A strong product rollout can set the tone for success and dramatically reduce the time needed to gain customer and market acceptance. Planning for this requires sufficient time prior to launch, choosing the best reference accounts, treating them well, and obtaining sufficient feedback from a well-run beta program. Rolling out a website or web-based business can be done more rapidly, but still requires testing and trials to see how consumers react to each piece of the website. Social media can play an important role in getting the word out and creating a following for your new offering.

Endnotes

1. Pebble Technology. (2015, March 11). "Pebble: E-Paper Watch for iPhone and Android." Retrieved from Kickstarter: https://www.kickstarter.com/projects/597507018/pebble-e-paper-watch-for-iphone-and-android.

2. "Where to Buy a Pebble Smartwatch." (2015, March 11). Retrieved from https://getpebble.com/retail.

3. "Pebble Launches Education Project for Schools and STEM Programs." (2013, December 16). Retrieved from releasd.com: http://releasd.com/0b02/.

4. Geoffrey A. Moore, *Crossing the Chasm* (New York: Harper Business, 1995), pp. 41-48.

5. Ibid., 37.

6. Ibid., 37.

11 Entrepreneurial Marketing for Building Teams

Anki: From Classmates to a Company

Mark Palatucci, a cofounder and the chief product officer for Anki, was a member of the winning team of the 2005 DARPA Grand Challenge, which races robots at high speeds across the desert without human intervention. Mark pursued this interest in artificial intelligence (AI) and robotics in a PhD program at the Carnegie Mellon University Robotics Institute. It was there that he met his cofounders of Anki, the company introduced in Chapter 7, "Distribution/Channel Decisions to Solidify Sustainable Competitive Advantage." Boris Sofman, CEO, and Hanns Tappeiner, president, joined with Mark to brainstorm concepts both while at school and after the three moved to the San Francisco area. The entrepreneurs were unified by the notion that they wanted to change the world through AI and robotics and apply these technologies to consumer products. According to Boris, "We wanted to work on difficult problems but only if they had an impact on the real world."

The three juggled school, jobs in industry, and product concepts for Anki over the next several years. Finally in 2010, the trio formally founded Anki and set about securing the human and financial capital required to build a viable and scalable AI robotics company. The cofounders' commitment to the vision was demonstrated by years of dedication and hard work, and they were able to leverage their work and technology to attract an incredible $50 million in early stage funding from several investors, including Andreessen Horowitz, a leading

Silicon Valley venture capital firm. Marc Andreessen, a general part-ner of the firm and Anki board member, emphasizes investing in sig-nificant engineering talent and vision, and Andreessen Horowitz was a perfect fit for Anki. The firm provided not only the capital, but also introductions to the talent required to bring Anki's first product, Anki DRIVE, to the market.

A complex AI robotics-based consumer electronic product com-pany requires a sophisticated combination of technology, creative design, manufacturing, supply chain management, sales and market-ing, as well as the leadership and administrative skills to manage this complex team and process. The founders excelled in technical tal-ent. Through a combination of their own networks, those of the ven-ture investors, and savvy recruitment, Anki built the complete team required to bring Anki DRIVE to market.

They brought Harald Belker on board to design the Anki DRIVE cars. Not only had Belker designed real-world autos for Porsche and Mercedes Benz, but he also created the futuristic designs of the Batmobile for the film *Batman and Robin* and vehicles for *Minority Report* and *Tron: Legacy.* In addition, Belker's work on Hot Wheels and other consumer products made him a perfect fit with Anki's vision for a "video game brought into the offline world."

Anki hired Gabriel Hebert, VP of operations, to manage the global supply chain and manufacturing of the complex electronics, track mats, and accessories. Likewise, the company added the talent to develop the complex relationships required to secure a technology partnership with Apple, exclusive distribution through Apple stores, and the eventual expansion into mass distribution via Amazon and Best Buy. And, finally, the team added the expertise for market plan-ning and launch, the very topics of this book. All of this is challenging enough to accomplish even with the right skills and experience. The team assembled by Anki's leadership brought the required industry and domain expertise required to build a great business.

Few companies can make the transition from founder/entrepre-neurs to a scalable company. Boris, Mark, and Hanns provided the compelling product, vision, and culture that attracted and engaged the right team; and they led that team to execute on a plan to build and scale the company. The results speak for themselves. Anki's first product not only was Apple's top-selling product in the 2013 holiday catalog, but was also Amazon's #2 selling toy during the 2014 holiday season (second only to Disney's *Frozen* doll). And the company sold out of product weeks before the holidays—a high-class problem to have![1]

Positioning for Talent

The three key items that fuel high growth are ideas, people, and capital. Section One, "Marketing Strategy—Refine Your Offering and Positioning," discussed generating and evaluating ideas, and the following chapter discusses the third key item, raising capital. This chapter focuses on the need of all successful companies for a continuing supply of great people to bring the ideas to fruition. Selling to potential recruits is a marketing problem like any other, and many of the same elements need to be considered. In fact, you can revisit many of the elements of this book in the specific context of building a winning team.

Great people want to work with winners. One of the key marketing challenges for the human resources (HR) group in a company is to generate the perception that your company is going to be the winner in your product/service space. This begins with a clear vision of what you are trying to accomplish and how you will have an impact on the world. Just as customers who share your vision may engage with you, prospective employees who find your vision compelling and worthwhile will want to work with you to achieve the vision. This vision is your positioning in the marketplace of companies competing for talent.

Segmentation: Understanding the Needs of Company and Employees

Almost every market segments itself along certain dimensions. The hiring market is no exception and may be segmented by functional specifications, by geography, by skill level, and by experience level required. In addition, the risk propensity of applicants causes the more conservative folks to shy away from entrepreneurial start-ups.

Start-ups often draw from the networks of the founding entrepreneur for early employees, those who can handle the inherent risk because they trust the founder. Early employees are often close friends and family because they have established relationships with founders built on trust. According to Noah Wasserman, in his book *The Founder's Dilemma*, it may be easier to start a business by drawing talent from this pool because these people are more likely to believe in the entrepreneur regardless of a lack of experience. In addition, this homogeneity of teams can contribute to the initial speed of venture development.

However, drawing from the pool of friends and families, and by extension, those with whom the founder has worked, has limitations. Heterogeneous teams offer benefits that may help a business grow and scale. In order to scale, companies often need a diverse set of skills and capabilities and can benefit from expanded networks and resources. Teams with varying background, and perhaps even conflicting views and approaches, are often more creative and innovative. These teams also expand the networks to a broader and more diverse pool of future employees. Add to this the benefits of drawing from the experience offered from the networks of investors, customers, and other stakeholders, and you see why the most successful companies have more diverse teams.[2]

Attracting and engaging diverse teams requires you to have a clear vision for what you are trying to accomplish and what the company needs to succeed. A portion of these needs is functional and requires bringing diverse skill sets together to achieve a common goal. Regardless of the common vision, you might need to market differently to attract different functional skills—accounting personnel look for different things in a company than manufacturing workers. And in the early stages of entrepreneurial companies, each person might have to take on several jobs and functions. The CFO may also run operations, be a purchasing clerk, and work on sales of company equity. It is hard to decide between a candidate with several years of direct experience as a CFO who has come up through the accounting and finance ranks, and someone with a CPA who has also been an operating officer or perhaps run his own business. Regardless, the best approach is to focus on the needs of the company, both short term and in the future.

Geographical segmentation is an especially difficult hiring hurdle to overcome. There are fundamentally different lifestyles in Boulder, San Jose, New York City, or Atlanta. People who are attracted to a particular place to live can color the applicant pool for your new venture. It is much easier to find people willing to work all day and night in Silicon Valley than in Atlanta—not that the Georgians are any less productive, just that their culture is built around more family time. Similarly, locating your office where most employees have long commutes (by train or auto) puts bigger limits on total in-office time.

Hiring people who have to change locations in a significant way is fraught with risks for both parties. For the applicants, there is great risk that they simply won't like the new location—or their accompanying family members won't. For the company, such employees are subject to the stresses of a young, fast-growing venture on top of the difficult home situation. Years ago, many Philadelphia-based start-ups found it difficult to recruit people into the Philadelphia suburban area. Even though candidates saw that the housing and school opportunities were far superior to other cities, they remained reluctant because there were too few other companies to go to if the venture did not succeed. Now, as more high-tech companies are locating in the region, and the ecosystem has expanded, it has become much easier to convince potential employees that, even if the job that moved them here doesn't work out, there will be ample opportunity for them in their specialty in the Philadelphia region.

Technology has allowed geographically remote employees to break the geographic boundary limits. With one or two visits a month to the corporate facility, the remote worker can retain enough personal contact and credibility for the rest of his work, which is arriving via e-mail or other remote technologies. Hiring remote workers means marketing to them where they live—on the Internet—and demonstrating a culture that integrates remote workers. However, as discussed later in the sections "Building a Team and Corporate Culture" and "Choosing the Prospect," it is still critical to develop personal and in-person relationships between recruits, the teams with which they may work, and the company.

Experience also segments the roles for team members. Entrepreneurial companies often have the luxury of hiring based on raw skill, rather than experience because they are going into business and product areas in which there may be no relevant experience. Inexperienced millennials, who can serve as Jacks or Jills of all trades, may be more responsive to the hiring message of a technology start-up than someone with five to eight years of experience and career track at a bigger company. However, there really is no substitute for experience. The less training a company needs to provide, the faster they can get their product to market. What is important in an entrepreneurial company is the right mix of experienced people, who have some idea of how things can be done, with entry-level talent, who know no limits to what can be accomplished. And what is most important is a team unified by a common mission—to build the company.

In short, there are many needs and ways to evaluate segments of recruits and match them with the needs of the company.

Differentiation: Setting Yourself Apart

The second part of positioning your venture in the competitive space for talent is differentiation—making sure that the most talented people will choose to work with you over other, competitive companies. People usually like to work in compatible environments—that is, they want to work with people who are more like them than not. Google, for example, has created the perception that the world's smartest people work there. To support this idea, they sponsor an annual global competition called Code Jam. Code Jam presents three difficult problems that must be solved correctly in 75 minutes. Google's 2014 Code Jam attracted over 25,000 applicants from around the world who competed in four rounds; 25 finalists together with the 2013 winner were selected to enter the competition. Code Jam serves both to raise Google's awareness as a seeker of highly intelligent engineers and to be used as a recruiting tool. As a result, they are able to hire many of the world's best minds—not just programmers, but also writers, marketers, salespeople, and so on.

Apple Computer, Inc., has fostered the perception that people who work there "think different" and are not afraid to challenge the status quo. Their consumer advertising campaign and their hiring speeches make the same point. When Steve Jobs was trying to lure

John Sculley away from his senior post at PepsiCo, he asked, "Do you want to change the world, or just sell soda the rest of your life?" Jobs successfully put forth the message of Apple in its hiring as well as its operations.

For other large companies, there are specific positioning messages designed to communicate differentiation and attract employees with whom the message resonates. McDonald's is "everyone's first job," and, as they try to hire more senior citizens, may be everyone's last job as well. Goldman Sachs, Disney, and McKinsey & Company are perceived as the best places to learn strategic thinking and to become part of the American corporate elite. Procter & Gamble is the place to learn all about brand marketing. All of these companies set themselves apart from the other employers.

For the high-growth company, differentiation for prospective employees should be simple and straightforward. They may have to work very long hours, with most of the rewards coming psychologically in the early stages, and through stock options exercised much later. This is why the company's mission and culture must be compelling and come through in a few sentences or images. Just as important as "the elevator speech" that you should be able to give to a prospective investor is your firm's positioning with a prospective employee. The prospective employee should know exactly why your company is a different and better place to work. But it is not just about messaging. Your vision and culture must be reflected in every interaction you have.

Building a Team and Corporate Culture

Although the company's mission might be a key differentiator, the company's culture might also set it apart from other prospective employers. Although every hiring decision is critical and needs to be looked at on an individual basis, the collection of early hiring decisions determines what type of team spirit and corporate culture will be created. At the start of a company, the culture is set by the founder's personality. As a company grows, it must adopt its own personality, separate from the founder and unique in its identity. There is no such thing as a good or bad culture, only a strong or weak culture.

Strong culture espouses the core values of the company in all aspects of the business and helps employees make decisions consistent with the goals of the company. Employees who behave in a manner consistent with culture are comfortable. Those who do not, in the words of Jim Collins, the author of *Built to Last,* "will be expunged like a virus."[3] Weak cultures breed inconsistency and eventually discontent.

W.L. Gore & Associates (Gore), founded in 1958, has a unique entrepreneurial culture based on a nonhierarchical meritocracy that cultivates innovation. Although the company has more than 10,000 employees in 45 locations around the world, they have no hierarchical structure. All Gore employees are "associates;" there are no managers, directors, vice presidents, or other hierarchical titles (although there are some used for external relationships only). New associates have mentors who help indoctrinate them into the culture. Projects are managed by teams of associates, and project "leaders" emerge from a concept of "followership," in which leaders earn followers. No Gore facility has more than 200 associates, to reinforce the collaborative, team-oriented approach. New products may be initiated by any associate, and other associates choose projects to work on based on interest and ability to contribute. Although resource allocations do require input from those with budgetary responsibility, every project must prove itself.

This structural approach is unique and is reinforced by four guiding principles developed by Bill Gore, the founder, and still in place today:

Guiding Principles[4]

- **Freedom:** The company was designed to be an organization in which associates can achieve their own goals best by directing their efforts toward the success of the corporation; action is prized; ideas are encouraged; and making mistakes is viewed as part of the creative process. We define freedom as being empowered to encourage each other to grow in knowledge, skill, scope of responsibility, and range of activities. We believe that associates will exceed expectations when given the freedom to do so.

- **Fairness:** Everyone at Gore sincerely tries to be fair with each other, our suppliers, our customers, and anyone else with whom we do business.

- **Commitment:** We are not assigned tasks; rather, we each make our own commitments and keep them.

- **Waterline:** Everyone at Gore consults with other associates before taking actions that might be "below the waterline"—causing serious damage to the company.

The only way for a 10,000+ person company to continue to thrive is if all employees are committed to and live by these principles. Although many believe that they would love to work in a company culture like Gore's, it is unique, and not everyone can live by and thrive in such an environment.[5]

In addition to a single, strong culture, growing a company requires different roles and personality types in your teams. You need entrepreneurs and visionaries who can work at the 50,000-foot level and not be deterred by small, uphill battles that occur each day. You also need people who enjoy the detail-oriented administrative tasks and those who will grind out the work. You also need those who can manage and integrate the people and processes of the organization. Showing a new recruit that your team works together with common purpose is a key marketing element in successfully hiring the best. Work to show recruits your company's personality to allow them to determine if they are a good fit with the community that they'll be joining.

Reaching the Prospects

Establishing your company's positioning and culture does not help you build the team, unless you get the message out and attract the talent. The same public marketing techniques discussed in Section Two, "Demand-Generation and Sales—Lead Your Customers to Your Offering," can be applied to marketing for talent. Tell your story through the media and all of your stakeholders to portray why your company is a winner, and recruits will flock to your door. Deliver on the promise of your story and provide fair compensation, and they will stay.

MetricStream, the enterprise Governance, Risk, and Compliance software company, proactively uses public relations to assist in recruiting, especially for their Bangalore, India, operation. As a venture-funded private company, they compete against large, well-known multinational firms for talent in a market where the brand of the company you work for is a key decision factor. Although Metric-Stream has a small customer footprint in India, they aggressively seek out interviews and article placements in Indian media. The sole purpose is to raise the company's awareness in a highly competitive hiring market. They also engage in high-profile activities. For example, MetricStream fielded a cricket team, complete with branded uniforms, that plays in intercompany tournaments. Cricket is a popular pastime in India, and these events draw huge crowds. MetricStream receives great branding for the cost of uniforms and entry fees. The strategy has paid off. The company has been able to grow their Bangalore research and development (R&D) division to over 400 employees in spite of the highly competitive environment. In addition, their attrition was less than half the market rate.

Although they may be effective, traditional want ads and classified job ads are rarely the mainstay of the start-up. Most of the candidates are reached via networking, job fairs, headhunters, and online media. Often, if the publicity surrounding the company is strong enough, résumés will flow in unbidden, from those who want to latch onto the hot new company.

Every employee, from the founder down, must be told to keep watch for any good talent and encourage those who qualify to apply, even when a specific job is not open. Your own employees are great judges of the "chemistry" fit of a candidate, and because one of the keys to successful organizations, and to job satisfaction, is having a best friend at the office, letting people recommend and potentially hire their best friends is a good way to ensure success. Such hires have lower turnover rates and better prospects. They also cost the company far less than standard headhunter fees.

Job fairs are an efficient way to focus your start-up on hiring. Post at local colleges and universities, advertise on the Internet, and hold an open house for two to three hours late some afternoon (typically 5:00 p.m.–8:00 p.m.). Many universities, including the University of

Pennsylvania (with whom the authors are affiliated), cultivate career opportunities for their students with start-ups. Start-up company-specific job fairs and job boards may help keep students apprised of opportunities.

Job fairs allow companies who have jobs an opportunity to engage those interested in positions. Similarly, the fairs may provide an opportunity for candidates to talk with people from many different functional areas in the company. In the Idealab incubators, where there are always 5–10 companies, they held job fairs in which each of these incubating companies, and the other 20 companies created that have moved away, set up a table with a few of their people. As a control mechanism, each applicant talks with a limited number of companies—usually 3–5. That way, the number of competing offers is limited, and the amount of duplicate processing is cut down. The applicants sort themselves by degree of risk averseness by the companies they choose to talk to because those who have been in business for years (such as CitySearch and GoTo.com) get the lower risk takers, and the ones who have started in the past week get the high risk takers.

Networking with local faculty members at a college or university near your company is crucial to seeing the best talent before it is pre-emptively taken off the market. If the professors know what you're looking for, they can recommend people to you long before they would think of themselves as being in the job market. One good way to get access to this talent pool is the use of students as interns. There are many well-defined tasks—market research, for example—that can be done by a student or student team during a semester course. This allows the student/prospect and the company to evaluate one another with no obligations and without having to make the hiring decision until after you have really seen both the work and work ethic of the candidate. In fact, this approach is the equivalent of adaptive testing for talent!

Choosing the Prospect

There are many people who play a role in the hiring process, and each needs to be trained in the marketing and sales function associated with recruiting. When the human resources person (or department, as a company grows) starts out, she should have the mission statement and position description clearly in mind. A key differentiator in entrepreneurial companies, however, is that whatever the position description says, there are likely to be other responsibilities because there are never enough employees to fill all the roles in a new venture. This message has to be put across to the recruit.

In the army, it is "unit cohesion," the sense of belonging to a small tightly knit group, which makes men and women willing to give their lives to save their fellow unit members. Entrepreneurial companies are also fighting key battles, and unit cohesion is critical. Hence, it is very important to have potential hires interview not only with HR and the specific workgroup manager, but also with most members of the group in which they'll work. Each of these members has to market not only the company's mission and vision, but also the ethos of their own unit and has to be convinced that the recruit will contribute to the cohesion and success of the unit.

In fact, create a hiring team of those in the company who understand both the role of the position and the core values and culture of the company. Focus your interviewing on the desired behaviors of the recruit. Create questions for candidates that pose situations and ask how they have handled similar situations in the past or situations that they believe demonstrated the approach they would take. Have each member of the interviewing team rate, evaluate, and even vote on the candidate according to the desired behaviors. The additional benefit of team-based behavioral interviewing is gaining buy-in of the recruit from key employees who are engaged in the hiring process. See Table 11-1 for a sample interview rating template and Table 11-2 for a sample candidate comparison matrix.

Table 11-1 Candidate Interview Rating (*Courtesy of Ellen Weber, Antiphony Partners, LLC*)

Position: _____

Date: _____

Name of Applicant: _____

Name of Interviewer: _____

The Technical/Job Skills to Be Evaluated	Very Strong Evidence Skill Not Present (1)	Strong Evidence Skill Not Present (2)	Some Evidence Skill Is Present (3)	Strong Evidence Skill Is Present (4)	Very Strong Evidence Skill Is Present (5)	Insufficient Evidence for or Against Skill Presence (N/A)

The Performance Skills to Be Evaluated	Very Strong Evidence Skill Not Present (1)	Strong Evidence Skill Not Present (2)	Some Evidence Skill Is Present (3)	Strong Evidence Skill Is Present (4)	Very Strong Evidence Skill Is Present (5)	Insufficient Evidence for or Against Skill Presence (N/A)
1. Integrity						
2. Customer satisfaction						
3. Passion and commitment						
4. Accountability, responsibility, trust						
5. Teamwork						
6. Communication						

RECOMMENDATION: Hire/Promote _____ Not Hire/Promote _____

JOB-RELATED REASON(S) FOR RECOMMENDATION:

Table 11-2 Candidate Comparison (*Courtesy of Ellen Weber, Antiphony Partners, LLC*)

Position: _____ Name of Interviewer: _____

Date: _____

Replace Candidate #1 with name of Candidate, etc. Then enter scores from individual Candidate Scorecard, and compare.

The Technical/Job Skills to Be Evaluated	Candidate #1	Candidate #2	Candidate #3	Candidate #4	Candidate #5	Comments

The Performance Skills to Be Evaluated	Candidate #1	Candidate #2	Candidate #3	Candidate #4	Candidate #5	Comments
1. Integrity						
2. Customer satisfaction						
3. Passion and commitment						
4. Accountability, responsibility, trust						
5. Teamwork						
6. Communication						

RECOMMENDATIONS: _____

Although these hiring practices are applicable to all candidates, each programmer has his or her own style. Development departments—so important to success in the technology industry—create their own sets of rules and conventions. Making sure that a new entrant into an existing group can work within, and perhaps extend, the group's style can be the difference between the success and failure not only of the recruit, but also of the company. In one open source software venture, the head of the group was a maverick who defied most standard programming rules to create a much more efficient e-commerce engine. When hiring for his group, he made sure that he kept a mix of mavericks and traditionalists so that the creative energy led to productive code, not chaos.

In addition to ensuring cultural fit and the appropriate behaviors, it also is important to test throughout the recruitment process, where possible, to determine whether the candidate has the relevant skills. Technical companies, both start-up and established companies like Google, will have a series of programming tests to ensure that the candidate has the required skills *before* proceeding further in the recruitment process. Many companies use assessments to determine organizational fit and approaches that recruits will take according to standardized frameworks. In addition, these same tools may be used upon hiring to continue to monitor and improve employee performance. Assessments like Myers-Briggs Type Indicator® (MBTI®) and DiSC® (DiSC stands for dominance, influence, steadiness, and conscientiousness) determine *how* a recruit approaches work and interactions with others. The Clifton StrengthFinder assessment helps identify a recruit's particular strengths and allows the company to further assess how a candidate might fit within the company and contribute to its needs.

Recruitment has even begun to adopt the trends in software services. Companies like SkillSurvey (a company in which one of the authors invested) use a cloud-based service and patented data analytics to improve talent hiring and management. One key premise of SkillSurvey, and hiring in general, is that past performance is the best indicator of future performance. Therefore, the better job you do of understanding the recruit's experience, skills, capabilities, and approaches, the more likely you are to make a good choice.

Compensation: Pricing Your Talent

One additional important consideration for talent is pricing, or compensation. Compensation packages at entrepreneurial companies are widely varied and usually balance cash compensation (including commission) and equity participation, which allows the employee to share in the upside potential of a company. Especially in the first few months of the company's existence, offers may be custom tailored to match the applicant's needs for cash, deferred compensation, equity, and other benefits. The *perceived* value of a package of salary, options, and perks will vary widely with the age, maturity, stage of life, and relocation status of the employee. As with the market's perception of the value of your offering, employee perception of the value of your compensation is critical to success.

A key consideration both for you and your potential hires is fairness, both in terms of fair market value for the job being performed and agreement by both parties that compensation is perceived as fair. It is common for many start-up companies to pay little (or nothing) and combine this with equity compensation. Although entrepreneurs may believe that paying in equity is "less expensive" than paying in cash, the exact opposite is true. It may conserve cash, but compensating in equity at an early stage is expensive. Because the risk associated with equity is at its highest, so too is the expected return. Therefore, to shift the risk to the employee (or an investor) requires you to pay a lot in the future value of the company.

From the employee's perspective, misunderstanding about the value and liquidity of equity can lead to tremendous conflict. If an employee believes that the 10,000 shares in a start-up she is being paid in lieu of cash can readily be sold for $100 per share when the company goes public next year, she will have a huge letdown if those expectations are not met. It is best for all parties for the company to pay fair market value for the job required and use equity as the compensation for the risk the employee is taking by working for a start-up. If you really want to use equity instead of cash, be sure the employee understands the risk she is taking and ensure that the amount of equity is commensurate with the risk.

One final word of advice about equity compensation is to use vesting schedules. Companies and their investors want significant contributors to share in the value they create in the company. However, they do not want to see equity leave with employees before that value is created. As a result, structure equity compensation to allow employees to earn the equity over time as well as reap the rewards of the equity earned as a company scales and succeeds.

Summary

Talent is the most valuable asset for a company. Attracting the best talent is a marketing challenge like any other. All the concepts for helping improve the interface between the company and its customers are also important for improving the interface between the company and its current and prospective employees. Start with a clear vision and positioning for the company and adapt as the company scales and the needs change. Understand the benefits and limitations of homogenous teams, and ensure you take advantage of the innovation and creativity that a diverse team can offer. As you identify talent, balance the needs to be filled with the experience, capabilities, and commitment of the talent you find. Use a combination of hiring team and assessment tools to better understand how a recruit fits and can most effectively contribute to your company. And, finally, remember that a strong culture can unify a team with core values and allow the right talent to deliver outstanding results.

Endnotes

1. Company website and personal interview with Mark Palatucci, 2014.

2. N. Wasserman, *The Founder's Dilemma: Anticipating and Avoiding the Pitfalls That Can Sink a Startup* (Princeton, NJ: Princeton University Press, 2012).

3. J. Collins & J. Porras, *Built to Last: Successful Habits of Visionary Companies* (New York, NY: Harper Business, 2002, p. 9).

4. Gore website: www.gore.com/en_xx/careers/whoweare/
   whatwebelieve/gore-culture.html.

5. Gore website and personal interviews with Gore associates, June
   2014 (J. Babin, Interviewer).

12————————————————

Marketing for Financing Activities

Pebble: Preserving Equity with Crowdfunding and Venture Funding

On February 24, 2015, Pebble Technology Corp., the company introduced in Chapter 10, "Create an Ecosystem to Maximize Product/Service Lifetime Profitability," launched its second Kickstarter campaign. The Pebble Time crowdfunding campaign shattered the record for fund-raising in a single Kickstarter campaign and redefined how crowdfunding can be used. Pebble began its start-up funding process in a common manner, participating in the Y Combinator accelerator program and securing $375,000 in angel funding. The company followed this with a Kickstarter campaign that raised an unusually high amount of $10.3 million. This demonstration of market demand and company capability helped the company raise a $15 million Series A round from Charles River Ventures, which allowed the company to scale its sales and distribution for the Pebble Watch as well as continue product design and development. Then Pebble returned to crowdfunding to launch its next-generation product, fund its working capital needs, and generate tremendous buzz.[1]

The Pebble Time Kickstarter campaign raised more than $20 million, breaking the record set by the Coolest Cooler, which in turn had bested Pebble's first record-breaking campaign. Although some have questioned Pebble's use of crowdfunding for follow-on product funding, the benefits to the company, customers, and product positioning are outstanding. Pebble raised a significant "round of investment" without diluting its current shareholders' equity. The campaign allowed Pebble to gauge the market's interest in its next-generation product, raised the working capital required to manufacture the product, and provided accurate estimates of demand to forecast revenues and profitability. Finally, the success of the campaign also allowed Pebble to watch the number of backers and funding increase while calculating the potential savings from decreasing cost of goods sold as larger volumes provided greater economies of scale.

The results and timing of the campaign delivered significant marketing benefits to Pebble and perceived value to its customers. As Eric Migicovsky, Pebble's CEO, shared that the "Kickstarter backers were the ones that cared the most so it wanted to reward their years of support."[2] The number of records the campaign set was impressive and further fueled the media attention. Pebble met its $500,000 funding goal in 17 minutes, was the fastest campaign to reach $1 million in funding (49 minutes), raised more than $5 million in one day, and broke its own $10.3 million funding record from its first Kickstarter campaign in 48 hours. One week later, Pebble made a new announcement for the campaign, launching a premium version of the product, the Pebble Time Steel, which further boosted the campaign, breaking the all-time Kickstarter campaign record. In addition to the Pebble Time Steel, the company announced Smartstraps, which further expanded the Pebble platform to allow developers to expand the ecosystem with capabilities built in to watchbands that interfaced with the Pebble and its apps.

The Pebble Time campaign was launched prior to Apple's March 9, 2015 event, during which it provided details about its upcoming Apple Watch. However, Pebble would deliver its Pebble Time to Kickstarter backers after the Apple Watch's planned availability. All of this well-timed and executed activity generated tremendous marketing buzz, causing a flurry of blogs, articles, and press in both the technology and general media. This, in turn, drove more campaign backers. Of course, only time will tell who will win in the burgeoning smartwatch market.

The Pebble Time Kickstarter campaign also was an outstanding value in terms of return on marketing investment and customer acquisition cost (CAC). When the campaign concluded on March 27, 2015, Pebble had achieved the following results:

- More than 78,000 backers
- More than 95,000 units (both Pebble Time and Pebble Time Steel)
- More than $20 million raised
- Average unit price of $200.00

Kickstarter's standard campaign fee is 5%, which means that Pebble's CAC for the campaign is $10/unit. Although Pebble probably could have sold the new products directly to its user community, 5% is a small percentage to pay for the incredible results and amount of free press received.*

The outstanding results of Pebble's crowdfunding campaigns are made all the more amazing when you realize that the company turned to crowdfunding initially because they could not raise funding from the venture capital community!

Financing: A Different Product for a Different Customer

One of the most important jobs of marketing is to help an entrepreneurial venture show its best side when raising money or maintaining stock price. Some of these concepts are applicable to early stage companies, some to later stage, and many to all companies, no matter what their stage of growth and financing. It is critical to note that when marketing to potential investors, your product is a share of stock (or debt instruments), not the product or service the company hopes to sell. Although investors may, at times, be customers also, their motivation for being a customer for stock is to maximize a risk-adjusted return. Hence, they are most likely to provide funds, at good valuations, to companies perceived as winners. It is marketing's job to position the company as a (the) winner, leader, most advanced, world-class competitor in its space. Being a leader will most often lead

---

*Although we have no direct knowledge of a discount, it would not surprise the authors if Pebble was able to negotiate a fee for the campaign that was less than 5%, which would make the marketing ROI even stronger.

to good financial returns on the products, which in turn will cause the company's valuation, in either public or merger transactions, to rise.

The other function of a good financial marketing plan is to create a sense of urgency, to counteract the oft-given venture response of "I'll put money in if you have a lead." The long-drawn-out "No," which is the response of most venture firms, is painful for a company that needs capital today for expansion, for growth of sales forces, or to complete product development. Because there is a natural tendency not to be the first one to jump into the pool, a great marketing plan will provide the incentives to act early. The right pitch aids in finding the lead investor, who will negotiate the specific terms, take a board seat, and help set direction.

In today's world, companies like Pebble may decide on a crowd-funding approach where appropriate. The success of crowdfunding usually depends on a great video and wide social media distribution to get potential crowdfunders to the site. Because some crowdfunding is based on product sales, it creates zero dilution. AngelList, Funder's Club, and others also let you sell shares directly to the public in the United States. Although this does create dilution, it can be a way to leverage a few influencers into a multimillion-dollar round. The Jumpstart Our Business Startups (JOBS), signed into law in 2012, may expand the potential sources of dilutive crowdfunding sources beyond the traditional accredited investor.

The marketing group, or individual in the early stages, must work with the CEO and whoever is taking on the CFO role to create an investor presentation that concentrates on the target market segment, which may include venture capitalists, banks, and strategic partner investors. The CFO needs to provide the detailed financial information, while marketing has to boil that down to two slides that help sustain the proper level of excitement. Too much hyperbole, and the pitch may lack credibility or generate legal liability. In a recent pitch, one of the authors heard a group start out with, "Our new Internet business will take over the users of Amazon, eBay, and Google because of our easier-to-use interface." Their financial projections were then based on taking tens of millions of users from these well-established leaders, all in the first year and a half of operation. With such total lack of credibility, none of the people present even heard much of the rest of the pitch.

At later stages, in preparation for an acquisition or initial public offering (IPO), marketing works with investment bankers to create a presentation for potential acquirers or investors. In these cases, there is a key role for the proper and legally limited ways to present the financial and product prospects for the company.

Product Versus Financial Marketing

There are many differences between product marketing and financial marketing, but the similarities are even more numerous. In both, you need to target the consumer of the goods and services by working through the chain of influencers and key decision makers, gatekeepers, and naysayers in order to have maximum impact. In both, getting key benefits understood by all is crucial.

One major difference between product and financial marketing is timing. Although the product marketing campaign can often be postponed to coincide with completion of a set of product features, failure to execute financial marketing may mean loss of funds and nowhere to turn—shutting down the business. The key elements of positioning, naming, and pricing still apply, but to the company and its stock, not the product itself.

A Financial Marketing Plan

Gust is a global Software as a Service (SaaS) funding platform for the sourcing and management of early stage investments. The service has helped to standardize across the early stage funding industry the type of information you should provide. See Table 12-1 for a summary of the Gust company profile. Because you only have a limited time to get your message across, figuring out how to sell your shares in this format is an important step. It gets at the product, the people, the prospects, and the finance all in one standardized document. This template provides a valuable lesson in how to pitch to entice a longer meeting. You should also look on www.kickstarter.com or www.indiegogo.com to see the type of videos used to generate crowdfunding.

Table 12-1   Gust Company Profile (*Adapted from gust.com*)

Company Name and Basic Information
- One-line pitch that highlights your unique selling proposition
- Stage, industry, location, year founded, number of employees, Website URL

Executive Summary
- Management team
  Who are the members of your management team, and how will their experience aid in your success?
- Customer problem
  What customer problem does your product and/or service solve?
- Products and services
  Describe your product and/or service and detail the key customer benefits.
- Target market
  Detail the geographic, demographic, and psychographic characteristics that define your target market.
- Customers
  Outline who your customers are and why you are targeting them.
- Sales and marketing strategy
  What is your customer acquisition and retention strategy? Detail how you will promote, sell, and create customer loyalty for your market offering.
- Business model
  What strategy will you employ to build, deliver, and retain company value?
- Competitors
  Describe the competitive landscape and your competitors' strengths and weaknesses.
- Competitive advantage
  What is your company's competitive advantage (for example, processes, patents, first-mover advantage, expertise, or proprietary technology)?

Financials
- Funding History (USD)
  Add any previous funding rounds.
- Current Funding Round (USD)
  Detail your stage of funding, the capital you're seeking, and your premoney valuation.
- Annual Financials (USD)
  Enter your financials for this year and last year, as well as projections for the following three years. Investors like to compare and evaluate financial performance over this time frame, so do your best to complete it.
- Annual revenue run rate
- Monthly burn rate

continues

	2016	2017	2018	2019	2020
Revenue driver					
Revenue $					
Expenditure $					
Profit (loss) $					

Additional Materials (Upload)
- Pitch deck to help investors evaluate your company (PowerPoint or PDF)
- Short pitch video similar to what you may find on Kickstarter or Indiegogo

The Buying Center

Just as every product marketer has a set of hurdles to jump through, so too do the CFO and CEO when selling the image of the company. There are several service professionals, other than the investors, who are involved in advising on investments. For many venture firms or investors, the first test is the analyst or associate who screens the business plan. They are hired to keep too many plans from cluttering the partners' desks or minds and get points for saying no early. However, they lose double points if a competitor gets a deal they should have bid on. Thus, telling the analyst at Firm 1 that Firm 2 is preparing a terms sheet can short-circuit the turndown. Be sure you are accurately reflecting the situation when communicating these messages.

After the analyst, the venture firms will often bring in outside "experts" to help them in fields in which they are not *au courant*. These consultants have their own agendas, along with the formal assignment from the venture fund. It is quite common for them to offer their services directly to the company after they have made a positive recommendation. They may facilitate the communications between a technically oriented founder and the financially oriented venture capitalist. The company should use its review time as an opportunity to gain valuable competitive intelligence because these experts have a broader view of the competitive space than most founders.

Segmentation of Investors

The customers for fledgling company stock fall into several categories: customers who might crowdfund, angels, venture capital companies, incubators and accelerators, corporate strategic buyers, or institutional investors. Each has a particular place in the investment food chain and is matched to certain types of companies and investments. Although the largest percentage of money invested in early stage companies come from venture capitalists, the larger number of investments and number of investors are in the friends, family, and angels category.

Crowdfunding

In today's open marketplace, companies can get money directly from individuals, sometimes without giving up any equity ownership. The main models are rewards-based crowdfunding, pioneered by kickstarter.com and indiegogo.com. Here, people give money to get rewards, which range from early product shipments, hats, T-shirts, placement in a movie or a book, and many more creative ones. In addition to the Pebble Watch campaigns discussed earlier, the virtual reality Oculus Rift raised almost $2.5 million before the company was bought for $2 billion by Facebook. Early product sales on the crowdfunding platforms can show angel and venture firms that there is real demand for the product or service and ease the path to additional funding.

A key element in a successful crowdfunding campaign is a video, showing how the product will look and act once it is completed. These can take serious time to produce, but are crucial in getting user attention. Once the campaign is started, social media is the main method of spreading awareness of the new product, drawing people to the crowdfunding page, and hopefully to contribute and be part of making your corporate dream come true.

Equity crowdfunding is quite different from rewards-based crowdfunding. On the equity crowdfunding sites—AngelList, Funders Club, CircleUp, and others—you are reaching out directly to accredited investors who will buy shares in the company. On these sites, a fully fleshed-out business plan is also critical, as well as a video and more detailed links.

On AngelList and Funders Club, not only can investors make their own decisions based on the material you provide, but they can also follow other, more experienced investors in what are called syndicates. If you attract the attention of a large syndicate, you can raise several million dollars in one fell swoop. The site is curated, and you must submit a plan or have an existing AngelList member post that she is investing—so getting that first angel can be crucial.

Whereas AngelList and Funders Club seem to specialize in tech companies, CircleUp specializes in consumer products, including foods, physical goods, and services companies. Try to understand which platform (and there are many others) has the right audience for the industry or market you are in.

On any of these sites, you have to be clear and concise about what your product or service does and how it benefits a particular customer base. You need a pitch deck that works when you're not there to explain or answer questions.

Given a number of changes in the securities laws post the 2008 financial crisis, angels and individual investors have more opportunity than ever, and you can now reach them through these networking sites.

Angels

Although angels may still be approached one at a time, the high-tech world has organized this channel so that it can be more easily reached. Angels now operate in clubs and formal funds to facilitate deal flow, due diligence, investments, and monitoring of companies. The New York Angels, formed in 2004, has a rigorous screening process for new business plans. In the second week of each month, a subset of the members sees quick pitches from about fifteen companies. They select three to four to present to the members during the last week of the month. Each of those companies gets some marketing help (presentation training and critique) during the week before the presentation. If some of the members like a company, due diligence sessions are held at the beginning of the next month. Many of the members offer not just money, but also access to their networks of contacts, which can be of great help in establishing market awareness of a new company.

The Angel Capital Association was formed in late 2004 to help share best practices among the hundreds of angel groups. Almost 800 groups have joined by now. Its website, http://www.angelcapitalasso-ciation.org/, has descriptions and contact information for angel groups throughout the world. The gust.com website also allows you to create and submit a plan for angel groups and some seed stage venture firms (see Table 12-1).

MIT Entrepreneur's Forums are held in several cities. Philadel-phia has the League of Retired Executives (LORE), Robin Hood Ventures, and a local chapter of the global Keiretsu Forum. Los Angeles has the Tech Coast Angels. In each of these, members agree to invest at least $25,000 in a start-up each year. They get to make the choice. Negotiating valuation with angel groups is very idiosyn-cratic and may result in higher valuations than the venture capital firms would provide.

To get the opportunity to reach these organized angel groups, a company should find a member to sponsor them; sponsorship may be required for some groups. Lawyers, accountants, professors, or other successful entrepreneurs can make the introductions for new start-ups that do not already have a link to this community.

Venture Capital Firms

The most visible and helpful investments come from the estab-lished venture capital firms. More than 350 funds belong to the National Venture Capital Association, and there are undoubtedly hun-dreds of other funds. The typical venture partnership has $50–$500 million to invest over a three- to four-year period and assumes that their initial investment will require at least as much in later rounds. Because the scarce asset of these firms is partner time, they need to put $2–$10 million into each deal. (The most recent megafunds are trying to put five or ten times that amount.) Firms such as Bench-mark Capital, Andreessen Horowitz, or Sequoia want to take an active role in helping the portfolio companies grow and provide a *keiretsu*

(Japanese for a corporate family) to help their companies help one another.

The largest venture firms now see tens of thousands of business plans each year and fund only a handful (typically less than one per month). How can a company work to maximize its chances with these 1,000-to-1 odds? First, almost all of the venture firms only fund plans that have been referred to them by someone they know and trust. This first screen is extremely important and requires that a company have an advisor (lawyer, accountant, technologist, professor) who is known to the venture firm. That person can make a telephone call or send an e-mail that describes the key business idea or differentiator in a few sentences. If the venture firm has any interest, it will then request either a plan or a meeting. Here, the entrepreneur's marketing skills are put to the test. A few slides and a prototype must tell the story, show how the market being attacked is large enough to be worth the venture firm's valuable time, and transmit the passion of the entrepreneur to the partners. Venture firms are looking for markets that can get to between $100 million and $1 billion in a few years, while angel investors can fund companies that may only do $25–$100 million.

In recent years, there has been a flood of seed funds created. These are smaller venture funds, often $15–$50 million, which focus on investing at the same stage as angels. They are often started by successful entrepreneurs who want to truly advise and mentor while they are investing, but they have enough other people's money to make $100,000–$500,000 investments and help you grow.

Incubators and Accelerators

The incubator or accelerator is a more recent innovation as a source of help, including capital. Traditionally, incubators were more focused on providing space, and that concept has expanded to the accelerator. Idealab, Y Combinator, Techstars, ERA, DreamIt, and a large number of universities are all providing business accelerators, which may provide space, infrastructure, educational services, mentoring, and funding to help entrepreneurs get a fast start. Pitching to these accelerators is similar to the venture capital presentation, but the business team does not have to be as well formed. An incubator often provides accounting services, general office services, and some technical consulting to the various companies, as well as overall business advice. Accelerators provide these services and usually offer funding in exchange for equity. In addition, accelerators usually take in a "class" of 10–20 companies for a defined period of time (usually three to four months). The accelerator runs some classes and hopes the companies can help one another. They typically have a Demo Day, where local angels and venture capitalists come in to hear pitches from each company. The funding success rate is quite high, including such stars as Airbnb and Dropbox. As a result, there are now 50–100 applications for each spot. Techstars and DreamIt now operate in many cities, so one can benefit even if not in Silicon Valley or New York. Many are funded through industrial development funds to try and heighten job creation in a particular region.

In the last few years, we have seen a boom in accelerators. There are now hundreds of accelerators, and they have begun to specialize in industries, for example DreamIt Health for healthcare IT companies only, or functional areas like HardTech Labs for manufacturing only. As with all investor types, not all accelerators are created equal, and you are best served finding the accelerators with the best track record in terms of success of graduates.

Corporate Strategic Partners/Investors

Many large corporations have started venture funds, partly for the financial gains that can be earned but mainly to keep a strategic eye on new developments in their sphere of interest. Many of the innovations that change industries start in the smallest, rather than the largest companies. Intel, Cisco, and even Samsung all have venture funds so that they can benefit from the technologies and business models that new companies have created.

If your entrepreneurial venture has received any visibility at trade shows, in the trade press, and so on, you may be contacted by these groups. They are often brought in as coinvestors by the established venture firms.

Institutional Investors

Finally, there are hundreds of investment bankers and finders who will try to help you raise money from qualified institutional buyers. These investors usually want to make large investments ($10 million and up). They are usually willing to pay placement fees. Early stage companies that do not have such large cash requirements may find this market hard to tap.

Naming

It is easier for people to remember who you are and what your company does if it has a well-thought-through name. At Idealab, names may be crucial—in more than one instance, the fact that a sufficiently catchy URL was not obtained stopped the investment into the company. The URL for Tickets.com, along with the 1-800-TICKETS phone number, were purchased for a substantial sum in order to get the benefits of quick consumer and investor recognition and remembrance of the company's business area. CarsDirect.com, for example, immediately says that you'll be dealing with a company in the automotive sector.

As with any nonfunctional name—for example, Google, eBay, Amazon.com—both the product and investor marketing are required to associate the business plan to the name in the minds of customers or investors. In some of these cases, there is high brand value to the name in both consumer and investor contexts. However, this brand value may take more time and financial resources to build. Chapter 13, "Building Strong Brands and Strong Companies," discusses how marketing and focus can build the value of your brand.

When naming an app, you need to make it easy to find in the App Store. With over a million apps in each the iTunes App Store and Google Play, this can be a challenge. Fortunately, you can create links to the download page so that customers and investors do not have to sort through 50 apps with the same name as yours.

In many cases, the name used to market to investors is quite different than the name used to market to customers. IAC (Barry Diller's InterActive Corp.) is well known to investors as the place to buy shares in a company that owns Ticketmaster, City Search, Expedia, Hotels.com, and about 40 other businesses. Internet Brands was chosen by CarsDirect.com when they expanded into mortgages, housing, and other businesses—each of which has multiple channels to the consumer. Those consumers are not the ones buying shares, and hence a name that makes more sense to the investment community was chosen.

Pricing—The Value of Your Venture

Just as product pricing is an art as well as a science, the pricing of offerings in companies is even more so. Once a company is public, and there is a "free market" for its stock, the price will be set in that marketplace. We will come back to this in the discussion of investor relations. In the private markets, the marketplace is extremely limited, and there are two types of prices—those set by the buyer or investor (low) and those set by the seller or company in the face of excess demand (high). What permits a company to get into the latter category is superior marketing of a strong company.

The key elements that need to be marketed to investors, in addition to the product, are the people (management team), the opportunity, the financial model, and any strategic relationships that the company may have entered into. Because the investor is buying a fraction of the company, not an instance of the product, it is the expected exit value that is most important. When there was an Internet stock mania, this value was projected high by some investors and lower by others. After the Internet stock crash, there was a period where no value was low enough, and the venture community stopped investing in all but the "sure things" that came their way. Currently, rationality has returned to the pricing process, and both entrepreneurs and investors have more realistic views of how to price their shares.

An idea from a new, untried entrepreneur and group of qualified engineers, marketers, and so on may be worth 20%–50% of the equity of a company for an initial cash investment of $250,000–$1 million. With a seasoned team of entrepreneurs, located in Silicon Valley, raising $5 million for 30% of the equity would not be unusual. There are regional biases in pricing of seed rounds, with the Bay area giving the highest premoney valuations, somewhat less in the New York and Boston markets, and less still in the rest of the country.

The marketing message around a successful team is clear—"They did it before; they'll do it again." Particularly, if the team has either taken a company public or sold at a good price to a major player (for example, Cisco), their "product" has a seal of approval. In addition, the success of Google and Yahoo! has led to them buying small technology companies, prerevenue, for about $1 million per engineer. It lets them get hiring done and prevents people from getting established and commanding much more money later on.

Many angel investors will invest in the form of a note that will convert to shares that are priced later by more professional investors. For example, the New York Angels often invest $300,000–$500,000 in a convertible note, which converts with a 25%–50% discount into the next round. There is also a cap on the price of that next round so that a giant success still yields what would have been a rational price at the time of the angel's entry. This also protects against the angels offering too high a price and then being "crammed down" by a later, lower valuation when the company next needs funding.

Venture Marketing

In the prepublic stage, reaching investors can be done by getting mentioned in the key influencer magazines (and online e-zines) such as *TechCrunch, Re/Code,* and *Wired.* The technology publications are also a source that many venture capitalists use to try to find deals. More recently, websites such as Producthunt.com have arisen, which mine data from the app stores for early signals that an app is going viral or growing at above-normal rates. If yours is an app like that, you may start getting unsolicited calls from investors.

In each region of the country, there are also weekly and monthly business magazines that cover start-up firms. *Crain's New York Business* and *Philadelphia Business Journal* are examples of publications that can get a young company noticed by potential private (prepublic) investors.

Initial Public Offering (IPO)

For many companies in the software and Internet world, much of the reason for going public is marketing related. The mantra for seasoned Internet entrepreneurs is: "The IPO is the premier branding event for an Internet or mobile company." In fact, the amount of publicity and brand recognition that can be generated by a successful, high-profile IPO is enormous. Planning for an IPO is an arduous task, and the actual road show and offering are several of the most grueling months that a CEO and CFO will ever face. But each meeting and luncheon presentation is selling the company's products, message, and positioning, as well as its stock.

The first part of getting the message out is accomplished during the underwriter selection phase. At this stage, the various investment bankers are trying to sell the company on choosing their firm to participate in the lucrative fees associated with the IPO. From the company's point of view, however, this is a chance to familiarize many of the Wall Street analysts who might later cover or be asked to comment on the company's business and stock prospects.

Too many companies make the mistake of talking to only a small set of bankers. If they want a "first tier" or "bulge bracket" firm, such as Goldman Sachs, Morgan Stanley, or Merrill Lynch, they may feel it is not worth their time talking with 10–15 smaller players that want to be part of the offering. In fact, just as you would not tell a potential good customer to go away without speaking to them, you should not do the same to the bankers. It is often best to hone the pitch that will be given to the first-tier folks on some of the other firms. Their analysts can constructively criticize the positioning, projects, and passion your company shows in its presentation. This feedback can be valuable in getting the highest valuation from these firms. It is common to have one or two smaller, boutique firms as part of the offering underwriters.

Just as you would not run a TV ad that was not professionally scripted and produced, the IPO road show pitch itself requires the same care and professionalism. We have observed Power Presentations' Jerry Weissman, whose company helps create road show presentations and then coaches the speakers in dealing with audiences—large and small—in the most effective way. Jerry says that he can help add a few dollars to the stock price, and we actually believe it. Nancy Duarte's books and her consulting firm have also been used by many companies in their search for the perfect pitch.

The buyers for the IPO fall into several groups: institutional investors focused on momentum, long-term institutional holders, retail holders, and flippers. A balanced mix of all of these types are needed to have the company's stock in strong-enough hands, yet trade enough to be interesting to market makers who support the stock.

Investor Relations

Once the IPO has been completed, a company has to communicate with its investors to keep them informed and to keep the stock price consistent with the company's performance and promise. Although there are a number of firms that can help, in the same way that traditional public relations firms help with product positioning, most companies should have an in-house designee to handle investor queries, provide copies of reports, and coordinate the company's release of information on a quarterly basis, as well as its conference calls with analysts.

The conference call gives the company a chance to present itself to 30–100 key influencers each quarter. Many of the analysts on the call will be writing a report or set of comments for their clients—recommending whether or not to buy, sell, or hold the stock. We recommend the following four simple rules for these communications, as follows:

- Tell the truth, the whole truth, and nothing but the truth.
- Tell the bad news first.
- Don't over "spin" the good news.
- Don't get on the message boards.

Although the first point should be obvious, the temptation to omit some of the bad news or to hold back or spin the positive news can sometimes feel overwhelming. Don't succumb! There is a large group of plaintiff's lawyers just waiting for any mis-statements they can use

to successfully sue you. (Note "successfully"—they'll often sue any-
way on bad news, whether or not you've been telling the truth.)

Dealing with bad news is never easy. Getting it out of the way
of the market so that its impact on stock price has been felt—and
then allowing the price to recover on good news—is far better than
wasting some good news immediately before the bad news comes
out. It is also important that everyone gets all the bad news at the
same time—avoiding the selective disclosure that could give an unfair
market advantage to those who hear before others. Most companies
schedule their press releases and conference calls outside of market
hours. Now that the markets are moving toward 24-hour trading, this
is becoming more difficult, but it still makes sense to schedule outside
the standard 9:30 a.m. to 4:00 p.m. (eastern standard time) window
when the bulk of the trading takes place.

Finally, it is also tempting to add some "spin" to good news. A
small contract may be touted as a harbinger of much bigger ones, or a
move from losses to break even may be spun as a major turnaround. It
is better to let the investors draw their own positive conclusions than
to force them on the market.

Over the past few years, there has been a dramatic rise in the
availability of information on public companies, which has been good
for investors. At the same time, the message board phenomenon has
cropped up. On Yahoo!, Raging Bull, Silicon Investor, AOL, Mot-
ley Fool, and other places, there are places where "investors" (usually rank amateur speculators) can post any comments they want
about your stock. Although there are occasional nuggets, most of it is
drivel—uninformed, meant to hype or cut the price when a smarter
speculator has gone short or wants to go long. The SEC has been
working with the providers to curb the worst of the abuses—outright
lies meant to manipulate a stock—but there is still far too much mis-
leading information on the boards.

When your Investor Relations executives read these, they, or
other employees or officers, may be tempted to correct the mis-statements. *Don't.* Once you start correcting, the public may feel that you
have taken on the obligation to always correct them, a task that the
company should not, and may not legally, be able to do. False merger
rumors, for example, abound on these boards. Companies must say

"No Comment" to any questions about unannounced merger activity, or (the courts have ruled) they must always respond accurately. This makes it difficult to have secret negotiations because any leaks would have to be dignified by the company's comments.

You can get help from Yahoo! and the other providers if there is harm being done. In one case, a message poster falsely took on the name of the company's CEO. Because Yahoo! generally allows anyone to get any unused e-mail address, they did not stop this until they were informed of the ruse. At that point, they took away the e-mail address. But the anonymous nature of posting makes it too easy to lie and deceive.

Summary

Each company has its basic product or service, and the separate product called *shares*. Treating the customer base for those shares with the same care and attention as those customers for products and services is crucial to success. In many young companies—including Internet, biotech, wireless communications, and other capital-intensive companies—far more cash comes in during the first five years through financing activities than through product sales.

Endnotes

1. CrunchBase. (2015). Pebble. Retrieved from CrunchBase: https://www.crunchbase.com/organization/pebble/funding-rounds.

2. Russel, K. (2015, March 3). "Pebble's CEO Discusses the Company's Second Product Launch." Retrieved from TechCrunch: http://techcrunch.com/2015/03/03/pebbles-ceo-discusses-the-companys-second-product-launch/.

13

Building Strong Brands and Strong Companies

Previous chapters have shown how to tackle all elements of the marketing mix for entrepreneurial marketers. All of these marketing mix chapters had similar formats. Regardless of whether the decision was pricing, public relations, advertising, distribution channels, sales force, or product or service design, the format of the decision-making process was similar. The process began with a given positioning—segmentation and differentiation—and then asked the role of the marketing mix element in furthering the positioning toward the target market segments and with the key points of differentiation. Each marketing mix decision process then described various paradigms for developing mix elements that contributed to the incremental revenue to the company in comparison to the incremental costs of the marketing mix element. Both revenue and costs are estimated over the lifetime of the impact of the marketing mix element. Each chapter emphasizes that the marketing mix elements must be justified based on revenue that they contributed over and above the incremental costs of gaining that revenue.

Given this orientation toward incremental revenue and incremental cost, a reasonable question to ask is: Do these marketing mix procedures contribute to the long-term health of the growing company? Are we performing marketing activities for the short term that help short-term sales for our products or services but that will hurt the long-term revenue and profit potential of our company? These are legitimate questions. To try to answer them, we turn to an expert on brand equity and building strong brands, David Aaker. Aaker has written two books and many articles on how to manage brands for the long term. His book, *Building Strong Brands*,[1] has as its goal to guide managers in how to build brands that are strong and will endure and prosper over time. This chapter examines two major concepts he uses in the book and looks at their compatibility with the entrepreneurial marketing approach we advocate. The two Aaker concepts this chapter examines are (1) why it is hard to build brands and (2) the ten guidelines for building strong brands. To make the examination come alive, this chapter uses two examples of entrepreneurial companies that have been successful in building a strong brand and strong company—Synygy, Inc., first discussed in Chapter 6, "Advertising to Build Awareness and Reinforce Messaging," and Victoria's Secret (VS), the largest subsidiary of L Brands.

Founded in 1991 by Mark Stiffler, Synygy began as a service to automate the analysis of sales data for pharmaceutical companies. Over time, the Synygy team developed a series of graphical reports that communicated extremely well to salespeople. Their experience kept building into better and better systems to handle compensation plan administration with an effective combination of computer systems and expert people. They now do the complete outsourced administration of incentive compensation plans. The only real competition to challenge Synygy (aside from in-house, homegrown solutions) has been the entry of enterprise software vendors who sell software but do not provide ongoing plan management services. From its beginnings in the pharmaceutical industry, Synygy has expanded into other industries that employ many salespeople and have incentive compensation as an important part of their plans. Since 1991, Synygy has grown fast enough to be on the Inc. 500 list of fastest-growing private companies for five years and is a member of Inc.'s Hall of Fame. In 2013, Synygy was named a Leader in the inaugural Gartner SPM Magic Quadrant for Sales Performance Management.

As this chapter examines how hard it is to build brands, it uses Synygy, Inc., as one example of a successful, strong brand. We try to understand why Synygy has been able to overcome the obstacles to building an enduring brand and an enduring company. In addition, we use the excellent brand-building example of Victoria's Secret, a subsidiary of L Brands that has been discussed throughout this book.

Why Is It Hard to Build Brands?

Aaker outlines eight reasons why many companies find it difficult to build strong, enduring brands. His orientation is more toward mass-market consumer products, but the concepts are appropriate for any entrepreneurial marketer to consider. Figure 13-1 shows these eight reasons.

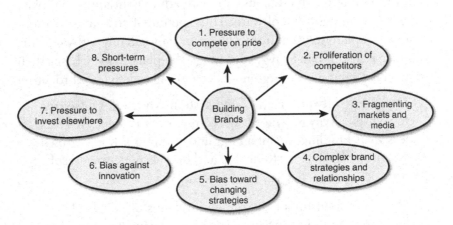

Figure 13-1 Why is it hard to build brands?[2]

We shall reinterpret these reasons from the viewpoint of the person who is beginning a new venture or has been operating a high-growth entity. The first reason, *pressure to compete on price,* can cause an entrepreneurial marketer to make decisions that are counter to building her brand. A lower price, all other things being equal, signals to the marketplace that the value of the product offering is going down also. However, if the perceived value of the offering compared with competition is not going down, then the entrepreneurial marketer should not change her price compared with the competition. Many high-tech market categories have price levels that are continuously decreasing as technology lowers costs for all of the players. However, the strong brands within the category will have aspects of their offering that add incremental perceived value versus the competition. This price premium compared with competition based upon perceived incremental value is the essence of what excellent entrepreneurial marketing enables. There is no reason to lower this premium unless something else in your marketing mix is changing the perceived value of your offering by the market participants.

Synygy really does not compete on price with anyone for the total outsourcing solution. They do compete with some enterprise software vendors for the software portion of the implementation. However, to capitalize on their distinctive competence in complete plan management, Synygy has partnered with their major software competitors to offer the implementation and ongoing administration of the plans using their competitors' software. Thus, potential customers can buy either a complete solution from Synygy, or they can buy software from someone else and pay Synygy to manage the plan. Synygy bases their pricing on a value-in-use argument. According to a Synygy brochure:

> Don't buy software. Don't build systems yourself. Outsource to Synygy. Synygy's incentive compensation solution costs less than building, maintaining, and running a home-grown system, or buying, customizing, and operating packaged software.

> Many of our customers have saved millions of dollars. That's because outsourcing to Synygy increases the top line, improves margins, cuts costs, and improves cash flow by eliminating the huge upfront investment in software and hardware.[3]

Victoria's Secret has been raising its prices as its positioning has become stronger in its target market. In a recent ten-year period, VS quadrupled its revenue and doubled its average selling price.

The second reason it's difficult to build strong brand is *proliferation of competitors,* which always makes entrepreneurial life interesting. However, if you are managing the perceived value of your offering versus your competitors, you should fare well. Also if your initial positioning strategy is soundly based on your distinctive competence that is the source of sustainable competitive advantage, then you should be ready for proliferating competitors.

Synygy was ready to compete when, late in 1998, major enterprise software developers such as Oracle Corp., Siebel Systems, and Trilogy began to offer software to manage incentive plans. Because Synygy's software and operating methods had been continuously improved by their experience and because the operational issues of actually managing the plans on an ongoing basis are so difficult, no competitor was able to challenge Synygy for the complete outsourcing solution. These new competitors did not find it easy to complete applications that are referenceable. However, that does not mean that Synygy could sit still.

In the early 2000s, Synygy experimented with repositioning their offering more as software and less as a total outsourced solution. They repriced their offering as a big up-front software purchase and hired a heavy duty sales VP from Oracle and a number of "software salespeople" to compete with their new competition. After a year and a half of this experiment, Mark Stiffler, the Synygy CEO, dismantled the "software" organization, fired the sales VP, and went back to "their roots."

According to Mark,

> I hated the culture and lack of teamwork; I hated the prima donna attitudes; I hated the lack of process and discipline. We are now back to our roots: focused on selling hosted and managed service solutions (with emphasis on people who understand client problems and improve their processes... the software is secondary... I say "demo our people not our software"). We also went back to pricing as a recurring subscription fee like I did for the first 10 years in business (after having gone down the path of upfront license fees).[4]

What Mark realized was that the enterprise software orientation was inconsistent with his desired positioning and was seriously hurting his perceived value. There were significant short and medium costs to going back to his roots, but they were worth it. He has recently introduced a one-year contract as his pricing vehicle, just like SAS. His clients can stop any time after a year if they are not satisfied. He has lost no clients, but it makes his service easier to sell if it is perceived as less risky.

To keep its competitive edge, Synygy invested money in web-based software that was essential to deliver the value in a way that was efficient for their clients. In addition to Enterprise Incentive Management (EIM) services, they added three new performance management solutions: referrals management, quotas management, and objectives management. EIM is still the focus, and other solutions are only sold as add-ons to EIM and not by themselves. Mark now realizes that EIM can be their enduring competitive edge, but it needs to always be improved to be perceived as better than the current and potential competition.

Synygy is continually concerned as to how the target markets *perceive* Synygy's offerings as opposed to how much better they actually are. In this situation, word of mouth from satisfied customers is the best weapon Synygy has. As long as Synygy continues to build its distinctive competence and increases its ability to be perceived as adding the most value to its target markets, it may be able to stay ahead of its competitors.

Similarly, Victoria's Secret actively manages and measures their market perception with ongoing consumer research. Because they own their own retail stores and have much clout with mall operators because of their association with other L Brands' mall stores, VS has not had major competitive threats in their core business.

We can combine the third and fourth reasons (*fragmenting markets and media* and *complex brand strategies and relationships*, respectively) for why it is hard to build brands for entrepreneurial marketers. These relate to keeping the positioning of the brand consistent regardless of which media or market is used and considering the brand's relationship to the firm's other brands. These reasons should typically not be very salient for most entrepreneurial marketers. Most successful ventures are targeting niche markets, not mass markets, so they should be using very targeted media vehicles and public relations. Most entrepreneurial ventures also have only one brand, their first. In many cases, their brand is their company. As they grow, some of these issues may become more salient.

For Synygy, a key strategic issue they faced was the best way to grow. They could expand their services to existing clients by performing other analyses on the same sales data they used for their incentive plan management or offer other plan management services such as the referrals, quotas, and objectives management services. They could alternatively expand their incentive plan management offering to other markets than pharmaceuticals. Both of the options were somewhat consistent with the firm's initial positioning and distinctive competence. However, the potential perceived value and distinctiveness of their incentive plan offering was much higher than the other services. Synygy correctly decided to prioritize the expansion of their core incentive plan management offering to other target markets. For their current users, they will do further analysis of the sales data or the other plan management programs as value-added services. However, Synygy's marketing budget and sales resources are used primarily toward expansion to new customers and new markets, leveraging their core distinctive competence. The tag line "The Incentive Compensation Company" was adopted after Synygy made this strategic decision to strengthen their company and brand. Please note that if Synygy would have known this strategy decision when they named their firm, it would have been more productive to name the company more consistent with its positioning. However, hindsight is clearer than foresight.

Remember that Chapter 5, "Promotion and Viral Marketing to Maximize Sustainable Profitability," shared the change in advertising copy that Synygy made that increased their short-term advertising productivity by over 15 times. This new advertising copy was still consistent with the basic positioning and segmentation strategies of the firm. The advertising just got the point across much more effectively.

As has been shown throughout this book, VS has done an excellent job of making sure that every marketing activity it does reinforces its positioning. That discipline has paid handsome dividends in its strategic position, financial returns, and market value.

The fifth—*bias toward changing strategies*—and sixth—*bias against innovation*—reasons are issues with which entrepreneurs constantly struggle. For many entrepreneurial companies, the issue of developing a scalable marketing-sales-business model is very difficult. The really successful firms succeed in developing a way of going to market, and getting and serving new customers, that becomes routine and scalable, like a formula. The founding entrepreneur no longer has to close each sale. The company's positioning and perceived value become known well enough in the market so that sales come somewhat easier. Growth can accelerate quickly when this happens.

However, the entrepreneur can become bored and lose focus. He might want the firm to move into other more interesting products or markets. This changing of strategies can seriously harm the venture, especially if the new products and/or markets are not leveraging the distinctive competence and positioning that have become the heritage of the company. Scarce resources need to be allocated to where they can provide the most long-term value to the firm, not necessarily to the most interesting new idea.

On the other hand, the entrepreneurial marketer cannot stand pat with the formula without continuously seeking to improve the firm's perceived value to its customers and leverage its distinctive competence. He must constantly keep ahead of current and potential competition. However, all the innovation should be leveraging the existing positioning and distinctive competence of the firm. If the marketplace needs are changing, then sometimes the positioning and associated product offering needs to adapt to the changing needs. However, adaptation to market changes should always be done to leverage the firm's distinctive competence relative to the competition.

Synygy's market needs and competition are constantly changing. We already discussed the new software competition. More and more, the market is also moving toward web-based systems and Software as a Service (SaaS) providers to solve information systems problems. The information technology officers at their potential client companies are causing this movement. Synygy is broadening its offering to include different ways of delivering its service. They will provide either a complete outsourced solution, be a SaaS provider, provide just the enterprise software for purchase, or provide the ongoing management and implementation of someone else's software. However, all of these options are consistent with its core positioning and leverage its distinctive competence. Synygy knows the nitty-gritty of implementing incentive plans to improve its customers' productivity better than anyone. All of its new, broadened offerings are consistent with and leverage that core competence.

VS has also continually innovated to reinforce its positioning. The "Pink" product line supporting breast cancer research and the Internet fashion extravaganzas are two good examples.

The seventh reason for brands being hard to build, *pressure to invest elsewhere*, might not be as salient for entrepreneurs whose companies or executives whose divisions typically have only one brand. The big problem is getting enough resources to invest in the company's main product offering. Many of the Internet companies of 2000 and 2001 were spending on their core brands, but spending ineffectively. They did not evaluate the incremental revenue due to the different marketing mix options they could use.

As discussed earlier, VS and the L Brands have shied away from big global investments because they were more confident that they could improve their competitive position with investments in their U.S. home market where they could leverage their large retail infrastructure.

The eighth and final reason Aaker posits for brands being hard to build is *short-term pressures*. It is sometimes very tempting to sacrifice positioning and the brand's perceived value to do some activity that will help short-term sales and profits. For consumer products, the activities that can cause the most problems are temporary price-oriented promotions. If these promotions are not reinforcing the product offering's targeted perceived value, they can harm this perceived value. If consumers see a brand as always "on sale," it may cheapen its perceived value. Even if such promotions cause some incremental short-term sales and profits, if they are not consistent with the positioning of the brand, they should not be done.

Chapter 7, "Distribution/Channel Decisions to Solidify Sustainable Competitive Advantage," documented what happened to Marantz when it brought in the discount stores to augment its then high-end retail distribution channels. The tactic was successful in the short term but ruined the company and brand for the long term.

Probably the most common short-term pressure for a company in business-to-business markets is from their salespeople to discount their product in order to "close the sale." Here, if the customer does not perceive enough incremental value to justify the normal price, then the salesperson has not done his job, or the customer is not in the target market. Unless the company can be confident that the "special" price reduction will not become widely known, then it does not make sense to reduce the price to "close" this one sale. The other potential customers who would have been willing to pay the normal price will no longer be willing if they learn that someone else has gotten a lower price. Thus, the price received will trend down to match the "special discounts" over time and hurt the long-term profitability of the venture. It is hard for most companies to lose sales, but sometimes it is the right thing to do, especially if the potential customer will not receive as much value as some other customers. As shown in Chapter 3, "Entrepreneurial Pricing—An Often Misused Way to Garner Extraordinary Profits," a good pricing policy implies that not every potential customer will buy the offering.

Synygy has been able to rapidly grow its business without having to resort to "special" price reductions to get certain clients. They have a given price list to which all companies are subject. Obviously, there are different prices for different numbers of salespeople and for the different levels of service that Synygy can provide. One of the reasons that Mark was unhappy with the "Enterprise Software" strategy was that the software salespeople were accustomed to giving discounts and negotiating special deals. Mark correctly was concerned that this was cheapening the perceived value of his offering and was dangerous.

In Chapter 3 we discussed how VS tested pricing, allowing them to increase their sales prices, even though in the beginning there was a short-term hit to profits when the constant price promotions were significantly reduced.

Can Entrepreneurial Marketers Overcome These Eight Difficulties in Building Brands?

The answer to this question should be obvious. If the entrepreneurial marketer has followed the prescriptions in the previous chapters, she will always be building the long-term health of her company and its brands while she simultaneously contributes to the venture's short-term revenue and profits. Every marketing mix activity—and, in fact, all venture activities—must be consistent with the perceived value the firm wants to deliver to its customers and potential customers. The venture must be dedicated to continuously improving this perceived value versus competition by building and leveraging its distinctive competences and communicating this value to its target markets.

One of the strongest brands built in recent years, Google, has followed these precepts. They have kept the identity and used the colorful logo in each of the offerings (Google Drive, Google Maps, Google Chrome, Google Photos, and so on). Occasionally, when Google acquires another company or product with a strong brand, like You-Tube or Nest, they retain that brand. They are continuously investing in the brand image, even as their dominance in search grows. And they know that the value for their customers (advertisers in the search marketing and end users) is best perceived through a strong brand.

Ten Guidelines for Building Strong Brands

Aaker also provides ten guidelines for building strong brands. These are good guidelines for entrepreneurial marketers in general; however, some of them need to be modified to the circumstances in which most entrepreneurs find themselves. The last guideline in particular merits significant modification for entrepreneurs. Following are the ten Aaker guidelines for building strong brands:[5]

1. **Brand identity**—Have an identity for each brand. Consider the perspectives of the brand-as-person, brand-as-organization, and brand-as-symbol, as well as the brand-as-product. Identify the core identity. Modify the identity as needed for different market segments and products. Remember that an image is how you are perceived, and an identity is how you aspire to be perceived.

2. **Value proposition**—Know the value proposition for each brand that has a driver role. Consider emotional and self-expressive benefits as well as functional benefits. Know how endorser brands will provide credibility. Understand the brand-customer relationship.

3. **Brand position**—For each brand, have a brand position that will provide clear guidance to those implementing a communication program. Recall that a position is the part of the identity and value proposition that is to be actively communicated.

4. **Execution**—Execute the communication program so that it not only is on target with the identity and position, but achieves brilliance and durability. Generate alternatives and consider options beyond media advertising.

5. **Consistency over time**—Have as a goal a consistent identity, position, and execution over time. Maintain symbols, imagery, and metaphors that work. Understand and resist organizational biases toward changing the identity, position, and execution.

6. **Brand system**—Make sure the brands in the portfolio are consistent and synergistic. Know their roles. Have or develop silver bullets to help support brand identities and positions. Exploit branded features and services. Use sub-brands to clarify and modify. Know the strategic brands.

7. **Brand leverage**—Extend brands and develop cobranding programs only if the brand identity will be both used and reinforced. Identify range brands and, for each, develop an identity and specify how that identity will be different in disparate product contests. If the brand is moved up or down, take care to manage the integrity of the resulting brand identities.

8. **Tracking brand equity**—Track brand equity over time, including awareness, perceived quality, brand loyalty, and especially brand associations. Have specific communication objectives. Especially note areas where the brand identity and position are not reflected in the brand image.

9. **Brand responsibility**—Have someone in charge of the brand who will create the identity and position and coordinate the execution over organizational units, media, and markets. Beware when a brand is being used in a business in which it is not the cornerstone.

10. **Invest in brands**—Continue investing in brands even when the financial goals are not being met.

These guidelines are self-explanatory and should be helpful to entrepreneurs as well as the consumer products corporate types to whom Aaker's book is directed. Guideline six, *brand system,* and seven, *brand leverage* to new products, may be overkill for most entrepreneurs who have one brand that keeps their hands full. Guideline eight, *tracking brand equity,* should be observed more in spirit by many entrepreneurs. They should remain close to their existing and potential customers to assess how their product offering's value is being perceived. They should put cost-effective means in place to check whether the perceived value of the offering is changing over time. Usually, this would be in the form of customer satisfaction surveys as well as getting periodic readings from potential customers on how they perceive the value of the offering versus its competition.

The last guideline needs some modification for entrepreneurial marketers. In fact, depending on how you interpret it, the guideline might not be consistent with research discussed in Chapter 6, "Advertising to Build Awareness and Reinforce Messaging." The guideline says to continue to invest in the brand even when the financial goals are not being met. We have discussed research that needs to be considered in this investment decision. That research (on TV advertising) basically said that *if the advertising didn't work in the short term, it had no long-term revenue impact.* It also said that *if the advertising worked in the short term, it had a long-term impact that more than doubled the short-term impact on the average.* There is no academic research that says this conclusion would be any different for other elements of the marketing mix, such as public relations or different media. Thus, the key determination that the entrepreneurial marketer needs to make is: Does the investment in my brand have an *incremental impact* on the short-term revenue of the product offering? This incremental impact must be determined relative to *what revenue would have been had the investment not been made.* If the brand would be going down if the advertising were not done, and its revenue would *go down less* with an advertising program, then the advertising program has a *positive incremental impact.*

Thus, for entrepreneurial marketers, we would modify the last guideline to read: *Continue to invest in the brand as long as the investment has a positive incremental impact on the brand's revenue.* If your brand-marketing investments are not impacting revenue compared with what the revenue would have been without the investment, then it won't help either the long-term or the short-term sales for the brand. The entrepreneurial marketing challenge is to continually find investments in the brand that will have short-term incremental impact. Chapter 6 outlined methods for managing these marketing investments so that they will more likely have the required impact.

Summary

This chapter has shown how the entrepreneurial marketer can simultaneously build short-term revenue and a strong company by following the prescriptions in the previous chapters. Entrepreneurial marketers cannot be satisfied to spend money just for "brand building" without having an impact on their revenue. Many advertising and marketing agencies would advocate this unproductive brand-building activity. The entrepreneurial marketer must resist this advocacy and insist on brand-building programs that have an incremental impact. If not, she is throwing away her money with a very high probability. During the Internet "bubble," many of the new Internet ventures were throwing away lots of money in brand-building spending but had no idea whether it was working or not. Effective entrepreneurial marketers should not let this happen.

Endnotes

1. David A. Aaker, *Building Strong Brands* (New York: The Free Press, 1996).

2. Source: Ibid, p. 27.

3. Synygy brochure, 1999. Bala Cynwyd, PA.

4. Personal communication of Leonard Lodish with Mark Stiffler, August 2005.

5. Source: David A. Aaker, *Building Strong Brands*, inside rear cover.

Index